FINANCIAL ACCOUNTING CASES,
3RD CANADIAN EDITION

FINANCIAL ACCOUNTING CASES, 3RD CANADIAN EDITION

Camillo Lento, Ph.D., CPA, CA, CBV, CFE
Associate Professor (Accounting), Faculty of Business Administration, Lakehead University

and

Jo-Anne Ryan, Ph.D., CPA, CA
Associate Professor (Accounting), Faculty of Management, Laurentian University

WILEY

Library and Archives Canada Cataloguing in Publication
ISBN 9781119594642

LCCN number: 2019027129

Production Credits
Executive Editor: Zoë Craig
Senior Marketing Manager: Anita Osborne
Editorial Manager: Judy Howarth
Content Management Director: Lisa Wojcik
Content Manager: Nichole Urban
Senior Content Specialist: Nicole Repasky
Production Editor: Umamaheswari Gnanamani
Cover Design: Wiley
Cover Image: © Aidan Campbell/Getty Images

Questions from the Uniform Final Examination have been reprinted (or adapted) with permission from the Chartered Professional Accountants, Canada (CPA Canada). Any changes to the original material are the sole responsibility of the author (and/or publisher) and have not been reviewed or endorsed by CPA Canada.

Printed and bound in the United States of America
V10012843_080819

John Wiley & Sons Canada, Ltd.

90 Eglinton Avenue East, Suite 300
Toronto, Ontario, M4P 2Y3 Canada
Visit our website at: www.wiley.com

CONTENTS

Section V Intermediate Accounting II Cases

Section VI Advanced Financial Accounting

Section VII Capstone Cases

Section VIII Integrative Cases

ABOUT THE AUTHORS

Camillo Lento is Associate Professor in the Faculty of Business Administration at Lakehead University's Thunder Bay, Ontario, campus. He received his Ph.D. in Accounting from the University of Southern Queensland and is a Canadian Chartered Professional Accountant, Chartered Business Valuator, and Certified Fraud Examiner.

Camillo teaches various financial accounting and auditing courses, including contemporary issues in accounting theory, integrative analysis of accounting issues, and, intermediate accounting. In addition, he is a facilitator and case preparer for CPA Ontario's Professional Education Program.

Camillo's research interests include various issues related to accounting education. Specifically, Camillo's research focuses on accounting students' use of technology inside and outside of the classroom, along with the impacts of technology and other factors on academic dishonesty. His accounting education research has been published in journals such as *Issues in Accounting Education, Journal of Accounting Education, and Accounting Education: An International Journal.*

Camillo has more than 10 years' experience working with a Big Four and mid-tier public accounting firm. His public practice experience includes a variety of assurance engagements, the valuation of privately owned businesses, corporate and personal tax compliance, the assessment of personal injury damages, and business interruption claims.

Jo-Anne Ryan is Associate Professor at Laurentian University in Sudbury, Ontario. She teaches accounting and assurance courses, from introductory to advanced. She has an HBComm in Accounting from Laurentian University and is a Chartered Professional Accountant and Chartered Accountant (Ontario), having articled with KPMG LLP. She earned a Ph.D. in Accounting from the University of Birmingham, United Kingdom.

Jo-Anne has over 16 years of experience in the classroom. She works closely with CPA Ontario and CPA Canada in various capacities. She has been a reviewer for the CPA Preparation Courses (PREP) and the National Facilitator for their Assurance Module within PREP. She has received several awards for excellence in teaching. Her academic research focuses on the use of investor relations websites to transmit accounting information to stakeholders and the impact of emerging technologies on organizations, auditors, and education.

Outside the classroom, Jo-Anne has been a guest speaker at several Rotary functions and has volunteered her time on several boards and at charity events.

ACKNOWLEDGMENTS

Camillo would like to thank his wife, Angela, and family for all of their support.

The authors would like to thank the following for their valuable contributions to the third edition of *Canadian Financial Accounting Cases*:

ALLAN FOERSTER
BRUCE MCCONOMY

The authors would like to thank the following for their valuable contributions to the second edition of *Canadian Financial Accounting Cases*:

JEFFREY BOTHAM
KRISTIE DEWALD
DARRELL HERAUF
NATHALIE JOHNSTONE
BRUCE MCCONOMY
RUTH ANN STRICKLAND

The authors also thank the following for their valuable contributions to the first edition of *Canadian Financial Accounting Cases*:

STEPHANIE MCGARRY
LAURA SIMEONI
SARA WICK
IRENE WIECEK

The authors would like to thank the following reviewers for their insightful suggestions on the current and previous editions of the casebook:

ROBERT DUCHARME, *University of Waterloo*
JOCELYN KING, *University of Alberta*
HEATHER SCELES, *Saint Mary's University*
RIK SMISTAD, *Mount Royal University*

The authors would like to thank JOEL SHAPIRO, *Ryerson University* for accuracy checking and reviewing the supplements.

INTRODUCTION

Introduction

The Case for Cases

Professional accountants continue to be recognized for their strong technical knowledge. A strong technical background is still a foundational trait for professional accountants in protecting the public interest. Professional accounting bodies across the globe are recognizing the increased importance of higher-order cognitive skills such as critical thinking, problem solving, and analytical ability. Many accounting professors continue to struggle to find ways to focus on the development of higher-order skills in undergraduate programs.

Case analysis is an important tool for developing these higher-order skills for financial reporting. At the introductory level, short case studies expose the students to a realistic situation and stress the importance that numbers do not always fit neatly into formulas. At the intermediate and advanced levels, more complex cases encourage integrated thinking. Not only do cases mirror real-life decision-making, they encourage critical thinking and help develop professional judgement. Furthermore, they allow students to test their true knowledge of journal entries and accounting theory by attempting to apply the latter in real-life situations.

Cases can be used to help students develop higher levels of knowledge as measured by Bloom's taxonomy.[1] For example, consider Table 1.1, which applies Bloom's taxonomy to accounting education.

In order to solve problems, memorized knowledge of journal entries and generally accepted accounting principles (GAAP) are important. However, Table 1.1 reveals that a student who has memorized this information has only climbed up half the mountain. Students must also be able to apply the knowledge in situations where there is uncertainty. This is where cases become important in developing problem-solving skills, critical thinking, and professional judgement.

What's in a Case?

What makes a case, a case? Many people have different views on this. Most cases involve some sort of real-life scenario where there are one or several issues or problems. You would be expected to identify the issues, understand the implications of the issue, analyze the issue, and then recommend a course of action. The cases may involve quantitative analysis, qualitative analysis, or both analyses.

What makes a case more challenging is the "required" information. Some cases will specify what you should do (e.g., calculate the future tax expense or identify which amortization method the company should use). Others leave the "required" section more open by requesting that you discuss the issues. In the latter, you must decide, for instance, if the future tax expense needs to be calculated in the first place or whether the choice of amortization methods is even an issue. Therein lies the challenge. What is the issue? How should the case be approached?

A successful accountant should not only be able to solve problems that have been identified for her, but more importantly, she should be able to identify the problems in the first place.

It is rare in real life that someone will present you with a problem and provide all the facts needed to solve it. In many cases, identifying the problem and gathering relevant information is a large part of the task.

Accountants are also required to communicate their findings and recommendations back to their manager, their partners, and their clients. Cases require you to determine who the report or memo needs to be addressed to and how to write this in an appropriate and professional manner.

---

[1]Bloom, B. S. (1956). *Taxonomy of Educational Objectives, Handbook I: The Cognitive Domain*. New York: David McKay Co Inc.

Table 1.1   Bloom's Taxonomy As It Applies to Accounting Education

Bloom's Taxonomy— Category	Example of Category	Example of Financial Accounting Knowledge	Educational Tools Available
Knowledge	Recall data or information	• Debits increase assets and decrease liabilities • Credits increase liabilities and decrease assets	• Matching (e.g., terms to definitions) • True and false questions
Comprehension	Understand the meaning, translation, interpolation, and interpretation of instructions and problems. State a problem in one's own words.	• Identifying the accounting issue	• Multiple choice questions • Exercises and problems on individual topics
Application	Use a concept in a new situation or unprompted use of an abstraction. Apply what was learned in the classroom into novel situations in the workplace.	• Recording journal entries	• Recording journal entries • Exercises and problems on individual topics
Analysis	Separate material or concepts into component parts so that its organizational structure may be understood. Distinguish between facts and inferences.	• Applying technical GAAP knowledge to specific situations	• Exercises and problems on individual topics • Cases (e.g., applying technical knowledge to case facts to analyze accounting issues)
Synthesis	Build a structure or pattern from diverse elements. Put parts together to form a whole, with emphasis on creating a new meaning or structure.	• Understanding how various accounting issues come together to make a significant impact on the users and preparers	• Cases (e.g., calculate or revise the earnings per share estimate based on an analysis of various individual accounting issues)
Evaluation	Make judgements about the value of ideas or materials.	• Developing professional judgement • Selecting between alternatives that are equally valid and within the boundaries of GAAP	• Cases (e.g., require students to analyze alternatives and make a recommendation based on the users and reporting landscape)

You must also learn to consider the impact of the environment on your decision-making, including the people involved, such as the financial statement preparers and users. Different people think in different ways depending on their own perspectives. What is right or good for one person may not be right or good for another. For instance, assume that two people are discussing the weather. Both comment that they hope the weather will be good tomorrow. One might be hoping it stays sunny because she has to drive to Montreal. The other might be hoping it snows because he plans to do a lot of skiing. They both want "good weather" but each one has a completely different definition of what "good weather" is at that time. "Good" financial reporting might mean one thing to one person and a completely different thing to another.

Cases sensitize you to these things. Because this way of thinking is often different from what you are used to, you may have problems analyzing cases at first. However, you will eventually catch on and find that the study of accounting is more fulfilling as a result of the use of cases. It is easier to approach this material with a completely open mind than to try to make it fit into a preconceived notion of accounting that may be more narrowly focused.

With cases, there is rarely a single acceptable answer or recommendation. There may be several, even for the same issue. The important thing is how you support your answer or recommendation.

For the most part, each case has a common set of learning objectives with the intent of developing problem-solving and critical thinking skills and professional judgement. The common learning objectives are as follows:

• To develop an ability to identify and assume an assigned role

• To identify and rank the importance of explicit issues

- To understand the importance of hidden (undirected) issues that arise from a detailed analysis

- To identify accounting issues (GAAP compliance issues), assess their implications, generate alternatives, and provide recommendations within the bounds of GAAP to meet the client's needs

- To understand how accounting standards affect financial measures (ratios, covenants, etc.)

- To prepare a coherent report and integrated analysis that meets specific user needs

In addition to the above noted learning objectives, each case will have its own additional learning objectives that are based on the specific technical accounting issues in the case.

The Purpose of This Casebook—Students and Instructors

The purpose of this casebook is to use cases to

- develop problem-solving skills, critical thinking abilities, and professional judgement;

- promote an understanding of the decision usefulness approach to accounting.

Accordingly, all of the cases require the student to understand the implications of financial reporting decisions on the users of the financial statements. A thorough user analysis is required for each case.

For the instructor

The casebook provides a wide variety of cases that can be used in several classroom settings. Some cases are short and focus on a few issues. These cases are well suited to be used as in-class discussion tools. Other cases are longer, more complicated, and deal with several issues. These cases are more suited to be used as assignments or exams.

What's new in this edition? All of the cases have been updated to reflect the most recent changes to the *Chartered Professional Accountants of Canada (CPA Canada) Handbook.* New cases have been added in each of the sections. A new section has been added with cases that provide integration across multiple competencies. Each case comes with a detailed solution and some case solutions have marking guides using an assessment opportunity approach.

New for this edition are cases that are financial accounting based with the additional added opportunity to be used to develop an audit plan. Cases with audit planning memos are designated in the casebook with an icon at the top of the case This will provide further flexibility in choosing cases for your classroom.

For the student

The cases allow you to assume a wide variety of roles and place you in different settings. Common reporting objectives, such as a focus on the debt to equity ratio, management bonuses, and purchase price calculations, are coupled with less common reporting objectives, such as government grant applications, debt versus equity investment decisions, and assessments of the creditworthiness of a company. Why is this important? As professionals, you will be faced with daily issues and decision-making. While it is not possible to provide you with this practice in actual situations, these cases will enable you to go beyond the numbers and integrate the quantitative applications you learn in your textbooks with the qualitative issues that ultimately occur in management decision-making.

Ultimately, the goal of this casebook is to enhance the learning in introductory, intermediate, and advanced accounting courses by exposing the students to situations that cannot be addressed in standard financial accounting textbooks.

Conclusion

This chapter presents the case for cases by introducing the purpose of and need for case analysis. Before attempting to analyze a case, students are encouraged to read the following three chapters. Chapter 2 provides a summary of the case framework approach. Chapter 3 provides a sample case and Chapter 4 discusses the critical aspect of debriefing.

2 The Case Framework Approach

There is no one way to answer a case, but there are some guidelines and tips that can assist you. The best way to improve your case writing is to practise! Developing your own personal case framework can help you to approach each case with confidence. In this chapter, we start with an illustration of a case-writing approach and then walk you through it. We end this important section with the same framework in a blank format. We encourage you to use this and develop your own approach that works. Let's begin by looking at that framework in Figure 2.1.

The Framework Explained

In order to answer a case study satisfactorily, we must first understand the environment within which the analysis takes place. A good question to ask is as follows: Is there anything about the environment or any background information that might cause us to identify different issues, or to view the issues differently, or to respond differently? Let's examine the sections in the framework more closely.

Step 1: Assess the Reporting Framework

1. **Identify the role that you are playing.**

   Usually, most cases require that you assume a role. Who are you in the case? From whose perspective will you be answering the case? Different people have differing opinions and views on things.

   If your role is that of an independent advisor (e.g., a chartered professional accountant hired by the shareholders), you might think differently than an employee who works for the company. As an employee, you might be concerned with keeping your job and, therefore, would want to keep your boss happy by giving her what she wants. As an outside professional, hired by the shareholders, you might focus more on keeping the shareholders happy. Keeping the boss happy and keeping the share-holders happy might not result in the same course of action.

   Consideration should also be given to ethics and legal liability. Outside consultants who offer advice might later be sued if the advice is relied on and results in a loss to the company, shareholders, or other users. Therefore, outside consultants must assess the risk of each engagement. For higher-risk engagements, they might take a more conservative position and give more conservative advice.

   Many situations involve ethical dilemmas where the individual must make decisions that either will harm himself or will harm others and a choice must be made. Sometimes, doing the right thing may result in personal loss. Humanize the analysis by thinking about what you would do in the situation. For instance, accruing a large loss might result in lower net income and, hence, a lower bonus for the controller. On the other hand, not accruing the loss may mislead users.

   Remember that the financial statements are a reflection of the successes and failures of the company and of management in that they reveal whether management is fulfilling its stewardship function. Therefore, in preparing the statements, management might be concerned about disclosing negative items.

   TIP – Put yourself in the shoes of the person whose role you are playing. Think about how you would react in a situation and what factors would influence your decision. Would you put your own needs ahead of those of other users?

   TIP – Preparers of financial information may be biased and this must be considered in any analysis.

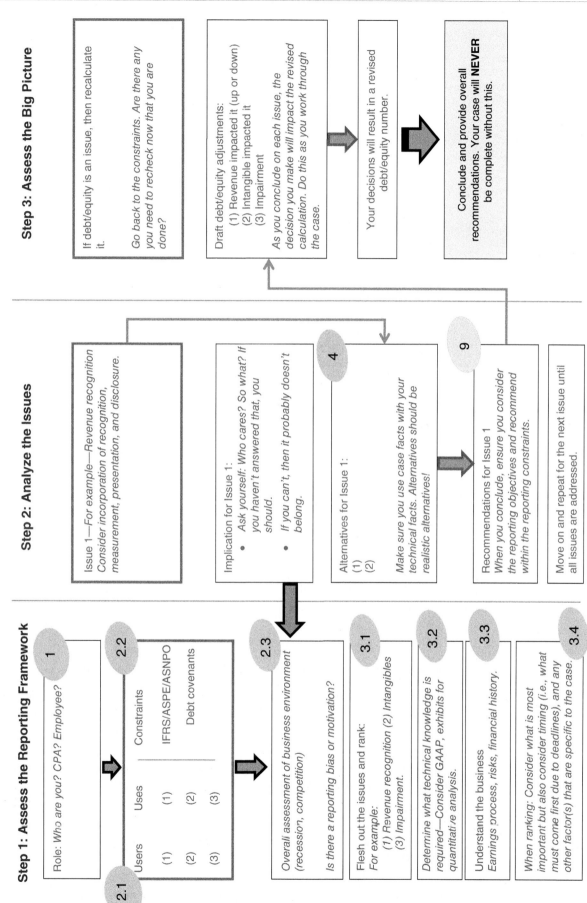

FIGURE 2.1   The Case-Writing Framework

Table 2.1   Users and Their Uses of Financial Statements

Users	Uses of Financial Statements

Banks and other creditors	• Predictive
	   ◦ Cash flow prediction for debt repayment
	• Feedback
	   ◦ Compliance with covenants (debt to equity ratio covenant, working capital covenant, etc.)

Potential equity investors	• Predictive
	   ◦ Cash flow prediction for dividend payments
	• Feedback
	   ◦ Performance evaluation (time series analysis over time and cross-sectional analysis against competitors)

Current equity investors	• Predictive
	   ◦ Cash flow prediction for dividend payments
	• Feedback
	   ◦ Assessment of management stewardship

Governments and funding agencies	• Predictive
	   ◦ Determine whether future funds should be provided
	• Feedback
	   ◦ Assessment of the use of funds provided (effectiveness and efficiency of funds provided)

Tax authorities	• Starting point for the assessment of taxable income
Suppliers	• Determine creditworthiness for extending credit for supplies
Employees	• Predictive ◦ Cash flow prediction for bonuses

2.   Assess the users and their needs and any constraints and assess the business environment.

2.1 Identify users and their needs.

There are unlimited numbers of potential users and uses of financial statements. Recall from your accounting studies the definition of relevance. Relevant information impacts a user's decision. Relevant information provides both feedback value (confirming past events) and predictive value (aiding in assessing future events).

Table 2.1 presents a brief summary of the most common users and their needs.

Preparers and Their Reporting Objectives

The preparers of financial statements may have different objectives than the users of financial statements and their objectives cannot be overlooked. Generally, the preparer is the senior management of the company, as opposed to the accounting staff.

The following is a summary of some of the major financial reporting objectives of senior management:

1. **Minimizing income tax:** Management of private entities that do not have any major creditors may have a primary reporting objective to minimize income taxes. Minimizing income taxes would help maximize shareholders' wealth.

2. **Smoothing income:** Management may try to smooth net income in order to reduce the company's perceived riskiness. Smoothing net income will also help management meet performance targets year over year.

3. **Maximizing net income:** Management may try to maximize net income for various reasons. For example, management may have a bonus based on net income (e.g., 10% of net income) and thereby try to maximize their personal wealth by maximizing net income. Alternatively, management may try to maximize net income in order to show strong financial performance to maximize an initial public offering price.

4. **Minimizing net income:** Management may try to minimize net income for various reasons. One reason may be that the company is experiencing significant political costs. For example,

large banks or oil companies may want to minimize net income in order to avoid political backlash or the potential for increased regulation and taxes. Alternatively, management may try to minimize net income in order to maximize net income in future periods. This is also known as taking a "big bath" as the books are cleaned up to allow for strong future profits. Consider management that is facing a poor year and will not earn a bonus. Management may decide to minimize net income by taking excess impairment writedowns and large contingencies in order to reduce future amortization and expenses, thereby increasing the possibility of earning future bonuses.

5. **Contract compliance:** Management may be confronted with various contracts that are tied to financial statement metrics. For example, loan covenants may restrict the ability to raise additional debt by limiting the debt to equity ratio. Working capital loans may be based on a percentage of accounts receivable and inventory. Not-for-profits that are charitable may be required to distribute a certain percentage of their net income. Government funding may require companies to incur a certain amount of wage expense.

TIP – For any question that requires professional judgement, always ask two questions: (1) who wants to know? and (2) why do they need this information; that is, what decision will they use this information for? That way, you may consider tailoring the information to help the users make their decisions.

TIP – Although ideally, the main objective of financial reporting is to provide information to users that is useful for decision-making, this does not always happen due to personal and corporate biases.

TIP – A good analysis will always look at the impact of the decision-making on the affected parties.

2.2 Identify any constraints.

It is important to keep in mind that preparers cannot meet their own needs or user needs without considering the constraints on financial reporting. In general, one of the following constraints will be present:

- Part I GAAP—International Financial Reporting Standards (IFRS): Publicly accountable enterprises will be constrained by IFRS and have no choice to adopt a different reporting framework.

- Part II GAAP—Accounting Standards for Private Enterprises (ASPE): Non-publicly accountable enterprises (e.g., private corporations) can choose either ASPE or IFRS. If a framework is not prescribed by the user (e.g., the bank), then management must assess which framework will provide the most benefit considering the costs.

- Part III GAAP—Accounting Standards for Non-Profit Organizations (ASNPO): Not-for-profit enterprises can choose ASNPO or IFRS. Again, if a framework is not prescribed by a funding government or contributor, then management must assess which framework will provide the most benefit considering the costs.

- Basis Other Than Generally Accepted Accounting Principles (GAAP): It is possible that financial reporting must comply with some other basis; for example, compliance with a specific contract for reporting lease revenues, or rate-regulated utilities, which have their own specific reporting standards.

TIP – If the question does not make it clear whether a GAAP constraint exists, then look to the main users. Normally, users would want GAAP financial statements since they are more reliable and comparable.

TIP – Acknowledging constraints upfront will help to keep you focused on the relevant analysis.

2.3 Consider the business environment and company and identify potential bias.

Is the economy in a recession or is the real estate market in a slump? This will affect your analysis because the company might be more prone to bias if it is trying to stay afloat in a sinking environment. Looking at other companies in the industry will give some background on how other companies are faring in the current times.

TIP – The environment will give some clues as to how information might be biased.

It is important to understand what the company does. How does it earn its revenues? Which costs must be incurred to earn revenues? What are the business risks? What is the financial history of the company; that is, have revenues been steadily increasing over time, or decreasing? What about profits? Does the company turn a profit every year? Were the results of this year predictable? What are the key ratios that are considered to be important in the industry? How do the company's ratios compare with industry norms and its own historical ratios? All this data provides a backdrop for the analysis.

TIP – Insight into the way the company operates and what is important to the company helps you understand why it might find certain financial reporting issues more sensitive than others and will help in understanding what is at stake in the decision.

Based on the above, determine the overall financial reporting objective.

This is a summation of the financial reporting landscape assessment. It helps you to focus the analysis and conclude in a manner that is consistent with the environment. For instance, assume that your role is a chartered professional accountant and that you will be providing information to a bank so it can make a lending decision. Your tendency will be to offer conservative advice and disclose more information (especially about risks and potential losses), rather than less. Hopefully, this will reduce the risk of a potential lawsuit should the bank suffer a loss. It will also give the bank the information needed to make a decision.

This is only one position or conclusion, and you might think that there are other overriding factors that are more important.

TIP – The conclusion or recommendation is a matter of judgement and there is usually no right or wrong answer, although certain cases may lean toward a certain interpretation.

TIP – Once the financial reporting objective is outlined, try to be consistent in your recommendations where there are multiple issues. For example, if you conclude conservatively on the first issue, the other issues should also reflect the conservative approach unless you explain why.

3. **Identify the issues, determine the technical knowledge required, and rank the issues.**

   3.1 **Keep in mind that an issue is a financial reporting problem that needs resolution.**

   Resolution is usually not straightforward but rather is arrived at through careful analysis of relevant alternatives. In financial reporting, keep in mind that most issues will relate to how to account for something or how to present it in the financial statements. Focus on relevant issues only.

   TIP – Although there might be issues that need to be addressed in other areas, such as tax or management accounting issues, try to keep focused on the financial reporting issues. Having said this, in real life, all important issues would be addressed.

   TIP – For more complex issues, the issue may not be any clearer than "How do we account for the transaction?"

   In cases involving complex issues, the following will help to clarify how to proceed with the analysis.

   1. Draw a diagram of the exchange, including all parties involved. This will illustrate the legal form.

   2. Try to answer the question: "What did the company give up and what did it get?"

   3. Attempt a journal entry or at least part of one.

   4. Try to identify economic substance. Note that management intent often gives a key to this.

3.2 Realize that identifying issues requires technical knowledge.

You cannot hope to spot an issue if you do not know GAAP. For instance, suppose a friend comes to you with the observation that his dog is shedding hair. He asks you if this is a problem. Is it? Unless you know something about dogs, and that particular breed, you will not be able to answer. The shedding might be perfectly normal if it happens every year and occurs in the spring. However, if this is a breed that normally does not shed hair at all, it may mean that the dog is sick. The point is that in order to spot a problem or an issue, you need to have specific knowledge in that area.

In the area of accounting, the specific knowledge you need to know is GAAP: the general principles, the available alternatives, the rules. Only then you can recognize if GAAP is not being followed, or advise a client how to account for something. Keep in mind that GAAP is not always legally required, or required by users of the financial information. In the latter case, you would be governed by providing the most useful information. This requires knowledge of what useful information is. It also helps to use common sense, as well, which is part of professional judgement.

TIP – Sometimes, if you cannot figure out the issues in the case, perhaps you need to reread the technical material assigned for that week or preceding weeks. After going over the material, reread the case again.

3.3 Understand the company's business.

What does the company do? How does it earn revenues? What costs must it incur? What are the business risks? All these questions and others must be understood. It is critical that you understand the business and the environment before you can offer any advice. Therefore, spend a few minutes figuring this out. This might include drawing quick timelines of the earnings process or diagrams of the business relationships; for example, who owns who.

TIP – If you do not understand the business, how do you ever hope to advice on how the business should be represented in the financial statements?

Realize that issues involve choices. Try to see if there is more than one way to look at a problem (i.e., from different perspectives). Look carefully at the preparer of the financial information (usually management) and the users of the information. Does good financial disclosure mean the same thing to management as it does to the shareholders? Often not. In the past, companies have often held the belief that the shareholders need only be told limited amounts of information. Furthermore, management might have a tendency to disclose only things that make the company and itself look good. Shareholders, on the other hand, may think that more information is better, especially information about risks and potential losses.

If you can see differing viewpoints, there is likely an issue. That is, one has a different idea of what the best accounting or presentation is than the other.

TIP – Look at the people in the case. Honestly attempt to put yourself in their shoes. This may sound silly, but you will find it to be one of the keys to successful case analysis. How would you feel about what is going on? How would you react? What would be important to you? After all, it could be you in the situation. If you see that the parties in the case may see things differently (remember the weather example), then there is a potential issue.

TIP – Most issues can be boiled down to four simple categories:

- **Recognition:** When should something be included in the financial statements?

- **Measurement:** How should the item be measured when it is initially recognized? How should it be measured going forward?

- **Presentation:** How should the item be presented in the financial statements?

- **Disclosure:** How much detail, if any, should be included in the notes?

Your issue identification statements should normally include at least one of recognition, measurement, presentation, or disclosure as the issue.

It is also important to note that the *CPA Canada Handbook* sections, in both IFRS and ASPE, are organized in the same categories noted above.

3.4 Keep in mind that some issues may be more important or less important.

It is essential to rank the issues and tackle the more important ones first.

An issue is generally more important if it involves large amounts, especially those that affect the calculation of net income (or some other sensitive number on the financial statements) or a sensitive financial ratio. This is a numeric application of the concept of materiality. Which numbers and ratios are more sensitive? That depends on the situation. Net income is almost always sensitive. That is, if net income changes by a material amount, it will usually affect user decisions. Other numbers and ratios are determined to be sensitive because the users will focus on them in that particular scenario. For instance, if the company has a loan, and part of the terms of the loan are that the working capital ratio be at least 1:1, then current assets and current liabilities would be sensitive numbers and anything that affects those numbers would potentially be an issue (e.g., classification of items between current and long term).

TIP – Rank issues and deal with the most relevant and material issues first.

TIP – Look for sensitive numbers or ratios in the case. If you see a potential reporting issue that affects these numbers, then you likely have an issue.

Step 2: Analyze the Issues

4. Develop relevant alternatives.

Only relevant alternatives should be looked at in your analysis. This is perhaps the most common mistake. Most students think in terms of right and wrong, black and white. When students are first introduced to case analysis, many are unable to look at an issue from more than one perspective. The tendency is to skip the assessment of the environment, skip the analysis, and give the "right" answer. Resist this urge!

Once enlightened that there may be more than one way of looking at the question, students often go to the other extreme and look for alternatives or different perspectives, even where none exist. Eventually, a happy medium is reached and they analyze only relevant alternatives. Be patient. Although to some of you, case analysis is intuitive, for many, this skill must be developed and it takes time.

What is a relevant alternative? A relevant alternative is one that is applicable given the reporting environment. It must make sense. There is no use suggesting an alternative if it is completely impractical or if it is impossible given the constraints. For instance, if GAAP is a constraint, do not suggest a non-GAAP approach as an alternative. It is not an option.

TIP – In order to train students to look at both sides of an issue or alternatives, we encourage them to start out an analysis with the words "on the one hand" and include "on the other hand" at some point later in the analysis. Otherwise the temptation to look at only one alternative is too great.

TIP – Looking at the issue from different perspectives is the key to identifying alternatives. Consideration should be given to the parties in the case. Imagine yourself as one party, and then as another. Would they see things differently?

TIP – Relevance is a function of the environment. Continue to ask yourself if your comment is pertinent to this specific case.

5. Consider qualitative and quantitative analysis.

Some cases lend themselves more to qualitative analysis, or quantitative analysis, or both. You must be sensitive to this. Cases with numbers in them may lend themselves more to quantitative analysis.

However, just because numbers are provided does not automatically mean that the information is relevant. Any calculations that you do must contribute something to the overall analysis. Do not just perform numerical analysis blindly.

Whether to present numbers in the case itself is an interesting dilemma that illustrates one of the shortcomings of case studies. In real life, you will always have numbers available to you—tons of them! You must choose which ones are relevant and then do the appropriate calculations to support or refute your analysis. You may choose to do many supporting calculations, or none at all. But usually, at a minimum, you should look at the numerical impact of the proposed alternative on net income and other sensitive financial statement numbers and ratios.

With cases, however, the authors of the cases cannot include all the numerical information that you would have access to in real life. They must choose which information to include in the case and, by doing so, it might be construed that they are making a statement that these numbers should be considered in the analysis. However, keep in mind that the numbers could be a "red herring" and also that time wasted on irrelevant number crunching is time that could have been spent on productive, qualitative analysis.

TIP – Just because numbers are included in the case does not mean that you should overemphasize quantitative analysis.

TIP – Keep focused by asking yourself the following questions: Will these calculations support or refute my analysis? Will they help in making the final decision? Will they provide additional information to help determine what the problem is and to arrive at a solution?

TIP – Try to strike a good balance between qualitative and quantitative analysis, assuming that quantitative analysis is warranted in the situation.

TIP – Remember that it is easy to get bogged down in numbers. If you are doing a case on a test, allocate some time for numerical analysis and stick to it closely. If you are not finished after the allotted time, then stop anyway, even if you know that the calculations are incorrect. In a test situation, it has been our experience that it is easier to go astray on quantitative analysis than qualitative. Also, once you go off on the wrong track, it's easy to get entrenched and waste valuable time. You become unable to pull yourself away from the calculations. Therefore, the best solution is to allot time and stick to it, no matter what!

TIP – Often some key numerical analysis opens up a deeper or more complex issue and might help explain certain things in the case. Issues may be disguised such that unless certain revealing analysis is performed, the issues will not reveal themselves and the resulting analysis may be shallow and without substance. To obtain a better answer, you may be expected to delve into a deeper level of analysis. This is difficult and comes with practice.

TIP – In most cases, a minimal quantitative analysis would include showing the impact of an alternative on key financial statement numbers and ratios.

While developing alternatives, and providing a balance of quantitative and qualitative analysis, consider the following additional points.

6. **Keep your analysis case-specific.**

Any discussions should make reference to the particulars of the case. Do not just regurgitate GAAP!

TIP – Try to start your sentences with the following: "In this case. . .". This will force you to focus on case-specific analysis.

TIP – Reread your analysis every couple of paragraphs. If any given paragraph or sentence does not have case-specific facts in it, reconsider your wording. One test to determine this is whether you could use that sentence or paragraph in another case analysis with the same issues without altering a word! If so, then you know that the sentence is generic and not specific to the case. Sometimes these types of sentences are unavoidable in that they are useful to set up a discussion. However, try to keep these to a minimum.

7. **Incorporate technical knowledge.**

You must indicate that you know the technical material (i.e., GAAP) by making reference to it in the analysis. This does not mean that you should be quoting reference sources or the *CPA Canada Handbook* by section number; however, you should be making specific reference to the key underlying principles.

TIP – Incorporate references to GAAP in your analysis; for example, revenues should be recognized when the goods are shipped because this represents the point at which the risks and rewards of ownership have passed. This illustrates your knowledge of GAAP in a case context.

8. **Do not blindly regurgitate case facts.**

Having discussed the importance of including case facts in the analysis, we will now stress the importance of not blindly regurgitating them, otherwise known as "dumping." The idea is to work selective case facts into your analysis, as opposed to just repeating case facts as a kind of introduction to the analysis.

There may only be a subtle distinction there, but the former results in a much tighter, more focused analysis. For instance, in a revenue recognition question, instead of taking up space by regurgitating the company's present policy word for word, you might say the following: "At present, the company's policy of recognizing revenue before shipment is a very aggressive policy since the risks and rewards of ownership generally do not pass until goods are shipped." Note how we have worked several items into that sentence. We have incorporated case-specific facts, displayed knowledge of GAAP, and made a judgemental statement by giving an opinion about the policy.

TIP – Try to make each sentence insightful, combining case facts and knowledge of GAAP with your analysis.

9. **Provide recommendations/conclusions.**

Recommendations should follow analysis of each individual issue. They should also be consistent with the overall financial reporting objective. For instance, if your role is the external chartered professional accountant providing information about a company to a bank, you may decide to offer advice that is conservative. Therefore, you would conclude, given alternatives, that revenues should be recognized later and costs recognized earlier.

Step 3: Assess the Big Picture

This is a critical part of a case analysis the students often overlook. The good students will find the issues, rank them and provide a satisfactory response. The excellent students will go back to the beginning and tie everything together. Was there an important overall factor that now needs to be reconsidered in light of your analysis? Based on your conclusions on each individual issue, what can you now conclude overall?

Conclusion

A blank case-writing framework is included at the end of this section. We encourage you to use it and personalize it to suit your writing style. Note that in this section, one approach to answering cases has been explored. As was stating at the beginning, there is no one way to answer a case. CPA Canada has information on its website that discusses the case approach. Students are encouraged to visit CPA Canada's site and explore their approach. The next chapter provides you with a sample case and then we end our case-writing analysis with a discussion on how to debrief a case.

A Walk-Through Example of Case Analysis

Let's look at the sample case of Bronwyn Boats. This case was chosen because it is of moderate length and difficulty so as not to either complicate or oversimplify case analysis. Read the case through to get a feel for what it involves.

Bronwyn Boats Limited

Bronwyn Boats Limited has been in the yacht-building business for the last 20 years. Bob, the owner, builds high-priced, customized boats that take on average two years to build. His reputation is such that Bob has never had to advertise. Rather, potential customers contact him, having heard of Bob through word of mouth. Bob has never had a dissatisfied customer and prides himself on high-quality workmanship.

In the past, Bob has always done his accounting on a cash basis; that is, expenses and revenues were recorded when cash changed hands. Also, Bob has never had to externally finance the boat construction since the business has always retained sufficient cash to internally finance the next boat to be built. Last year, however, Bob stripped all the excess cash from the business when he purchased his dream "cottage," a mansion on Lake Muskoka.

As a result of this, Bob found that he did not have enough cash to finance the construction of the next boat to be built and had to go to the bank for a loan. The bank told Bob that it would be happy to lend him the money as long as it could take his cottage as security. Also, the bank informed Bob that it wanted ASPE financial statements (accrual-based) and required that the debt to equity ratio not exceed 2:1. Bob reluctantly agreed to pledge his cottage as security and promised ASPE financial statements.

Bob was not very worried about repayment of the loan since he had just received some very large orders. As a matter of fact, he had to hire several assistants to help him get the boats built on time. Bob also rented an additional barn in the area so that he could work on the boats at the same time. The barn that he normally rented was not big enough to house all the boats. Bob also hired a secretary to help keep up with the filing and the paperwork.

For the first time, Bob had a customer who placed a large order and signed a written contract. Bob felt that the contract was required due to the size of the boat and the expensive special materials that had to be ordered. All other agreements were verbal. The key terms of the contract are as follows:

»	Purchase price:	$500,000
»	Delivery date:	June 30, 2022 (approximately two years)
»	Down payment:	$50,000 upfront; $100,000 on June 30, 2020; rest on delivery
»	Insurance:	Bob must cover the cost of insurance while the boat is being built. (Bob just included this as a cost of building the boat and passed it on to the customer anyway.)
»	Acceptance:	Purchaser can test the boat prior to making the last payment. Purchaser can refuse to accept it if not satisfied (within reason).

At December 31, 2020, Bob had completed about two-thirds of the work on the boat and was ahead of schedule. However, on the other boats, work was behind and they were only 10% complete.

Bob has come to you, his friend, a professional accountant, for advice on how to prepare the financial statements according to ASPE. Prepare a report to Bob regarding the financial accounting issues.

Cases Versus Exercise Questions

This case could have been a straightforward exercise question on revenue recognition. It could have simply asked the following question and not bothered to create a case scenario: When should revenues be recognized?

The above type of directed question asks for regurgitation of memorized facts (i.e., revenues should be recognized when the risks and rewards of ownership have passed from the seller to the buyer and when measurability and collectibility are reasonably assured).

Instead, the question is complicated by disguising it within a scenario or case. Firstly, revenue recognition must be identified as an issue and once identified, the question then becomes when should revenues be recognized in this scenario? The memorized knowledge must be applied to the facts of this specific situation. You must recall revenue recognition principles and ask yourself the following questions:

- What are the risks and rewards of owning/building a boat?

- When do they pass to the buyer?

- When is the earnings process substantially complete?

- Can revenues and costs be measured?

- What are the costs associated with these revenues?

- Are there any collectibility problems?

The trick here is to identify the issue and then to apply knowledge instead of merely regurgitating memorized information. That is the true test of whether you have absorbed and understood the material.

Tackling the Case

For most students, the initial challenge is being able to identify the issues. Then, once that is mastered, the challenge becomes how to analyze the issues in a meaningful way that will result in a reasonable recommendation or conclusion.

There are many different ways to approach case analysis, but most have a similar underlying structure that may be adapted in different situations. The material that follows is one method of case analysis.

Applying the Case Analysis

Assessing the Financial Reporting Landscape

With Bronwyn Boats Limited (BB), who are you? From what perspective will you be discussing the case? What is the reporting environment? Are there any constraints that will limit your analysis? These items will all affect your answer.

Your Role

It would appear that you are a professional accountant and friend of Bob's. How will that affect your analysis? As a professional accountant, you would want to ensure that your advice is professional, unbiased, and sound. However, you would want to make sure that any advice you gave would not leave you open to future lawsuits (e.g., if someone like the bank relied on the financial statements and suffered losses).

Identify the Users and User Needs

Who are the main users of the financial statements? What decisions (uses) will the users be making? An understanding of the users and their needs will help you further identify issues, and rank the importance of issues. (For example, some issues will affect users' decisions more so than others.)

In this case, it appears that the bank is going to be one of the main users. What does the bank want? Does that matter? Again, yes it does. The bank is going to be using the financial statements to assess financial performance of BB and compliance with the debt to equity ratio. Therefore, knowing that the bank would rely on the statements in order to advance funds to Bob, you would likely be conservative in your advice to Bob.

In addition, Bob will be using the financial statements in order to determine BB's compliance with the loan agreement. What does Bob want? Does this matter? Of course, it matters. He is the one who has hired you to do the job and is a friend of yours. Bob does not appear to know what he wants; however, he likely wants the statements to look good so that the bank will give him the financing he needs.

Would the fact that you are friends with Bob affect your answer? Perhaps. You might be tempted to give Bob the answer that he wants, although this would be weighed against your professional responsibility and the bank's reliance on the statements. What would you do in this situation?

Remember that, ideally, the objective of financial reporting is to provide information that is useful to users. The bank is the key user of these financial statements. It will use the statements to determine whether to lend money to Bob. The bank will, therefore, want reliable information using the accrual basis of accounting, since net income is presumably the best indicator of future profits and the ability of the business to pay off the loans.

In conclusion, you will likely be conservative in any advice given to Bob (assuming that you have decided as a professional not to let your friendship influence the advice given).

Constraints

Can you make any accounting recommendation that will maximize the debt to equity ratio? Are there any constraints on how the statements will have to be presented? Are the statements constrained by the recommendations of IFRS (Part I GAAP), ASPE (Part II GAAP), ASNPO (Part III GAAP), or some other reporting framework?

In this case, ASPE will be a constraint since the bank will want reliable information. Since ASPE is a constraint, you will have to follow the accrual basis of accounting.

Identifying the Issues

The overall issue is how to prepare the financial statements since this is the first time they will be presented on an accrual basis. Remember to keep focused on financial reporting issues.

Bob has a simple operation. He generates revenues by building boats and incurs costs in the process. He obtains the contracts upfront and then builds each boat according to the qualifications specified in the contracts. A key business risk is that customers can refuse the boat at the end if they are not satisfied. However, Bob has never had any problems.

Recall that accounting issues can be boiled down into four groups: recognition issues, measurement issues, presentation issues, and disclosure issues. Therefore, the issues here would appear to be fairly straightforward:

1. When to *recognize* revenues

2. When to *recognize* the costs associated with the revenues as expenses

Why are these issues? First, there appears to be some choice as to when revenues could be recognized. The earnings process is not a traditional one whereby goods are produced, sold, and then shipped. Here goods are sold first, then paid for, produced, and finally delivered. Second, there is the question of whether costs can be deferred or whether they should be recognized immediately since it is not clear which costs relate directly to the revenue-generating activity.

The preceding paragraph requires knowledge of ASPE/IFRS. If it is not clear to you, then read the chapter in your accounting textbook on revenue recognition, or better yet, refer to the *CPA Canada Handbook* section.

Assessing the Implications of the Issues

How do the accounting issues affect the financial statement users? For example, does the period that revenue is recognized affect the users? How about the expense recognition? If the issue identified has no implication, it is most likely not an issue!

In this situation, earlier recognition of revenue will positively affect the debt to equity ratio.

Analyzing the Issues

The analysis of issues requires developing reasonable alternatives that are within the identified constraints (ASPE, IFRS, etc.).

Revenue Recognition

Usually for revenue recognition questions, it is wise to go over the earnings process. Draw a timeline depicting the process. This helps to identify alternative points where revenues may be recognized. Keep in mind that Bob likely wants to recognize revenues earlier (which is a more aggressive treatment) in order to make the statements look better (by benefiting the debt to equity ratio). Also, remember that you would rather wait to recognize revenues since you are adopting a more conservative stance. Since ASPE is fairly flexible, there is some judgement in determining when the revenues may be recognized and there will be a more aggressive and a more conservative position.

You will likely present both positions to Bob since he will want to see the more aggressive stance and since you know that you will recommend the more conservative one. Alternatives that require waiting until cash is collected are not really relevant here since no information has been given to indicate that there are collection problems.

Make sure that your discussion is case-specific and try to incorporate knowledge of ASPE. For revenue recognition, the following concepts should be worked into the solution:

- Risks and rewards of ownership
- Performance complete
- Earnings process
- Measurable expenses and revenues
- Reasonably collectible revenues

Ensure that your recommendation is consistent with the overview. For instance, in this case, earlier recognition is justifiable, but probably not as early as Bob would like. Therefore, the recommendation will be to conclude on the conservative side.

Costs

The key issue is whether the costs should be expensed immediately or deferred or treated as inventory costs to be matched to revenue when recognized. Deferral of costs will presumably help maximize net income, and therefore, positively affect the debt to equity ratio. Key technical knowledge to be worked into the answer is as follows:

- Matching principle: matching costs with revenues
- Direct costs versus indirect costs
- Inventoriable costs versus period costs

Again, keep the discussion case-specific by making reference to the facts of the case whenever possible.

Your recommendation will depend on the conclusion for revenue recognition since the costs must be matched with the revenues. This is not so much of an issue if the revenues are recognized bit by bit, as the boats are completed, since all costs will be recognized in the period incurred anyway along with a corresponding portion of revenues. However, if the conclusion is to wait until the boats are delivered, this would be a bigger issue since costs that vary directly with the production could be deferred.

For both costs and revenues, the answer given is only one suggested solution. Numerous others would also be acceptable, including ones with different financial reporting objectives, different alternatives, and different conclusions. That is the beauty of case analysis. As long as the answer makes sense and the position taken is defensible within the context of the case, the answer is acceptable. Work toward a defensible position!

Suggested Solution

Assessing the Financial Reporting Landscape

User Analysis

Users	Uses	GAAP Consideration
Bob	Performance evaluation and obtain bank loan	ASPE
The bank	Evaluation, loan repayment, and covenant compliance	ASPE
Canada Revenue Agency	Tax determination	Income Tax Act

The main user of these financial statements will be the banker who will provide the financing to Bob. The banker will look for Bob's ability to repay the loan and whether he has a successful business. Bob will want to maximize revenues and profits. ASPE is a requirement since the bank has requested it. Bob must switch from cash-based to accrual accounting.

As a professional, you are aware that the statements will be used by the bank to make a decision as to whether a loan should be granted and, therefore, if there is exposure. If the statements are overly aggressive and make the business look better than it really is, there is the risk that the bank will rely on the information and later suffer a loss if Bob is unable to pay. If this is the case, there is the potential for the bank to sue you.

Therefore, although you would like to help Bob get the loan, you must consider your professional obligations. Any advice that you give will be conservative, emphasizing full disclosure such that the bank has the information that it needs.

The following is a suggested report you could prepare for Bob.

Bronwyn Boats Limited Report To BB Management Regarding The Financial Accounting Issues

Revenue Recognition

Issue

When should revenue be *recognized*?

Implication

The timing of revenue *recognition* will impact the debt to equity ratio and the financial performance of BB. Early recognition will be more favorable.

Analysis and Alternatives

In order to determine when the earnings process is substantially complete (critical event) and when the risks and rewards of ownership pass, the earnings process must first be identified as follows:

- Agreement/contract signed/down payment
- Supplies purchased
- Construction
- Deposits
- Boat completed
- Delivery
- Purchaser tries out boat to see if satisfied
- Final payment

Alternative 1—Recognize Revenues Earlier

- Earlier recognition would be supported by the following:

    ○ The agreement is made upfront (i.e., the boat is presold).

    ○ Some cash is received upfront as evidence of the contract.

- ○ Bob has never had a dissatisfied customer.

- ○ Bob is very experienced and is capable of finishing the boat once a customer is found.

- Therefore, we might conclude that the signing of the initial agreement is really the critical event in the earnings process. At this point, revenues are measurable, being agreed to, and costs are estimable, given that Bob has been in business a long time and knows what it will cost. Many of the boats use special materials, which Bob appears to order upfront anyway.

- There is no information that would indicate collectibility is not reasonably assured and it appears as though Bob has always been able to collect in the past.

Alternative 2—Recognize Later

- On the other hand, the following would support later recognition:

  - ○ Purchaser has the right to not purchase the boat if not satisfied (really, the contract is just conditional).

  - ○ Bob insures the boat up to this point, indicating that he still has the risks and rewards of ownership.

  - ○ The customer does not really indicate acceptance until the final payment.

- Measurement is not necessarily estimable since the sales price may change if Bob has to alter the original plan for the boat or the purchaser is not satisfied. Costs may also not be estimable since each boat is different and Bob will not know what the price of materials is or their availability until he actually purchases them.

Alternative 3—Recognize Revenues As the Boats Are Constructed

- This is more like a continuous earnings process since the earnings process is made up of many significant events.

  - ○ It makes sense to recognize revenues before delivery due to the binding contracts and Bob's past reputation.

  - ○ A percentage of revenues and profits could be recognized as costs are incurred.

  - ○ Total costs are estimable since Bob has had a great deal of experience.

- In this case, Bob would prefer earlier recognition to make the financial statements look better, especially since the bulk of the boats under construction are only 10% completed.

- The bank might not be so concerned that revenues are recognized later if it can see the contracts in order to assess cash flows. The problem is that most of the agreements are verbal and, therefore, the bank will not be able to verify them.

Recommendation

Given all of the above, it would seem more desirable to recognize the revenues earlier rather than later. Although this may be less conservative, it is justifiable due to Bob's track record. (He has been in the business for 20 years and has never had a dissatisfied customer.) Likely, revenues will be recognized bit by bit based on percentage complete, since full recognition prior to the boat being built might be considered to be too aggressive. There is still uncertainty as to whether Bob will indeed finish the boat and whether the customer will be satisfied.

Full note disclosure of the revenue recognition policy will be made so that the bank is aware of its impact.

Costs

Issue

When should the expenditures be *recognized* as an expense?

Implication

The timing of expense *recognition* will impact the debt to equity ratio and the financial performance of BB. Later recognition will be more favorable.

Analysis

Bob must decide which costs are period costs, which are deferrable, and which are inventoriable. If the costs are inventoriable, they will be recognized when the revenue is recognized, which is more desirable than showing them as period costs, especially in years with little or no revenues.

The following costs would clearly be inventoriable since they were incurred directly in the production of the boats: payroll for assistants working on the boats and materials used for the boats.

There are other costs that may be inventoriable. To back up a bit, the boats would be considered inventory and the *CPA Canada Handbook* states that inventory should be costed using absorption costing, which includes an applicable share of overhead. Although the latter is not clearly defined, Bob could easily consider capitalizing overhead costs that vary with production, such as rent and presumably heat, light, and power for the barn. If Bob was not constructing the boats, he would not incur these costs. Therefore, there is a direct relationship.

Other costs, such as the secretary's salary, are more clearly period costs and do not relate even indirectly to the construction of these specific boats.

Recommendation

In conclusion, it would be in Bob's best interest to treat any costs that vary with construction, such as direct labour, materials, and variable overhead (like the incremental rent on the barn), as inventoriable costs. These costs would be recognized on the income statement when revenues are recognized under the matching concept.

Earlier revenue recognition would require estimation of some of these costs, especially if the 10% complete boats were recognized as sales. This might pose some estimation problems. Recognition of revenues, bit by bit based on percentage complete, makes this a nonissue since the percentage of revenues recognized would be based only on actual costs incurred to date (as a percentage of total estimated costs).

Other Issues

- Regardless of when the revenues are recognized, Bob should consider providing the bank with information on the sales orders taken, as this will help the bank assess future cash flow.

Conclusion

This chapter walked you through a typical case and how you should analyze it after you write your answer. The next chapter details what happens after the case is written.

The case analysis was adapted from "The Case Primer" accompanying Kieso, Weygandt, Warfield, Young, and Wiecek: *Intermediate Accounting,* Ninth Canadian Edition (Toronto, ON: John Wiley & Sons Canada, Ltd., 2010).

4

What Happens After the Case Is Written: The Debrief

What's a Debrief and Why Do It?

Any student who has gone through the accounting professional designation process will tell you that debriefing the cases that you have written is just as important as writing the case to begin with. Why? Well let's look away from cases and think about how we learn accounting to begin with (or at least how we should be learning accounting!). We begin with fundamental accounting concepts, such as reading about what the accounting equation is all about, what journal entries are, and what debits and credits are. We then usually complete some technical questions in the area, come back to class, and check our answers against the suggested answers. Why does this result in a better learning experience? When you check your answers against the suggested solutions, you find out where you went wrong. If you are doing this the right way, you'll then go back and find out why you went wrong. By doing this, you are more likely to do the question better the next time.

Debriefing your cases after you have written them is just as important. In some ways, debriefing is even more important for cases than for problems. Recall that cases are not just about the numbers. The calculations are just one component of the case. You need to be able to identify the issues, generate and discuss alternatives, and provide recommendations.

So what is debriefing? Consider an elite sports athlete. They train hard physically during the off season, and before games they'll study the videos of opposing teams to try to get tips about how best to approach the upcoming game. They prepare beforehand so that when it comes to game time, they give themselves the best opportunity to perform well. Now, what do they do after the game? Well, the weekend athlete is more apt to shower and move on with their day. But athletes who want to be better will analyze their performance. They'll reflect on what they did well and what they could have improved upon. They'll reflect on the feedback given to them by their coaches: Could they have run faster? Was their accuracy off? In summary, they'll debrief their performance so that they can learn about what they did well and what they didn't do well so that next time, they'll hopefully be better. That's what we do when we debrief a case. Writing a case is only half the learning experience. The other half is learning about what we did right and where we can improve so that the next time we write a case, we can do a little better. Learning to do a good job at debriefing will improve your case writing over time.

Debriefing a Case

Debriefing can be performed in different ways by different individuals. Ideally, you should develop your own approach to debriefing that is suited to your unique learning style.

However, there are some common elements to debriefing a case. Debriefing is not merely reading the solution and rewriting your response. Although these could be considered as components of debriefing, they are of very little use in isolation. Rather, debriefing should be a much more proactive and reflective process, where you do the following.

- Understand the main issues in the case and where in the case the concepts are that give rise to these issues.

- Evaluate your performance to determine what was done well and what was done poorly.

- Determine actions to correct the identified weaknesses with your case-writing skills.

Although there is no single approach or standard methodology to debriefing a case, the following is a suggested approach:

1. Summarize your feelings about the case.

2. Read the solution and teaching notes.

3. Compare your response against the solution and identify any deficiencies.

    • Determine if the deficiencies are related to case-writing skills (e.g., reading, issue identification, ranking).

    • Determine if the deficiencies are related to technical skills (e.g., lack of GAAP or generally accepted auditing standards knowledge).

4. Rewrite and edit your response (e.g., using track changes) so that it is sufficient to meet the expectations.

5. Prepare and update your list of technical weaknesses and required corrective actions.

Your corrective actions should be a function of the weakness identified. For example, consider the following:

• Did not understand an issue?

   ◦ This could indicate that you lack the technical knowledge required to fully understand the issue in the case.

• Did not see an issue?

   ◦ This could suggest that the weakness lies in your reading skills. Go back and try to identify which words in the case are the triggers for the issue.

• Saw an issue but did not address it?

   ◦ This could be the result of various weaknesses. It could be a problem with ranking and time management. Try to develop and stick to a time budget. In addition, it could be a technical problem in that you did not have the technical knowledge to adequately deal with the issue.

• Identified an issue but incorrectly addressed it?

   ◦ This is more than likely a technical issue. Consider reviewing the technical material in your textbook or the *CPA Canada Handbook*.

As a general rule of thumb, the debriefing process should take between one to two times the time that it takes to write the case.

Experiment with a debriefing system that works for you but try to be consistent with it. Remember that the cases are often a prelude to the examinations. Consider creating an electronic list that tracks the issues and technical questions that you are exposed to and an honest assessment of how you did. This list can then be used as your starting point for your final examination preparation.

Conclusion

Good case writing takes practice and like anything else, you get better when you sit back and assess what you did. If you spend the time to determine where you had problems, not only will your case-writing skills improve, but you will also find that your overall examination-writing skills will improve.

Step 3: Assess the Big Picture

Conclusion

Step 2: Analyze the Issues

Step 1: Assess Reporting Framework

The Case-Writing Framework

Financial Statement Preparation and Analysis

Poirier Holdings

Mitch Poirier is considering an investment in a multiple-unit, residential building. The building has 30 units, which are all currently rented to tenants. Further details on the apartment building are provided in Exhibit I. If Mitch decides to proceed with the investment, he will purchase the apartment through a newly formed holding company (Poirier Holdings).

The apartment building, and required initial working capital, will require an investment of $1 million ($900,000 for the building and $100,000 for working capital). Mitch is contemplating various alternatives by which the apartment could be financed. The following four options are available:

1. Borrow $950,000 from the Bank of Calgary, with the remaining $50,000 being financed through personal equity. The loan would be repaid on a monthly basis over a 20-year term with an effective annual interest rate of 6%. The bank would require that the debt to equity ratio not exceed 3.75:1.

2. Borrow $750,000 in the form of an interest-only note from a local, wealthy businessperson, with the rest coming from personal equity. The loan would require annual interest payments, but no principal payments until the end of the 15-year term. Interest is payable at a rate of 7% per annum. The loan covenant stipulates that the debt to equity ratio not exceed 2.75:1.

3. Borrow $600,000 from the Bank of Edmonton, on a 15-year loan with an effective interest rate of 5%. The bank would require a debt to equity ratio of 5:1. An additional $300,000 could be obtained from issuing preferred shares to Joe Poirier, Mitch's brother. The preferred shares would be cumulative, with a 6% dividend yield. Mitch would finance the remaining $100,000 through common equity.

4. Allow Joe to become a shareholder, whereby both Mitch and Joe would invest $500,000 in common share, equity financing. In this scenario, there would be no long-term debt taken by the Poirier Holdings.

Mitch has contacted you, CPA, in order to provide assistance regarding the possible financing alternatives. Mitch would like you to assess the impact of four alternatives on the return on common equity, debt to equity ratio, and ability to pay dividends at the end of each year. Mitch will not proceed with the investment if the debt to equity covenant is likely to be violated, or the return on equity is below 10%. In addition, he would like to be able to draw out dividends of at least $20,000.

Required

Prepare a report that addresses the concerns of Mitch Poirier by assessing the four financing alternatives and recommending a source of financing. A pro forma statement of financial position under each alternative for the future periods should be included in your report.

| *Exhibit I* | Details Regarding the Operations of the Apartment Building |

- The apartment building has a total of 30 units, all of which are currently rented to tenants. The average rent of a unit is $550 per month.
- Historical financial statements reveal the following operating expenditures (they do not include any financing expenses):

	Last Year	Two Years Ago	Three Years Ago	Four Years Ago
Advertising	$ 1,500	$ 1,250	$ 2,250	$ 1,760
Depreciation	23,333	23,333	23,333	23,333
Bad debt expense	0	550	0	0
Insurance	4,450	4,450	4,250	4,250
Office	5,500	5,700	6,700	4,200
Professional fees	2,500	2,250	2,250	2,000
Property management fees	30,000	30,000	30,000	30,000
Repairs and maintenance	23,550	45,375	17,075	17,500
Wages and benefits	5,575	5,275	4,775	5,735
Total operating expenses	$96,408	$118,183	$90,633	$88,778

- Historically turnover is about one tenant per year. When someone leaves, it normally takes about three months to replace the tenant, during which the unit is vacant.
- The nature of the business is such that most revenues and expenses are paid for on a cash basis. Accordingly, there are very few accounts receivable or accounts payable at year end. Therefore, Mitch has said that it is safe to assume that all revenues are received when earned and all expenses paid when incurred.
- The building is expected to have a useful life of 30 years, with a residual value of $100,000.
- The working capital should not decrease below $100,000. This amount is required in order to pay for emergency repairs, and so on.
- Property management fees are expected to increase in the future by $5,000 over their four-year average.
- Assume that Poirier Holdings has a tax rate of 30%.

Prodigy Systems Ltd.

An Introduction to Financial Statement Information

Prodigy Systems Ltd (PSL) was created by Jesse Gemmel, a third-year undergraduate business student. Unable to find work in a business setting, Jesse started up his own business during the summer months. Jesse was able to secure the services of his uncle, Pierre Chalut, to incorporate the company.

Prior to attending university, Jesse was involved in various athletic activities. In addition, Jesse has taken many kinesiology courses during his undergraduate studies. Jesse has always had a passion for fitness and athletics and spends more time in the gym than in class! Therefore, Jesse is trying to turn his passion into his business by incorporating PSL with the purpose of developing and distributing fitness-related products.

PSL began operations in April 2020, and continued until the end of August 2020, at which point Jesse had to return to university to complete his degree. Jesse invested $2,500 of his savings into PSL, and also took out a loan of $1,000 from his father.

During its first summer of operations, PSL designed and sold DVDs for beginners. Jesse recorded the videos with the help of a friend, a professional videographer, who was paid $750 by PSL. The videos focus on basic stretches, workouts, and diet tips. The DVD cover was designed by a professional in the community for $500. Jesse purchased 250 high-quality DVDs for $5 each, including the jewel case, and made copies of his video on his personal computer and packaged the videos to be ready for sale. PSL incurred $200 in printing costs for the front and back covers. The business has a credit card it used to pay for certain expenses, but the credit card had no balance at the end of September.

A total of $2,000 was used to purchase new gym equipment for the video shoots. The equipment can be used for at least another three years to produce videos. In addition, PSL spent an additional $400 on the appropriate software to copy the videos.

Jesse promoted the video at local gyms, and virally on YouTube and Facebook. During the course of the summer months, PSL sold all 250 copies of the DVD for $30 each. A local gym has purchased 100 copies of the DVD to give away to its members, but promised to pay PSL in December 2020.

It is now September 1, 2020, and Jesse is reflecting upon the first five months of PSL's operations. Given that the new semester is about to begin, and tuition payments are coming due, Jesse would like to know how PSL performed. He is fairly excited because PSL sold $7,500 worth of DVDs, which he believes could be used to cover his tuition and book costs. As of today, Jesse received $1,500 from PSL for his services, which he paid himself at the end of August.

Required

As Jesse's best friend, who is majoring in accounting, you have been asked to prepare a report on PSL's financial performance over the past five months. Specifically, Jesse has asked you to consider the following:

(a) Prepare PSL's balance sheet and income statement.

(b) Given that PSL is a corporation, how could Jesse receive funds from the corporation?

(c) What does the accounting information say about Jesse's management abilities? If he did not start up PSL, he could have found a summer job at a grocery store and earned $3,000.

(d) PSL is applying for a bank loan in the near future to expand operations and develop a new video. How can the accounting information be used by the bank to decide whether credit should be provided to PSL? The bank has said that it will only provide a loan if the business has twice as much equity than debt.

(e) Jesse would like to know if the bank will accept the financial statements as prepared by PSL, or whether the statement will need to be audited. What benefit does an audit provide to the bank?

Sky Watchers Ltd.

Sky Watchers Ltd. (SWL) is a manufacturer of telescopes and binoculars, offering products to amateurs and professionals. The company has experienced significant growth in the past five years due to an increase in the popularity of star gazing, combined with an effective branding campaign and enhanced distribution network.

The company has applied to the Bank of Winnipeg for a $1-million long-term loan in order to finance further expansion plans. Specifically, the funds would be used to purchase additional capital assets.

SWL's application and financial statements have been provided to Peter Sparks, a newly hired junior analyst with the Bank of Winnipeg. Peter has been asked by his supervisor, Maria Simms, to conduct a preliminary review of SWL's financial statements and determine whether SWL should proceed further into a more detailed analysis. Maria has asked Peter to document his recommendation and supporting analysis in a report that will be maintained in SWL's file.

MARIA: "SWL has provided us with a copy of their most recent statement of financial position and income statement (Exhibit I). I know that this may not be enough to make the final decision, but it should be more than enough for you to get started."

PETER: "Yes, I can obtain much information from these two statements."

MARIA: "Okay, that's great. I took a quick look at the statement of financial position and am wondering what has caused the change in cash. Cash is needed to pay back the loan. Although I haven't done any rigorous analysis, it is a bit concerning to see the cash decline by such a large amount."

PETER: "I can definitely look into the decrease in cash."

MARIA: "It may also be useful to give some thought to what the statement of financial position may look like if the loan is approved. Historical statements are fine, but they will not be able to provide you with this information. Additional information on the use of the loan is provided in Exhibit II."

PETER: "That is a great point. I will take this into consideration."

MARIA: "Alright. Let me know if I can be of any further assistance. I look forward to reading your report. If you recommend to proceed with future due diligence, can you prepare a list of additional information that would be useful in making our final decision?"

PETER: "Yes, I can most certainly do that. I will get started right away."

Peter is excited about his first assignment and wants to impress Maria. Peter begins to conduct some preliminary research by searching the bank's database for industry comparables. Peter has located various industry ratios that can be used as a benchmark (Exhibit III).

Required

Assume the role of Peter and prepare the report.

Exhibit 1 | Financial Statements

Sky Watchers Ltd.
Statement of Financial Position

As at December 31	2020	2019
Assets		
Current		
Cash	$ 35,359	$ 134,550
Marketable securities	145,780	457,206
Accounts receivable	223,450	174,930
Inventory	425,770	355,790
Prepaid expenses	17,500	19,500
	847,859	1,141,976
Property, plant, and equipment, net	2,956,950	2,492,655
	3,804,809	3,634,631
Liabilities and shareholders' equity		
Current		
Accounts payable	294,305	95,700
Accrued and other liabilities	237,595	244,760
Current portion of long-term debt	375,900	345,900
	907,800	686,360
Long-term debt	1,280,330	1,601,500
Common shares (50,000 outstanding)	595,817	595,817
Retained earnings	1,020,862	750,953
	1,616,679	1,346,771
	$3,804,809	$3,634,631

| Exhibit I | Financial Statements (Continued) |

Sky Watchers Ltd.
Income Statement

For the year ended December 31	2020	2019
Sales	$2,975,990	$2,575,990
Cost of sales	1,368,955	1,184,955
Gross profit	1,607,035	1,391,035
Expenses		
Amortization	155,490	125,490
General and administrative	134,500	102,800
Marketing and sales	175,680	155,600
Interest expense	76,820	96,090
Office expense	295,980	255,000
Wages and benefits, administration	315,000	315,000
Total operating expenses	1,153,470	1,049,980
Operating income	453,565	341,055
Gain (losses) on marketable securities	25,475	9,800
Impairment loss on capital assets	0	0
Income (loss) before taxes	479,040	350,855
Provision for (benefit from) income taxes	134,131	98,239
Net income	344,909	252,615
Opening balance—retained earnings	750,953	573,338
Net income	344,909	252,615
Dividends	75,000	75,000
Closing balance—retained earnings	$1,020,862	$ 750,953

| Exhibit II | Information About the Use of the Loan |

- The loan will be used to purchase $1 million in additional capital assets. The additional assets will result in an increase in revenues of 20%.
- The loan will bear interest at 6%. Principal payments of $200,000 per annum will be required.
- The company will withhold any dividend payment during the foreseeable future in order to support the debt-to-equity ratio.
- The capital assets are expected to have a useful life of 15 years with no residual value.

- All other fixed expenses are expected to remain consistent.
- The existing loan will require a principal payment of approximately $375,900 during the upcoming fiscal year. The payment for the following fiscal year is expected to be $300,000.
- Accounts receivable, inventory, prepaid expense, and accounts payable will all increase by 40% as a result of the increased sales.
- The marketable securities will be converted to cash at the beginning of the year.

Exhibit III	Industry Benchmark Ratios

	Ratio	Industry Average
	Profitability	**2020**
1	Return on equity	15.0%
2	Return on assets	8.0%
3	Financial leverage percentage	7.0%
4	Earnings per share	$ 4.40
5	Quality of income	75.0%
6	Profit margin	10.0%
7	Fixed asset turnover	2.00
	Tests of liquidity	
8	Cash ratio	7.0%
9	Current ratio	1.00
10	Quick ratio	0.75
11	Receivable turnover	13.00
12	Average days in accounts receivable	28.08
13	Payable turnover	19.00
14	Average days in accounts payable	19.21
15	Inventory turnover	6.50
16	Average days in inventory	56.15
	Solvency and equity position	
17	Times interest earned	5.40
18	Cash coverage	6.30
19	Debt to equity ratio	1.35
	Miscellaneous	
20	Book value per share	$29.00

Shutterbug

Contributed by
Ruth Ann Strickland
King's University College, Western University
London, Ontario

James Ling had loved photography ever since he received his first camera as a gift from his grandmother for his fourth birthday. When he was young, he took pictures of everything that interested him, and he stored them in virtual photo albums that he enjoyed looking at. He continually challenged himself to take better and better pictures. At one point, he took 100 pictures of lily pads and made an entire exhibit of them. He spent so much time taking pictures that soon his nickname became Shutterbug. It was a name that he loved.

By the time James was in his final year of university, he was asked to take pictures at so many events that he decided to start a business and he began charging for his services. On July 1, 2018, James officially launched his business, which he immediately named Shutterbug. He has now graduated and runs Shutterbug on a full-time basis. Information about the business is in Exhibit I.

It is now the beginning of July 2020, and James would like to know how Shutterbug has done during its second fiscal year. He knows that he has been busy, and he knows that he has had fun, but he also wants to know about the financial success of his business so that he can make some important decisions about whether to expand during the upcoming fiscal year. He would also like to know how much he will have to pay in tax, at a rate of 30%. Throughout the year, James withdrew a personal salary of $2,500 per month.

James is eager to see the financial results of the year ended June 30, 2020, his second year of business. He has provided you with a trial balance of his accounts at June 30, 2019 (Exhibit II) and has asked you to prepare journal entries for all transactions, as well as any adjusting or closing entries, for the year ended June 30, 2020. He would also like you to prepare T accounts and financial statements. Please do your very best work so that James will be impressed and will ask you to prepare his financial statements again next year.

Required

Prepare:

- **(a)** all journal entries, including closing entries
- **(b)** a T account work sheet for all of the transactions
- **(c)** a statement of income
- **(d)** a statement of financial position
- **(e)** a memo to James indicating how much he will have to pay in tax

Exhibit I **Information on Shutterbug**

Operating Expenses

James operates Shutterbug out of his home and allocates 30% of the total space to his business. He pays rent on the last day of each month for the following month. On January 1, 2020, his rent increased from a total of $1,400 to a total of $1,500 per month.

One part-time employee, Karen, helps James during busy periods. Karen earns $16 per hour and was paid cash for 1,400 hours that she worked during fiscal 2020. Prior to year end, she worked an additional 11 hours that had not yet been paid. Karen also receives a 10% commission on sales that she personally makes. During fiscal 2020, Karen was personally responsible for 20% of Shutterbug's gross photography sales. (Gross photography sales were $94,500. Commissions are paid on the last day of each fiscal year.)

Photography supplies were purchased on account during fiscal 2020 for $1,750. (All accounts payable for operating expenses are paid at the end of the current month. Use a separate journal entry.) At the end of June, $400 of supplies were still on hand that had not yet been used. Shutterbug has a telephone service plan that costs $80 every month for telephone service. On January 1, 2018, James had purchased a 12-month insurance policy. When it expired, he paid for another 24 months and received a 10% discount off the original price.

Because this was a highly mobile business, a major expense for James was operating costs for his car. During fiscal 2020, James drove his car 40,000 km. He kept careful records of all costs and determined that the operating expenses for the car totaled $0.15 per kilometer. These costs were paid in cash as incurred. All of the mileage driven was for business purposes. James has a separate vehicle that he uses for personal purposes.

On September 15, 2019, James paid $3,600 for 12 months of advertising in a local photography magazine. The ads were scheduled to start on October 1, 2019.

Property, Plant, and Equipment

On July 1, 2018, James had paid $20,000 for a Smart Car that was specially designed for his business. He expects to use this car for a total of five years and calculates depreciation based on an expected 160,000 total kilometers.

When James started Shutterbug he already owned $6,000 worth of camera equipment that he contributed for exclusive use by the business. Depreciation for this equipment was done on a straight-line basis. On April 28, 2020, James traded this equipment in on some newer equipment offered by a local vendor. Because of the excellent condition of James's equipment, the vendor gave a trade-in allowance of $4,000, which was the fair value of the equipment. The vendor also extended delayed payment terms by having James sign a $9,000, 4%, 12-month note payable. (All accounts payable for operating expenses are paid at the end of the current month. Use a separate journal entry.) Due to possible rapid obsolescence, James decided to use double declining-balance depreciation for the new equipment, which has a useful life of 10 years and an expected residual value of $3,000. As a condition of the note, the vendor requires a copy of James's fiscal 2020 financial statements once they

are completed and requires that James not incur any other debt until the note is repaid. An additional requirement is to maintain a current ratio of at least 2:1.

Shutterbug also has $4,000 worth of computer equipment that is being depreciated on a declining-balance method. For this equipment, there is $300 residual value expected at the end of its useful life.

Intangible Assets

On July 1, 2018, James had paid $5,000 to register the name Shutterbug as a trade name that has an indefinite life. On the same day, he had also paid $8,000 for a five-year patent to protect his unique photography process. On June 30, 2020, the patent had a fair value of $3,000.

Photography Revenue

Many of Shutterbug's customers are university students who pay by cash or credit card for services as they are received. Students who pay cash receive a 3% discount. Students who pay by credit card do not receive a discount. James pays a 2% service fee to the bank for all credit card transactions. For accounting purposes, credit card purchases are treated as cash.

James also does work for schools and for businesses. He calls these "corporate" customers and allows them to pay later, with generous credit terms of 3/30, net 60. Corporate customers never pay with credit cards.

Shutterbug's gross sales for photography services in fiscal 2020 were $94,500. Of these sales, 78% were to corporate customers; 65% of the corporate customers paid within the discount period. For the remaining sales, 25% were in cash.

All unearned revenue from fiscal 2019 was earned during July 2019. (No discounts or credit card fees applied to this revenue.) All accounts receivable were collected in the month following the sale, except as noted in Exhibit III.

Camera Sales

James's customers often commented on his great skill and the wonderful pictures he took. When they asked him his secret, he said it took years of practice and great equipment. He identified a camera he really liked that sold at a retail price of $450, and he began selling them to interested customers. He found that they were particularly popular as Christmas and Valentine's Day gifts.

James was able to purchase the camera he liked from CamPro for $325 each if he ordered at least 25 at a time. Otherwise, he paid $350 per camera. Credit terms from CamPro were 2/15, net 60. Shipping was FOB shipping point and was paid by the correct party. The shipping cost was $4 per camera for orders under 40 cameras and a flat rate of $160 on orders of 40 or more. See Exhibit I for a list of camera purchases.

Five of the cameras from the November 15 purchase had defective lenses. James had already paid for these cameras before he realized that they were damaged. He called the supplier and arranged to

Exhibit I **Information on Shutterbug (Continued)**

return them and to get a full refund for all of his costs. The supplier also agreed to pay for the shipping cost for returning the cameras.

In December 2019, James needed 10 extra cameras for a customer who wanted them for holiday gifts. CamPro was unable to provide them quickly enough, so James had to order them from SnapShots, a supplier in the United States, at a cost of C$400 each. SnapShots did not offer any credit terms and shipped overnight at a cost of C$10 per camera. Duty of 8% was also charged on gross purchase price. Shipping terms were FOB destination. In March 2020,

James ordered five more cameras from SnapShots for the same customer, under the same terms as the previous order.

James sold a total of 100 cameras during fiscal 2020, and had 15 in ending inventory at the end of the year. Most of the cameras sold at the regular selling price of $450; however, the customer who wanted the special-order cameras from SnapShots paid $500 for each of them. She had paid for them and had received them prior to the end of fiscal 2020. Periodic inventory with a FIFO cost flow was used for the rest of the cameras. All camera sales were for cash at the time of the sale.

Exhibit II **Financial Statements**

Shutterbug Trial Balance
June 30, 2020

	Debit	Credit
Cash	$26,200	
Accounts receivable	1,044	
Allowance for doubtful accounts		$ 150
Prepaid rent	420	
Prepaid insurance	600	
Supplies	200	
Inventory	7,080	
Camera equipment	6,000	
Accumulated depreciation—camera equipment		1,500
Vehicle	20,000	
Accumulated depreciation—vehicle		3,750
Computer equipment (Note 1)	4,000	
Accumulated depreciation-computer equipment		2,000
Patent, net (Note 2)	6,400	
Trade name	5,000	
Accounts payable (Note 3)		7,080
Unearned revenue		600
Wages payable		300
J. Ling, Capital		61,564
	$76,944	$76,944

Note 1. Acquired on July 1, 2018.
Note 2. Includes $1,600 of accumulated amortization.
Note 3. All accounts payable relate to inventory purchases.

| Exhibit III | Photography Sales and Collections—Corporate Customers |

August 1, 2019	James received a cheque in the mail from a business whose account had been written off in January 2018. The cheque was for 30% of the $4,000 that had been written off.
September 5, 2019	The London High School called to complain that some of the pictures James had taken for a school function were not the right type. The school had already paid its bill, so James sent them a $200 refund.
December 12, 2019	Stanley Company declared bankruptcy, and James decided to write off its outstanding balance of $1,700.
February 10, 2020	The Business Company, a corporate customer, called to ask that their $2,000 outstanding account be converted to a note. James agreed to convert the account receivable to a 12%, three-month note receivable. The note was paid in full on May 9, 2020.
March 9, 2020	Sterling Corporation called to ask James if he would be available to take pictures at a family fun day they were planning for August 2020. James agreed to take the pictures, and told Sterling the cost would be $1,500. Sterling gave James a deposit of $500 and will pay the balance when the services are performed. This $500 was not included in the gross sales figure for the year.
June 30, 2020	At the end of the fiscal year, the balance in Accounts Receivable was $3,150. James believes that 4% of outstanding accounts receivable at the end of the year will not be collectible.

| Exhibit IV | Camera Purchases |

Purchase #	# of Cameras	Date Shipped	Date Delivered	Date Paid
1	20	June 20, 2019	July 2, 2019	July 10, 2019
2	45	Nov. 15, 2019	Nov. 28, 2019	Nov. 29, 2019
3	10	Dec. 10, 2019	Dec. 12, 2019	Dec. 15, 2019
4	30	Feb. 1, 2020	Feb. 12, 2020	Feb. 20, 2020
5	5	Mar. 28, 2020	Mar. 30, 2020	Apr. 1, 2020
6	10	June 25, 2020	July 5, 2020	July 6, 2020

The London Tour Company

Contributed by
Ruth Ann Strickland
King's University College, Western University
London, Ontario

The London Tour Company (LTC) organizes tours of scenic and historic places of interest for visitors and new residents of London, Ontario. The company was started by Andrew Zhang after he moved to London from Chongqing, China. It has an April 30 year end and uses ASPE. After a successful first year, Andrew is eager to find out how his business did in May 2020, the first month of his second year. He has asked you to create financial statements and has also informed you that the bank will require copies of the statements as part of the conditions of a bank loan obtained in May 2020.

Andrew has provided you with a trial balance at April 30, 2020 (Exhibit I). Additional information about LTC is found in Exhibit II.

Andrew has asked you to prepare the financial statements for May 2020 for his own use and for use by his bank. He would like you to provide a copy of all of your T accounts so that he can get a good idea of how his business is doing. He has reminded you that his income tax rate is 30%. ASPE was used for the first year of business, but now Andrew wonders if this is still appropriate as the business grows and adds external users. Please provide your very best work, so that Andrew will be impressed and will ask you to do his financial statements again next month.

Required

Prepare the financial statements according to Andrew's instructions.

Exhibit I	Trial Balance

London Tour Company Trial Balance April 30, 2020

	Debit	Credit
Cash	$18,200	
Accounts receivable	6,630	
Supplies	5,240	
Prepaid insurance	750	
Furniture	5,000	
Accumulated depreciation—furniture		$ 1,000
Equipment	8,000	
Accumulated depreciation—equipment		4,000
Accounts payable		6,400
Unearned service revenue		1,900
Capital shares, A. Zhang		20,000
Retained earnings		10,520
	$43,820	$43,820

Exhibit II	Additional Information

Operating Expenses

Andrew has two tour guides who work for him. Each guide is paid $500 wages per week for working five days, Monday through Friday. Payment is made on Friday each week. During May, Andrew paid $3,600 for wages. Assume that May 31 was on a Tuesday and that the employees have worked for two days for which they have not yet been paid.

Supplies were purchased on account on May 10 for $800. A 12-month insurance policy had been purchased for $1,800 on September 30, 2019, Andrew pays $1,000 cash each month for office rent. In May 2020, he made an additional payment of $800 to rent extra space for June 2020. He knew that he would need extra space because of the large number of tourists who would be in London in June.

Andrew pays $50 per month for basic telephone services. This covers up to 600 minutes per month of cell phone use. Extra charges of $0.05 per minute apply if Andrew uses more minutes. On June 2, Andrew received the May invoice for 700 minutes. Payment is due on June 28.

On May 10, Andrew paid the accounts payable balance from April 30. On that day, he also withdrew a personal salary of $5,000 from the business. At the end of May, $1,200 of unused supplies were still on hand.

Operating Revenue

Andrew charges $100 per person for each tour. This includes a full day of travel around London, lunch at a very nice restaurant, and stops at two museums. Most customers pay in cash on the day of the trip; however, some groups arrange tours and are given up to 30 days after the tour to pay. During May, 125 individuals paid cash for tours and four groups arranged tours of 30 people each. One of the groups

had not yet paid by the end of May. All customers who owe London Tour Company money at the end of each month pay in full during the following month.

Some groups request special tours that they pay for in advance. On May 25, one group paid cash for a special tour for 50 people at $150 each. The tour will take place on June 7. All revenue that is not earned by the end of each month is earned in the following month.

Capital Assets

Office furniture had been purchased on May 1, 2019, when Andrew first started his business. The furniture is expected to have a residual value of $500, and double declining-balance is used for depreciation.

Andrew uses special double-decker tour buses to conduct his tours. In the past, he always rented busses, but on May 1, 2020, he decided to purchase his own bus at a cost of $35,000. An additional $5,000 was paid to the dealer for customization of the bus. Andrew paid $10,000 cash and signed a one-year 4% note payable for the rest of the cost. Interest and principal are due on April 30, 2021. As a condition of the loan, the bank requires monthly financial statements. LTC will use the bus for five years and will drive it an expected 175,000 km. In May 2020, it was driven 3,000 km. The bus has a residual value of $5,000. Depreciation is based on the number of kilometers driven.

LTC also uses video equipment to record the tours it conducts. Andrew gives customers a copy of the video at the end of the tour so that they can remember their fun day. On May 1, Andrew traded in his old equipment for new, better equipment worth $16,000. The dealer allowed a trade-in value of $6,000 for the old equipment, which was its fair value. The balance of the purchase price was paid in cash. The new equipment will be depreciated on a straight-line basis over five years and has an expected residual value of $1,000.

The Louisiana Grill

The Louisiana Grill (TLG) is a restaurant in Toronto. TLG is a regional restaurant created and operated by Alex Ventresca, a former football player from New Orleans. The company was established in 2016 and has experienced steady revenue growth since inception. The restaurant's success can be attributed to its variety of dishes.

Currently, there is only one restaurant, which is located in downtown Toronto. Alex is looking to expand the business by opening another restaurant in Mississauga, Ontario. Alex estimates that it will cost upward of $1 million to open a new location. Alex has approached Diane Drapeau, a managing partner at a venture capital firm, about the potential opportunity. Alex has proposed two alternatives to finance the new restaurant:

1. Extend credit to the business: Lend TLG $1 million in debt financing. The bond would be secured by the building and equipment purchased with the funds. Alex would like the interest to accrue at 5% per annum, with the loan repayable with blended monthly payments over a five-year term. In exchange for the low interest rate, the bond will be convertible in common shares at the rate of nine common shares per $1,000.

2. Purchase an ownership interest: Purchase 10,000 shares in the business (50% interest). The funds will be used to start up the new location. Depending on the purchase price, any deficiency in the funds required will be obtained through traditional bank financing.

Of course, Alex is aware of the fact that Diane can choose neither of the options and walk away from the opportunity.

In order to help make a decision, Alex has provided Diane with TLG's historical income statements and statements of financial position since inception (Exhibit I). In addition, Diane had a long discussion with Alex. (Notes from the meeting are in Exhibit II.)

Diane has asked you, a newly hired junior analyst, to prepare a preliminary report that provides a recommended course of action. Your report should be based on a thorough analysis of TLG's historical financial performance. As it is one of your first assignments, Diane reminds you that a well-prepared report of this nature should include, at minimum, the following:

- The preparation and analysis of the statement of cash flows for the five-year period
- An analysis of financial ratios and common-sized financial statements
- A preliminary valuation of the common shares (note that a common share earnings multiple for similar franchise restaurants ranges from 4 to 6 times normalized net income)
- Based on the estimated share value, the value of the conversion feature over the life of the bond
- A comparison of the rate of return on the equity versus debt investment.

Required

Prepare the report for Diane. For simplicity, ignore any financial reporting issues related to the bifurcation of the debt and equity components of the convertible bond.

| Exhibit 1 | Financial Statements |

The Louisiana GRILL
Statements of Financial Position
for the Year Ended December 31

Assets	2016	2017	2018	2019	2020
Current assets					
Cash and cash equivalents	$ 0	$ 0	$ 53,297	$ 76,969	$ 199,051
Accounts receivable	71,584	110,272	67,042	91,175	122,647
Inventory	107,664	129,680	76,408	114,630	139,310
Prepaid expenses	20,419	17,414	11,558	16,240	26,387
Total current assets	$ 199,667	$ 257,366	$ 208,305	$ 299,014	$ 487,395
Fixed assets (net)					
Land	$ 165,000	$ 165,000	$ 165,000	$ 165,000	$ 165,000
Building	618,213	556,391	500,752	450,677	405,609
Computer and equipment	46,750	32,725	22,908	16,035	11,225
Furniture, fixtures, and equipment	94,500	75,600	60,480	48,384	38,707
Kitchen equipment	233,750	163,625	114,538	80,176	56,123
Total fixed assets	1,158,213	993,341	863,678	760,272	676,664
Total assets	$1,357,878	$1,250,707	$1,071,983	$1,059,286	$1,164,059
Liabilities					
Current liabilities					
Bank indebtedness	$ 100,900	$ 175,000	$ 0	$ 0	$ 0
Deferred revenue	186,789	190,949	202,075	205,601	219,276
Payables and accruals	154,631	97,325	122,885	176,544	177,636
Income taxes payable	17,071	15,706	35,070	35,289	69,708
Total current liabilities	$ 459,391	$ 478,980	$ 360,030	$ 417,434	$ 466,620
Long-term debt					
Long-term debt	860,204	710,623	550,570	379,315	196,071
Total liabilities	$1,319,595	$1,189,603	$ 910,600	$ 796,749	$ 662,691
Shareholders' equity					
Capital stock (10,000 shares issued)	$ 10,000	$ 10,000	$ 10,000	$ 10,000	$ 10,000
Retained earnings	28,283	51,105	151,383	252,537	491,368
Total shareholders' equity	38,283	61,105	161,383	262,537	501,368
Total liabilities and shareholders' equity	$1,357,878	$1,250,707	$1,071,983	$1,059,286	$1,164,059

Exhibit I | **Financial Statements (Continued)**

The Louisiana GRILL
Statements of Income
for the Year Ended December 31

	2016	2017	2018	2019	2020
Sales	$3,579,208	$3,675,730	$3,943,656	$3,964,108	$4,229,192
Cost of sales	2,290,693	2,315,710	2,464,785	2,497,388	2,579,807
Gross profit	$1,288,515	$1,360,020	$1,478,871	$1,466,720	$1,649,385
Expenses					
Administrative	$ 209,117	$ 214,608	$ 293,408	$ 302,173	$ 318,119
Advertising	127,368	127,083	131,906	155,140	148,005
Depreciation and amortization	92,538	164,871	129,664	103,405	83,608
Computer	3,074	5,464	6,944	4,687	6,844
Credit card	53,688	55,136	59,155	59,462	63,438
Bad debts	716	0	2,011	0	613
Equipment rental	25,269	12,271	1,456	1,726	2,206
Freight	16,035	16,210	17,253	17,482	18,059
Insurance	13,113	10,022	12,300	13,079	13,855
Interest and bank charges	5,021	4,248	3,421	2,536	1,588
Interest on long-term debt	63,556	53,770	43,299	32,095	20,108
Janitorial supplies	40,425	48,373	33,565	43,483	39,084
Office and restaurant supplies	144,962	132,242	133,784	124,079	129,500
Professional fees	3,909	4,186	4,299	4,683	4,481
Repairs and maintenance	74,152	75,952	48,455	49,564	47,560
Royalty fees	125,272	128,651	138,028	138,744	148,022
Taxes and licences	1,682	1,682	1,682	1,682	1,682
Telephone	9,338	9,919	10,248	10,239	10,195
Travel	10,319	8,031	6,475	3,957	9,113
Utilities	92,058	115,562	135,738	129,403	145,347
Wages and benefits	95,000	95,000	95,000	95,000	95,000
	$1,206,612	$1,283,281	$1,308,091	$1,292,619	$1,306,427
Other income	3,450	1,788	4,569	2,341	5,580
Earnings before income taxes	85,354	78,528	175,349	176,443	348,538
Provision for income taxes	17,071	15,706	35,070	35,289	69,708
Net income	68,283	62,822	140,279	141,154	278,830
Retained earnings, beginning	0	28,283	51,105	151,383	252,537
Net income	68,283	62,822	140,279	141,154	278,830
Dividend	40,000	40,000	40,000	40,000	40,000
Retained earnings, end	$ 28,283	$ 51,105	$ 151,383	$ 252,537	$ 491,368

Exhibit II | Notes from the Meeting with Alex

Historical Financial Results – Toronto Operations

- The menu of dishes was created by a celebrity chef, who regularly visits the restaurant. The chef is paid a royalty fee of 3.5% of gross revenue.

- The original cost of the current assets are as follows:

    Fixed assets (net)
Land	$165,000
Building	650,750
Computer and equipment	55,000
Furniture, fixtures, and equipment	105,000
Kitchen equipment	275,000

- The capital assets are depreciated in the same manner as their capital cost allowance (CCA). The following CCA rates are used: building, 10%; computer equipment, 30%; furniture, fixtures, and equipment, 20%; and kitchen equipment, 30%.

- Deferred revenue represents the value of gift cards sold, but not yet redeemed.

- The company initially obtained a $1-million loan, which was repaid with blended payments over a five-year period, with interest of 7%.

- Alex has been paying himself an annual dividend of $40,000. He would like this dividend to continue into the future. In addition, Alex draws an annual salary of $95,000, which reflects the fair market value of the services he provides.

Future Financial Results – Mississauga Operations

- The Mississauga location is expected to generate the same revenues, and net income, as the Toronto operation.

To Lend, or Not to Lend?

You are sitting at your desk, contemplating your first client file. As a recently hired commercial credit officer at a large Canadian bank, your job is to assess the creditworthiness of businesses to determine how much, if any, credit should be extended to potential and existing clients.

Your first engagement is Extreme BXM Ltd. The Company has approach your bank seeking long-term financing. Your job is to determine the following:

1. Should any credit be extended to the Company? If so,

   a. How much credit should be extended?

   b. What would be an appropriate interest rate for the loan?

   c. Should any covenants or restrictions be included in the loan agreement?

You are deep in thought regarding the decision because even though your bank has a credit extension policy (Exhibit I), you know that these are general principles as opposed to hard and fast rules. You want to make the right decision, based on a sound analysis, in order to impress your supervisor and receive a favourable performance review.

Just before you begin to prepare your report, you decided to review the credit file you have prepared, which includes:

- Statistics regarding the current economic conditions (Exhibit II);

- Additional information obtained from a discussion with management (Exhibit III);

- The Company's financial statements (Exhibit IV);

Required

Prepare a report that outlines your research and recommendation regarding the extension of credit.

| Exhibit I | Excepts from the Bank's Credit Policy Manual |

1. Factors to Consider When Determining to Extend Credit

Credit decisions must be based on sound, economic analysis, and research. In general, the analysis should be conducted with the intention of determining whether the business will be able to generate sufficient cash to repay the loan and interest.

The following factors should be considered as part of the credit analysis.

I. Historical Financial Statement Analysis

1. Ratio analysis should form a significant portion of the analysis. As a general guideline, credit should not be extended when the following ratios exceed the noted thresholds:

Current ratio:	2:1
Debt-to-equity:	2.5:1*
Acid test:	0.75:1
Profit margin	5%
Return on assets	10%
Quality of income	100%
Days-in-receivable	30 days
Days-in-inventory	90 days
Times-interest-earned	5 times

*The debt-to-equity ratio should not be exceeded after considering the loan to be provided.

2. Trend analysis and common-sized financial statements should also be considered as a supplement to the ratio analysis.

II. Pro Forma Financial Statement Analysis

1. In addition to historical financial statements, it may be prudent to consider pro forma (forecasted) financial statements. Forecasted statements could be based on historical statements, adjusted for:

a. The impact of one-time, extraordinary, or discretionary items;
b. The impact of the economic conditions going forward;
c. The impact of the loan on the future of the company;
d. Any other relevant future factors.

III. The Management Team

1. Management should have the abilities, based on a combination of past experience and education, to lead the business.

2. Resumes from the management team could be requested for review.

IV. The Purpose of the Loan

1. The purpose of the loan must be for legitimate business purposes. The following table presents the common purposes of a loan[1]:

Land and Building	Vehicles	Computer Hard/ Software	Other Machinery	Working Capital	R&D	Debt Consol.	Intangibles	Purchase Business	To Grow Business
20%	24%	11%	32%	45%	5%	8%	6%	8%	36%

2. Factors to Consider when Determining the Extent of Credit to Issue

1. Loans are generally issued in increments of $100,000.

2. The extent of the loan should be based on the business' debt loan, post loan. In determining the maximum debt load, postloan debt-to-equity, times interest earned, etc. should be considered.

3. If the client's loan request is too much to grant, the bank may offer the client a lower loan amount.

3. Factors to Consider when Determining an Appropriate Interest Rate

1. Interest rates should reflect the risk commensurate with the loan. Generally, the interest rate will be prime, plus an appropriate percentage for additional risk factors.

[1] *Survey on Financing Small and Medium Enterprises,* Statistics Canada, Small Business and Special Survey Division, March 2009, Table 5, page 8.

Exhibit II	Current Economic Conditions

1. Canadian Interest Rate Environment[2]: The following is a summary of the interest rates in Canada, from the Bank of Canada website:

- Bank rate (V121785):   1.25
- Prime corporate paper rate, 1 month (V121809):   1.06
- Prime business ('prime rate') (V121796):   3.00
- Guaranteed investment certificates—1-year (V121771):   0.98
- Guaranteed investment certificates—3-year (V121772):   1.43
- Guaranteed investment certificates—5-year (V121773):   1.98
- Government of Canada marketable bonds— average yield—3 to 5 year: 2.00
- Government of Canada marketable bonds— average yield—5 to 10 year: 2.70
- Government of Canada marketable bonds— average yield—over 10 years: 3.40
- Average bond yields (Scotia Capital)— Provincial—Mid term (V121792):   4.88
- Average bond yields (Scotia Capital)—All corporate—Mid term (V121762):   5.37

2. GDP Growth in Canada (2008–011)[3]: The following chart, from Statistics Canada, displays the real GDP trend from 2008 to 2011.

Real gross domestic product unchanged in April

billions of chained (2002) dollars

All industries

3. Bankruptcies in Canada[4]: On average over the last 18 years, there have been approximately 12,000 business bankruptcies per year in Canada. In the 1990s, they gradually increased from about 11,000 to a peak of more than 14,000 in 1997. Since then, business bankruptcies have been on the decline, to about 6,700 in 2009.

4. Survival Rates[5]: Survival is defined as the percentage of new firms that continue to operate when they reach a given age. Survival rates for small businesses in Canada decline over time. About 96% of small businesses (1–99 employees) that enter the marketplace survive for one full year, 85% survive for three years and 70% survive for five years.

   Looked at another way, though, smaller businesses fare less well than bigger ones. Businesses with revenues of less than $30,000 had significantly higher business failure rates than those observed for businesses with revenues of more than $30,000. Of those businesses with revenues of less than $30,000 that started in 2001, 55.0% survived after three years and only 36.1% survived after five years.

5. Reasons for Selecting Credit Suppliers[6]: The following table presents the reasons why small and medium sized enterprises (SME) selected credit suppliers:

SME by ↓	SME by →	Only Credit Supplier in the Area	Other Credit Suppliers Would Reject the Application	Credit Supplier Would Offer the Lowest Interest Rate	Credit Supplier Would Offer the Best Credit Terms and Conditions
Employment by Size	All SME	5%	11%	42%	58%
	1 to 4	6%	11%	44%	62%
	5 to 9	4%	7%	41%	59%
	20 to 99	6%	5%	43%	64%
	100 to 499	2%	3%	55%	60%

6. Requested and Authorized Credit[7]: The following table presents the credit requested by SMEs and the amount that was authorized:

| SME by ↓ | SME by → | Total $ (000,000) | | Average | |
		Amount Requested	Amount Authorized	Amount Requested	Amount Authorized
Employment by Size	All SME	59,424	50,830	310,102	296,175
	1 to 4	14,811	12,631	198,413	187,085
	5 to 9	17,399	15,675	n/a	n/a
	20 to 99	12,906	11,545	738,254	737,800
	100 to 499	2,073	2,025	1,239,104	1,236,524

7. Reasons for Rejecting the Loan[8]: The following are the reasons why credit has be refused in the past:

Credit Supplier Gave No Reason	Insufficient Sales, or Cash Flows	Insufficient Collateral	Business Plan Was Rejected	Poor Credit History	Business Operates in Unstable Industry	Business Is Too Young	Other
22%	24%	25%	3%	11%	14%	25%	43%

8. Credit Terms[9]: The average interest on authorized loans to SME is 7.3%, with an average term of 67 months.

9. Although no recent study has been completed in Canada, among 272 risk managers surveyed at banks in the United States, "60% said they expected approval rates for small-business credit and loan applications to stay flat or decline in the months ahead. Over the same period, 73.8% said demand for credit from small business would likely rise, while only 46% said credit extended to these firms would increase, the survey found. Another 28.1% expected delinquency rates by small-business borrowers to ease, compared to 36.2% in the first quarter, while 33% expected the rates to rise"[10].

---

[2] http://www.bankofcanada.ca/rates/
[3] The Daily, Gross domestic product by industry, June 30, 2011, Statistics Canada.
[4] *Key Small Business Statistics – July 2010*, Industry Canada, page 13.
[5] *Key Small Business Statistics – July 2010*, Industry Canada, page 14.
[6] *Survey on Financing Small and Medium Enterprises*, Statistics Canada, Small Business and Special Survey Division, March 2009, Table 4, page 7.
[7] *Survey on Financing Small and Medium Enterprises*, Statistics Canada, Small Business and Special Survey Division, March 2009, Tables 8 and 8a, pages 10 and 11.
[8] *Survey on Financing Small and Medium Enterprises*, Statistics Canada, Small Business and Special Survey Division, March 2009, Tables 10, page 14.
[9] *Survey on Financing Small and Medium Enterprises*, Statistics Canada, Small Business and Special Survey Division, March 2009, Tables 11, page 15.
[10] Loten, Angus. *Bankers: Credit Tightens for Small Firms*, Wall Street Journal, July 12, 2011.

Exhibit III	Discussion with Company Management

Discussion of the Company's Background

1. Extreme BXM Ltd "EBL" Ltd. is a new company that designs, manufactures, and markets approximately 20 premium-priced ($1,500 and up) bicycles throughout all of British Columbia and Ontario. The product line includes seven mountain bikes, seven juvenile BMX, and six road and specialty bicycle models.

2. In addition to the bicycles, EBL sells a wide variety of parts and accessories, ranging from helmets, water bottles, locks, and apparel. EBL also services their own bikes, and bikes sold by other manufacturers.

3. Headquartered in Vancouver, British Columbia, the Company is managed by its sole owner, Michael Bourne, a former X-Games champion. The Company began in Michael's garage, as he felt that he could design a better product than what was being offered in the market. Since then, the Company has grown to have sales of approximately $600,000 and over 10 employees.

4. EBL does sell their bikes and accessories through larger retailers, along with their own storefront locations. The storefront locations offer the bike repair services.

5. The Company's first full year of operations was in 2012, and it was a successful year as the bikes were well received by the market. Fiscal 2011 and 2010 were mostly a start-up years, with various one-time expenses and start-up costs. However, some income was earned during these two years.

Most of these one-time costs were eliminated by the end of fiscal 2011.

Discussion of the need for the loan

6. The Company requested $500,000 in long-term debt to expand their operations into Saskatchewan and Alberta. If this expansion is successful, the Company will expand into the rest of Canada, and eventually the United States.

7. EBL's business plan suggests that the loan will be used to double their sales (operating capacity) by expanding their existing plant, purchasing additional machinery, and help finance additional working capital needs. The allocation would be as follows:

Buildings	$175,000
Equipment	$250,000
Office equipment	$15,000
Furniture and fixtures	$10,000

8. The new sales would cause working capital requirements to increase. Management expects that accounts receivable, inventory and accounts payable will double. A total of $50,000 from the bank loan will help finance the increase in working capital.

9. The gross margin on the new sales will be consistent with the current gross margin. However, advertising expense would

Exhibit III	Discussion with Company Management (Continued)

likely increase to $2,000 per year from its current level in order to attract the new business.

10. Management has informed you that if the loan is granted; the related party note receivable will be collected and a portion of the proceeds will be used to repay the related party note payable, due to shareholder and current long-term debt. Management feels that this will clear the balance sheet of all creditors aside from the bank.

11. Management employed a low price strategy as they entered the market. However, their products are know well known and in demand. Accordingly, management has decided to raise selling prices. Sales prices for both divisions are expected to increase by 5% in the next year and continue into the indefinite future.

Discussion of the Historical Financial Statements

12. The management and administrative wages include $20,000 of severance pay for an employee that was not working out with the Company. The employee was let go and replaced immediately with an employee that fit the position much better.

13. The cost of goods sold is expected to remain consistent with the most recent fiscal year. Because of synergies, administrative costs are expected to remain the same.

14. The 2012 vehicle expense includes a $5,000 relating to a vehicle accident that was not insured.

15. The 2012 fiscal year includes $3,500 in shop supplies expense that resulted from inefficiencies in start-up operations.

16. The fair value of the capital assets is different that the historical cost. Management's best estimate of the fair value in use of the equipment is $400,000, while an orderly liquidation would result in $250,000 being obtained for the capital assets.

17. Michael's wage is included in the operating and administrative wages (management wages). He has taken a minimal salary in the first few years in order to reduce the drain on cash and help internally finance the Company. Michael expects that his wage will increase by 50% from his 2013 compensation within the next year or so in order to reflect the fair market value of his services. In addition, he would like to pay himself a $100,000 to make up for his lack of appropriate compensation in prior years.

Exhibit IV	Financial Statements

Extreme BXM Ltd.
December 31, 2013

Contents

	Page
Audit Report	47
Statements of Earnings and Retained Earnings	48
Balance Sheet	49
Statement of Cash Flows	50
Notes to the Financial Statements	51-53
Schedule of Sales and Cost of Sales	54
Schedule of Operating and Administrative Expenses	54

Audit report

To the Shareholders of
Extreme BXM Ltd.

We have audited the accompanying financial statements of Extreme BXM Ltd. which comprise the balance sheet as at December 31, 2013, the statements of earnings and retained earnings and cash flows for the year then ended, and a summary of significant accounting policies and other explanatory information.

Management's responsibility for the financial statements

Management is responsible for the preparation and fair presentation of these financial statements in accordance with Canadian generally accepted accounting principles, and for such internal control as management determines is necessary to enable the preparation of financial statements that are free from material misstatement, whether due to fraud or error.

Auditor's responsibility

Our responsibility is to express an opinion on these financial statements based on our audit. We conducted our audit in accordance with Canadian generally accepted auditing standards. Those standards require that we comply with ethical requirements and plan and perform the audit to obtain reasonable assurance about whether the financial statements are free from material misstatement.

An audit involves performing procedures to obtain audit evidence about the amounts and disclosures in the financial statements. The procedures selected depend on the auditor's judgment, including the assessment of the risks of material misstatement of the financial statements, whether due to fraud or error. In making those risk assessments, the auditor considers internal control relevant to the company's preparation and fair presentation of the financial statements in order to design audit procedures that are appropriate in the circumstances, but not for the purpose of expressing an opinion on the effectiveness of the company's internal control. An audit also includes evaluating the appropriateness of accounting policies used and the reasonableness of accounting estimates made by management, as well as evaluating the overall presentation of the financial statements.

We believe that the audit evidence we have obtained is sufficient and appropriate to provide a basis for our audit opinion.

Opinion

In our opinion, the financial statements present fairly, in all material respects, the financial position of Extreme BXM Ltd. as at December 31, 2013, and its financial performance and its cash flows for the year then ended in accordance with Canadian generally accepted accounting principles.

Lento and Lento, LLP

Thunder Bay, Ontario
February 14, 2014

Chartered Accountants
Licensed Public Accountants

Extreme BXM Ltd.
Statements of Operations and Retained Earnings

Year Ended December 31	2013	2012
Sales (Page 9)	$ 579,913	$ 587,196
Cost of sales (Page 9)	441,682	469,793
Gross profit	138,231	117,403
Other and interest income (Note 5a)	5,931	7,099
Loss on disposal of property and equipment	(15,459)	(314)
	128,703	124,188
Operating and administrative expenses (Page 10)	97,670	133,546
Earnings (loss) before income taxes	31,033	(9,358)
Income taxes (Note 9)	9,534	(645)
Net earnings (loss)	$ 21,499	$ (8,713)
Retained earnings, beginning of year	$ 237,631	$ 246,344
Net earnings (loss)	21,499	(8,713)
Retained earnings, end of year	$ 259,130	$ 237,631

See accompanying notes and schedules to the financial statements.

Extreme BXM Ltd.
Balance Sheet

December 31	2013	2012
Assets		
Current		
Cash and cash equivalents	$ 30,433	$ -
Receivables	38,903	44,383
Inventories	88,817	100,090
	158,153	144,473
Note receivable from related party (Note 5a)	85,211	87,783
Property and equipment (Note 3)	146,386	182,635
	$ 389,750	$ 414,891
Liabilities		
Current		
Demand loan (Note 4)	$ -	$ 42,476
Payables and accruals	38,873	36,395
Income taxes payable	9,530	646
Current portion of long term debt	5,982	5,012
	54,385	84,529
Note payable to related party (Note 5b)	14,321	14,397
Due to shareholders (Note 5c)	19,287	29,286
Long-term debt (Note 6)	42,626	49,047
	130,619	177,259
Shareholders' Equity		
Capital stock (Note 7)	1	1
Retained earnings	259,130	237,631
	259,131	237,632
	$ 389,750	$ 414,891

On behalf of the Board

_____ Director   _____ Director

See accompanying notes and schedules to the financial statements.

Extreme BXM Ltd.
Statement of Cash Flows

Year Ended December 31	2013	2012
Cash and cash equivalents derived from (applied to)		
Operating		
Net earnings (loss)	$ 21,499	$ (8,713)
Amortization	10,790	12,720
Loss on disposal of property and equipment	15,459	314
Change in noncash working capital items (Note 8)	28,115	(7,681)
	75,863	(3,360)
Investment		
Purchase of property and equipment	-	(10,117)
Proceeds from disposition of property and equipment	10,001	43,017
	10,001	32,900
Financing		
Repayment of long-term debt	(5,451)	(7,839)
Decrease (increase) in note receivable from related party	2,572	(4,460)
(Decrease) in note payable to related party	(76)	(133)
Advances from shareholders	(10,000)	(517)
	(12,955)	10,384
Net increase in cash	72,909	39,924
Cash and cash equivalents (bank indebtedness)		
Beginning of year	(42,476)	(2,552)
End of year	$ 30,423	$ (42.476)

See accompanying notes and schedules to the financial statements.

Extreme BXM Ltd.
Notes to the Financial Statements
December 31, 2013

1. Nature of operations

The company sells motocross bicycles and accessories and provides general bicycle repair services.

2. Summary of significant accounting policies

Cash and cash equivalents

Cash and cash equivalents includes cash on hand, balances with bank, and short-term investments with an original maturity date of three months or less. Bank borrowings are considered to be financing activities.

Revenue recognition

Bicycle and accessory revenues are recognized upon delivery to customers and service revenues are recognized as repair service is completed.

Inventories

Inventories are valued at the lower of cost and net realizable value as determined on the specific identification method.

Property and equipment

Property and equipment are recorded at cost and amortization is provided on the declining balance basis at the following rates:

Building	4%
Equipment	20%
Office equipment	30%
Furniture and fixtures	30%

Use of estimates

In preparing the Company's financial statements, management is required to make estimates and assumptions that affect the reported amount of assets and liabilities at the date of the financial statements, and the reported amounts of revenues and expenses during the reporting period. Actual results could differ from those estimates.

Impairment of long-lived assets

Long-lived assets are reviewed for impairment upon the occurrence of events or changes in circumstances indicating that the carrying value of the asset may not be recoverable, as measured by comparing their net book value to the estimated undiscounted future cash flows generated by their use. Impaired assets are recorded at fair value, determined principally using discounted future cash flows expected from their use and eventual disposition.

3. Property and equipment

	Cost	Accumulated Amortization	2013 Net Book Value	2012 Net Book Value
Building	$ 170,359	$ 42,656	$ 127,703	$ 133,024
Equipment	62,020	47,804	14,216	17,769
Office equipment	7,434	6,893	541	774
Furniture and fixtures	40,739	36,813	3,926	31,068
	$ 280,552	$ 134,166	$ 146,386	$ 182,635

4. Demand loan

The Company has an authorized operating loan of $500,000, of which $nil was used at year end ($40,833 in 2012). The operating loan is payable on demand. The loan is not to exceed 75% of accounts receivable plus 50% of inventory. As security, the Company has provided a general security agreement, first claim on receivables and inventory, and a postponement of any claim by shareholders. Interest is calculated at prime plus 1/2% and is paid monthly.

Extreme BXM Ltd.
Notes to the Financial Statements
December 31, 2013

5. Related party transactions

a. The note receivable from 1359528 Ontario Inc., a common controlled company, bears interest at 5%, is unsecured, and without terms of repayment. During the year, interest of $4,057 ($4,180 in 2012) was charged to this related party. The Company does not expect to demand repayments during the coming 12 months. During the normal course of operations, the Company had sales of $18,462 ($20,495 in 2012) to and purchases of $15,913 ($20,392 in 2012) from this related party. Receivables include $85,211 ($87,783 in 2012) from this related party. The Company also paid $6,250 ($6,250 in 2012) to this related party for services rendered.

b. The note payable to Antique Automotive Restoration, a common controlled company, is interest free, unsecured, and without terms of repayment. Since the related party has confirmed that it will not demand repayment during the coming 12 months, the note has been excluded from current liabilities.

c. The loans payable to the shareholders are unsecured, interest free, and without terms of repayment. Since the shareholders have confirmed that they will not demand repayment during the coming 12 months, the loans have been excluded from current liabilities.

d. Related party transactions are measured at exchange amount.

6. Long-term debt	2013	2012
FedNor loan payable, bearing interest at 5.25%, repayable in blended monthly payments of $854. As security, the Company has provided a general security agreement, and postponement of claims by shareholders. The loan can be repaid in full without penalty or fee.	$ 48,608	$ 54,059
Less: current portion	5,982	5,012
	$ 42,626	$ 49,047

7. Capital stock	2013	2012
Authorized:		
Unlimited number of common shares		
Unlimited number of special shares.		
Issued:		
360 common shares	$ 1	$ 1

8. Supplemental cash flow information	2013	2012
Change in noncash working capital items:		
Receivables	$ 5,480	$ 1,349
Inventories	11,273	7,300
Prepaids	-	2,777
Payables and accruals	2,478	(15,366)
Income taxes payable	8,884	(3,741)
	$ 28,115	$ (7,681)
Income taxes paid	$ 685	$ 4,727
Interest paid	$ 4,857	$ 5,777

Extreme BXM Ltd.
Notes to the Financial Statements
December 31, 2013

9. Income taxes	2013	2012
The Company's reported income tax rate on operating earnings differs from the statutory rate as follows:		
Income tax rate at the combined basic federal and provincial tax rates	36.1%	36.1%
Small business deduction	(20.5)	(20.5)
Amortization claimed versus capital cost allowance	4.2	(19.5)
Loss on disposal of property and equipment	18.0	(1.2)
Nondeductible expenses	7.1	(1.8)
Effective tax rate	30.7%	(6.9)%

10. Financial instruments

The Company's financial instruments consist of cash, receivables, bank indebtedness (including demand loans), payables, amounts due to (from) related parties, and long-term debt. Unless otherwise noted, it is management's opinion that the Company is not exposed to significant interest, currency or credit risk arising from these financial instruments. The fair value of these financial instruments approximate their carrying values, unless otherwise noted.

Extreme BXM Ltd.
Schedule of Sales and Cost of Sales

Year Ended December 31			2013	2012
	Bicycle and Accessory Sales	Servicing	Total	Total
Sales (Note 5a)	$ 479,873	$ 100,040	$ 579,913	$ 587,196
Cost of sales				
Opening inventory	100,096	-	100,096	7,396
Purchases (Note 5a)	247,311	-	247,311	395,872
	347,407	-	347,407	403,268
Ending inventory	88,817	-	88,817	100,096
	258,590	-	258,590	303,172
Other direct expenses				
Labour	119,134	54,717	173,851	157,376
Freight	9,241	-	9,241	9,246
Cost of sales	386,965	54,717	441,682	469,793
Gross profit	$ 92,908	$ 45,323	$ 138,321	$ 117,403

Extreme BXM Ltd.
Schedule of Operating and Administrative Expenses

Year Ended December 31	2013	2012
Expenses		
Advertising	$ 252	$ 1,238
Amortization	10,790	12,720
Bad debts (recovery)	(1,136)	(2,209)
Insurance	5,453	6,787
Interest and bank charges	5,936	4,547
Interest on long-term debt	4,287	5,777
Office	3,797	6,352
Management wages	34,607	54,530
Professional fees	1,944	1,470
Property taxes	5,482	4,928
Shop supplies	9,927	14,124
Telephone	2,013	1,799
Travel	2,717	2,433
Utilities	5,166	5,565
Vehicle	6,434	13,485
	$ 97,670	$ 133,546

Introductory Cases

Button Productions[1]

Francine Smeritt founded Buttons Productions (BP) in 2020. BP is an entertainment facility located on 5 acres of land near a major Canadian city. The first and major attraction that has been set up is a haunted house where both young and old can go to be frightened to death (or entertained depending on your fright tolerance level). There are two different paths to take in the house; one for those who wish to be less frightened than others. At the end of the "tour" customers exit the house into the gift shop where survivors can purchase souvenirs before they leave.

While Francine has the creativity to make BP a success, her accounting skills are not quite as strong. She has kept a summary of all of her activities to date and has asked you for help in preparing her statements. BP opened to the public on October 1st, and the year end is December 31st.

While she is incorporated (because her father told her to), she isn't really sure about what that means and has asked you, in addition to preparing the journal entries and statements, to also discuss the different types of ways of operating a business.

Required

The transactions for the year will be provided to you in a separate document. Once you receive the transactions, complete the following:

1. Journal entries for all the transactions (show your work when required)
2. Final trial balance in good form
3. Statement of income (income statement) for the period ended December 31, 2020, in good form
4. Statement of financial position at December 31, 2020, in good form
5. A memo to Francine addressing her other concerns

---

[1] Note: Further information that is required to complete this case will be provided to you by your instructor.

Glacier Beverage Company

Your partner, Siddig Fleming, has just dropped a mountain of files and other paperwork on your desk and left instructions for you. You notice at the top of the instruction sheet that he has marked the request *urgent*. As a result, you put your other work aside and begin to sift through the information.

Your firm has been a consultant for Glacier Bay Beverage Company (GBB), a publicly traded company located in Torbay, Newfoundland, and founded by James McCarthy. GBB manufactures the famous McCarthy's beverage, Glacier Bay Iced Tea. Your firm has been their consultant for five years. GBB's year end is December 31. You are the brand new lead consultant for GBB. You were not originally assigned to GBB but you were given the task after the original consultant suddenly left for a job in the Caribbean.

GBB is currently in the process of a major expansion and it is looking into financing alternatives for the acquisition of manufacturing equipment to be used in its beverage-making facilities.

GBB is currently in a cash crunch, although its sales and production have expanded considerably over the past 10 years. All of its other key ratios are in good order, which is allowing GBB to look at a variety of ways to finance its next expansion. The founder and major shareholder, James, is concerned about maintaining a healthy current ratio and debt to equity ratio as he believes this will be important in the future and the minority shareholders have shown some concern over these ratios in the past.

In addition, in order to fully understand the situation, GBB would like you to prepare journal entries for the first year for alternatives one, two, and three and the potential impact they will have on GBB's ratios.

Your firm has been hired by GBB to assist it in exploring the various alternatives as described in Exhibit I. They would like your detailed analysis. This analysis should incorporate calculations, impact on financial statements, and more qualitative impacts as you deem appropriate in the circumstances (such as impact to corporate structure, overall leverage, advantages, and disadvantages).

You have been made aware that the auditors will be arriving in a few months and GBB has asked you to ensure that all accounting recommendations are consistent with GAAP. In addition to the proposed machine acquisition, GBB has a few other accounting items that management would like you to comment on prior to the auditors' arrival (Exhibit II).

Required

Prepare the draft report to GBB.

Exhibit I	GBB Details

Machine Details

- The equipment in question is an ALPHA8K9—Type II Beverage Bottling Machine capable of bottling 100 cases of iced tea per minute. The fair value of this machine is $1.5 million.

- The machine is expected to have a useful life of 10 years after which it could be sold for $100,000.

- Technological obsolescence is a factor in this type of machine as manufacturers are always making them better, stronger, and faster.

- *Note: You may assume that the purchase of the equipment and the issuance of the debt or equity will take place on January 1, 2020.*

Acquisition Arrangement #1

- GBB could finance the purchase of the machine by issuing bonds.

- $1,000 bonds would be issued totaling $1.5 million, for 10 years and a coupon interest rate of 6%.

- The current market rate for similar bonds is 4%.

- Interest would be paid semi-annually with the bonds being issued January 1, 2021.

Acquisition Arrangement #2

- GBB could purchase the asset for $1.5 million and obtain a secured loan from its bank.

- The terms of the loan call for principal payments each year beginning January 1, 2021, of $150,000.

- The interest is to be paid annually each January 1st and is fixed at 8%, which is consistent with the market rate of this type of loan.

- GBB is required to maintain a specified debt to equity ratio or the loan will become immediately payable.

Acquisition Arrangement #3

- GBB could issue common shares or preferred shares to finance the acquisition of the machinery.

- GBB is a public company with the founding member owning 51% of the common shares currently outstanding (currently there are 4.5 million shares outstanding in total).

- The current market price per share is $15.

| Exhibit II | Other Details |

- During the year, a visitor to the facility slipped and fell on some spilled iced tea and broke their leg. They have subsequently sued GBB for $800,000. GBB's lawyers do not believe that the $800,000 lawsuit will be successful, but do believe that there is a 20% chance it will be dismissed, a 60% chance that GBB will have to pay $200,000, and a 20% chance it will have to pay $400,000.

- GBB intends to put on a contest this year with a coupon attached to each tea product. Any customer who collects five coupons may send them to GBB and redeem them for a GBB T-shirt. GBB would like some guidance on how to account for this.

Hallaway Greens

Hallaway Greens (HG) makes custom and generic golf clubs. HG primarily sells the clubs to several large golf retailers in Canada. HG owns two manufacturing plants and has its head office located just north of Moncton, NB. While it employs a large number of manufacturing staff, HG operates its administrative department with a lean staff. HG experienced some administrative staff turnover this year with the accounts receivable clerk, accounts payable clerk, and controller all leaving to take positions at other companies. While HG looked into hiring, the receptionist stepped in and posted cash receipts, set up new vendors when required, and processed payments. The owner of HG, Maria Stewart had a stronger presence at the office during this time and signed all of the cheques.

While you were hired as the new controller in December 2020, no one has yet been hired to replace the accounts payable or receivable clerks. It is now after year end (early January 2021) and you are in the process of ensuring that all entries with respect to receivables are in order (Exhibit I), and that the December 31 bank reconciliation is complete (Exhibit II). Maria has also come to you and has suggested that perhaps they don't need to hire anyone to replace the two clerks since the receptionist seems to be doing a good job. She has asked you to prepare a memo to her that first completes the bank reconciliation with journal entries and then assesses the accounts receivable.

Required

Prepare the memo for Maria. Provide your comments on her suggestion along with your recommendations and/or concerns.

Exhibit I ‖ **Accounts Receivable Details**

HG uses the balance sheet approach based on aging, in accounting for its doubtful receivables. The balance in the allowance for doubtful accounts on December 31 was a debit of $43,000. In previous years, the allowance account was always in a year-ending credit position and you note that this seems excessively high. In analyzing the receivables, you note the following:

Receivables outstanding less than 60 days amounted to $144,000, 60–90 days amounted to $198,000, and greater than 90 days amounted to $89,000. Previous experience shows a doubtful percentage of 2%, 11%, and 60%, respectively.

Exhibit II ‖ **Bank Reconciliation Details**

- The unadjusted balance per the bank on December 31 was $91,500.

- A cheque dated May 25, 2020, for $120 has not yet been cashed and is now stale dated.

- Monthly bank service charges amounted to $110.

- The unadjusted balance per the books on December 31, 2020, was $89,436.

- Cheques outstanding and not yet cashed amounted to $4,500. (This does not include the stale-dated cheque above.)

- One cheque was returned by the bank due to nonsufficient funds. The cheque was written for $265.

- Deposits placed in the night deposit box but not recorded by the bank amounted to $2,200.

- A cheque was recorded by HG as $680 but was actually written and cashed in the amount of $661.

Hilton Chalets

Hilton Chalets (HC) was founded by Jacques Clouthier in the 1970s and was operated primarily as a small local ski hill. For the next 20 years, the ski hill was very popular and made significant profits. By the 1990s, the ski hill was caught up in the recessionary times, Jacques retired, and the hill was closed down. In 2019, Madison Campbell, a multimillionaire entrepreneur, purchased all the assets of what was left of HC after Jacques' estate put it up for sale. The total cost of the assets was $5 million, with 90% of this allocated to the land and the other 10% allocated to the one building that remained on site. All other equipment had long since been removed. Madison was able to keep the name and the private company HC was resurrected.

Throughout 2019, Madison slowly began to rebuild the small ski hill and she hired an accountant to track and record all of her expenses. In addition to the original purchase, Madison spent a further $10 million before the ski hill opened. The allocation of the $10 million was as follows:

Grading, prepping the hill for use	$300,000
Ski lift (four-year life)	1,000,000
Restoration of chalet on site	2,000,000
Lights for night skiing (10-year life)	800,000
Snow-making machine (10-year life)	2,200,000
Other ski hill equipment (eight-year life)	1,200,000
On-hand rental equipment (three-year life)	400,000
Office equipment (five-year life)	300,000
Operating costs (all prior to opening)	1,800,000

The chalet, which was restored with a complete overhaul, is expected to have a useful life of 20 years. One half of the costs above were funded through Madison's initial infusion of cash when she purchased HC ($5 million total). The balance was raised through a business loan at the Regal Bank. Madison was asked to personally guarantee the loan. Details of the loan are in Exhibit I.

Revenues for 2019 were very small, with the ski hill opening mid-December of that year. January and February 2020 produced record snowfall in the area and the ski hill was at near capacity. Details of ski operations can be found in Exhibit I.

During the summer of 2020, Madison began to design phase two of her dream recreational facility: cottage rentals. By November, Madison had created on paper a 15-chalet development. Her plan was to eventually create a year-round recreational facility where people could bike and hike during the summer and ski, snowshoe, and snowtube in the winter. The budget for the 15-chalet development was set at approximately $5 million and Madison was aiming to begin the development during the summer of 2021. In order to do so, she will need to raise the money and is interested in knowing what options are available. In order to do this, she really needs to know where her cash flow is.

The accountant has been very reliable but retired on January 1, 2021. Before he left, he completed the unadjusted financial statements for HC for 2020 but was not able to post any of the adjusting entries.

Required

It is now January 14, 2021, and you have been hired as the new accountant for HC. As a recent CPA graduate, Madison believes you are ideally suited to help her. She would like you to complete the following tasks:

(a) Prepare the required adjusting journal entries based on the information that you are given in Exhibit I and update/correct the draft financial statements in Exhibits II and III.

(b) Prepare the operating activities section of the Cash Flow Statement from the revised financial statements.

(c) Write a memo to Madison discussing some of the financing options available to her regarding the $5.0 million needed for the 15-chalet development. In this discussion, include your thoughts on (i) advantages and risks for HC of completing the planned expansion and (ii) advantages and risks of three different financing alternatives [Hint: when considering financing alternatives, you should consider whether financing the $5.0 million using debt or equity would be preferable, and why].

Exhibit I	Other Information

- Lift ticket prices are affected by demand, with more popular ski hills in the area charging premium pricing. Most ski hills sell season passes and single lift tickets. Often single ticket prices are based on age and time of day. For ski hills in the same category as HC, single ticket prices can range from a low of $8 for a child 6 and under to a high of $55 for an adult.

- HC made the decision during the 2019/2020 season to charge a lift ticket flat price of $30 in order to attract attention to the new ski hill. A child ticket price was set at $10 for children 12 and under. At any one time, the percentage of adult tickets is 90% and child tickets 10% of those in attendance.

- The ski hill operates from 9 a.m. to 9 p.m. and has a capacity of approximately 2,500 skiers at any one time.

- During the month of December 2019, HC operated for 10 days, with a consistent attendance of 800 skiers. During the months of January to March 2020, this increased to a daily average of 950 skiers. Total paid tickets for the three months before closures was 85,500 skiers in the same age breakdown noted above.

- 2020 was not a good start to the snow season, with record warm temperatures. Despite HC's attempts at making snow, it was unable to open until December 29. As a result of the extremely warm temperatures, skiers were waiting to ski at a moment's notice. For the final three days of December, HC maximized its capacity with the same age ratios as anticipated.

- There was some controversy from some customers about the pricing at HC. While average adult ticket prices remained much better than competitors, HC does not have student pricing, which is generally for students 12–18 years. This category makes up 50% of the adult ticket category and typically is provided a discount of $10 off the lift ticket price at competitors' hills.

- Costs to operate the ski hill during 2019 were as follows:

Seasonal salaries	$125,000
Hydro	30,000
Internet	3,000
Insurance	12,000
Other	50,000

- Minimal costs are required during the off season because most workers are seasonal workers. HC has three full-time time workers who are paid a combined salary of $135,000 per year earned evenly throughout the year. Full-time employees were hired on June 1, 2019.

- Full-time salaries remained the same during 2020 and all other costs tripled as a result of a full year of opening. Unpaid salaries on December 31, 2020, amounted to $8,500 and were not recorded in the unadjusted statement of financial position. There were no salary accruals for 2018.

- The chalet has a food venue area. In order to remove this from HC's operation, Madison negotiated with a local restaurant. The restaurant fully operates the food venue, including inventory and salaries, and keeps all revenues. In return, the restaurant pays HC a rental fee of $2,000 per month for the months of December, January, February, and March. Madison believes this is the most cost-effective way of providing food services to patrons at the moment.

- HC's loan calls for equal principal payments over a 20-year period, with the first payment due on January 1, 2021. Interest was negotiated at 4%, with the loan arrangements and terms being up for renegotiation in five years. The loan was provided to HC on June 30, 2019, and HC was required to pay all accrued interest from June 30, 2019, to December 31, 2020, and then yearly thereafter.

- HC adopted the accounting policy of taking a full year of depreciation in the year of acquisition and none in the year of disposal. Straight-line depreciation is taken on all assets with no salvage value.

- HC had outstanding payables of $15,000 in other expenses that was included in the expenses noted above for 2019. For 2020, there were unrecorded payables of $30,000 related to other expenses.

- It is expected that the warm winter season will continue through 2021. In fact, the ski hill had to be closed as of January 5, 2021, due to a lack of snow.

- Industry trends are showing that there will be fewer adults and more young skiers under 12 in the future, with the ratio being closer to 65% over 12 and 35% under 12.

- You are to ignore income taxes.

Exhibit II	Income Statements

Hilton Chalets
Income Statement
for the Year Ended December 31, 2019

Sales		
Ski lift revenues	$	224,000
Ancillary revenues		2,000
Total		226,000
Less:		
Salaries	$	203,750
Depreciation expense		893,333
Hydro		30,000
Internet		3,000
Insurance		12,000
Interest expense		100,000
Other operating expenses		50,000
Net income (loss)		$(1,066,083)

Hilton Chalets
Income Statement
for the Year Ended December 31, 2020 (UNADJUSTED)

Sales	
Ski lift revenues	$2,394,000
Ancillary revenues	8,000
Total	2,402,000
Less:	
Salaries	$ 510,000
Depreciation expense	0
Hydro	90,000
Internet	9,000
Insurance	36,000
Interest expense	0
Other operating expenses	150,000
Net income (loss)	$1,607,000

| Exhibit III | Statement of Financial Position (Unadjusted for 2017) |

Hilton Chalets
Statement of Financial Position
December 31, 2020 (UNADJUSTED)

	2020	2019
Assets		
Cash	$ 3,349,250	$ 1,732,250
Land	4,800,000	4,800,000
Property, plant, and equipment	8,400,000	8,400,000
Less: Accumulated depreciation	(893,333)	(893,333)
Total assets	$15,655,917	$14,038,917
Liabilities and Shareholders' Equity		
Accounts payable	$ 15,000	$ 5,000
Interest payable	100,000	100,000
Long-term bank loan	5,000,000	5,000,000
Common shares	10,000,000	10,000,000
Retained earnings	540,917	(1,066,083)
Total liabilities and shareholders' equity	$15,655,917	$14,038,917

Kelowna Brick and Cement Company

Kelowna Brick and Cement Company (KBCC) is a medium-sized company that specializes in providing cement for construction sites, primarily in the Kelowna/Kamloops area. KBCC had sales two years ago of $10 million and sales for the year just ended were $12 million. At present KBCC is solely owned by Joel Hatchuk, who founded the private company in 1980. KBCC follows the Accounting Standards for Private Enterprises. Despite its revenues, KBCC operates with few administrative staff, currently employing 12 individuals in addition to Joel, who is there every day.

Joel is considering expanding his operations into the Vancouver area. In order to do so, he will have to look into financing options. He is contemplating two debt options: traditional bank financing or bonds. He is also considering selling some of his common shares to five of his friends and relatives. He is unsure of how these options would impact him and the current organization of his company.

In December of this year, one of KBCC's trucks carrying cement was in an accident. The substance spilled into a local river, contaminating the water supply. KBCC's lawyers have stated that the local residents have filed a lawsuit for $2 million. They expect that KBCC will be found guilty but the settlement will be between $1.0 million and $1.6 million. KBCC had let its insurance policy expire and therefore does not have any coverage.

On December 31, four of KBCC's trucks were loaded with customer freight and were shipped the same day, FOB shipping. The goods were delivered to the customers on January 5 and 6, respectively. The revenue of $80,000 was recorded in the books on December 31.

Joel knows about the importance of internal controls but believes he needs a refresher. He had an individual from finance leave earlier this year and is now using the accounts receivable person to receive the cash and cheques, post them to the accounts receivable subledger, and complete the monthly bank reconciliations. He is beginning to think that this is a good idea as it would save one salary. On the other hand, he does want to maintain controls and is interested in eliminating all potential problems. He would like your recommendations about how he should deal with this including what could go wrong.

KBCC purchased equipment on January 1 five years ago for $190,000 and estimated a $10,000 salvage value at the end of the equipment's 10-year useful life. On March 31 of this year, the equipment was sold for $95,000. The last entry to record depreciation was at December 31 of the prior year. No entries for the sale have been made yet.

KBCC is a client of your accounting firm and you are the CPA in charge of the engagement. The year end for GBCC is December 31. It is now April 20 and you have been asked to provide a memo to your partner that can be used as the basis for discussion with Joel that addresses the issues that concern you and Joel. You must address all of the issues in depth and provide recommendations on how to account for them.

Required

Prepare the memo.

Play Tennis Now Inc.

Contributed by
Laura Simeoni
*Sysim Consulting Limited, Director and Professional Development
and Training Consultant, Oakville, Ontario*

Martina Fabcic's dream, ever since she was the national tennis champion in the under-14 girls' division, was to own and operate her own tennis club. After earning her business degree with a major in marketing, Martina decided to work for a local club as its general manager. She saw this as a stepping stone to her real dream. Martina was responsible for all operating aspects of the club except for the preparation of the monthly financial statements. These were prepared by the bookkeeper and audited annually by a local CPA firm.

After five years at the local club, Martina decided it was time to start her own tennis club. She began to research the surrounding area in order to decide where to locate her new business. Within a year, Martina decided to open a new tennis club in a growing area in the north end of the city. She had $60,000 of her own savings and decided to invest $50,000 of it into the club. Based on her business knowledge and experience in the tennis industry, Martina estimated that she would need another $100,000. She approached a private investor, Michael Riggio, who had played professional tennis in his early years. He was keen to see a new club in the area and agreed to lend Martina the money with an option to buy into the club in five years. The terms of the loan require Martina to repay the full amount over the five years through monthly principal and interest payments. In addition, the business has to prepare and submit to Michael an audited set of financial statements within 60 days of year end. Also the terms require that the financial statements be prepared in accordance with Accounting Standards for Private Enterprises.

On February 1, Martina incorporated her business, Play Tennis Now, Inc. She then began the hard work of getting her office, staff, and facilities ready for opening day. On May 1, Martina successfully opened her doors to local tennis enthusiasts.

Now that the peak tennis season is over, Martina is thinking about the need to prepare her first set of annual financial statements. Although she is somewhat familiar with accounting processes based on her previous job, Martina did not have a good grasp of accounting policies suitable for this kind of business. She decided to contact her good friend, Professor Mark Phed, to ask for a reference for someone who could help her decide on the most appropriate policies for Play Tennis Now Inc. Professor Phed teaches at the local university and was pleased to help Martina with this request. Professor Phed quickly thought of you, since you had recently earned the highest mark in his accounting class.

When Martina contacted you, you were excited to take on this role as accounting advisor. Here was a chance to earn some extra money and finally use all that accounting knowledge in a real situation. You agreed to meet with Martina to learn more about her tennis club.

On November 2, you met with Martina at her office at the back of the tennis club. A summary of your notes is found in Exhibit I.

Required

Assume the role of accounting advisor and top student. Provide Martina with your advice and recommendations on the accounting policies that would be appropriate for Play Tennis Now, Inc. for its first year end. Provide any other advice that you think may help Martina as she begins this new business venture (e.g., advice regarding general internal controls would be an ideal starting point).

Exhibit I	Notes from Meeting with Martina

1. In order to promote the new club, Martina took out a full-page advertisement in the local paper. She paid $1,000 for this advertisement, which ran weekly in four local newspapers during the months of May and June. Martina felt that it was important to spend this amount of money and "get the word out" as the benefits could last over several years if players visited the club and then agreed to join as members.

2. On May 5, Martina had an open house. She offered healthy drinks and fruit trays for those people dropping in. It gave her a chance to meet potential players who would hopefully join the club. She had about 150 people drop in that day to meet her, the two office staff (the receptionist and the bookkeeper), and the tennis pro, Johnny Mac. The cost for the open house was about $250.

3. Martina explained that part of the $50,000 that she invested in the club was used to purchase office furniture, two computers, and some club house furniture such as two couches, and a table and chair set. In addition, tennis nets, tennis balls, and a ball machine were purchased. The ball machine will be made available to players, who can rent the machine on a first-come, first-served basis.

4. The funds received from Michael, the private investor, were primarily used to build four "hard courts," the most common tennis surface. The money not used for the building of the courts was set aside for ongoing court maintenance. Martina confirmed that she spent about $80,000 to build the courts. Of the amount remaining, $10,000 will be used to repaint the lines or resurface the courts about every three years. The remainder will be used for emergency repairs.

5. Martina explained that she had hired a web designer to set up a web page as well as an online booking system. In this way, members or potential members could easily access the site to learn more about the club or to book courts.

6. By mid-May, 100 people had joined the club. Per the terms of membership, each new member paid $900 for a nonrefundable annual membership. The membership could be paid all upfront or at a monthly rate of $75 without any interest charges. The membership fee allows each player the right to book courts at any time. At the current time, Martina is not selling court time to nonmembers. In addition to the membership fee, court time is charged at $22 per hour for peak play and $18 per hour for nonpeak play.

7. Martina introduced me to the tennis pro. He was well known among local tennis players. In order to encourage Johnny Mac to join the club, Martina included the following terms in his employment contract:

   (a) A fixed annual salary
   (b) A commission based on court bookings where the pro is asked to play in. These bookings can be made online or by other acceptable methods; that is, call in or in-person bookings
   (c) A bonus if the club membership exceeds 250 members within one year of opening and remains at this level for 30 days after it is reached.

   Johnny Mac receives 12 equal monthly payments to cover his annual salary. Payments are made the last Friday of the month. The commission is paid one month after the commissions are earned since the amounts need to be verified against the online and manual booking systems.

   The bonus will be paid 10 days after the bonus is considered earned.

   Martina indicated that Johnny Mac was excited about the potential for this club. She felt that Johnny Mac would most likely earn his bonus given that the club had almost reached 50% of the total goal in the first two weeks of operations.

8. Martina also opened a small pro shop that carries tennis racquets, tennis balls, tennis clothing including tennis shoes, and other tennis accessories. Club members are particularly sensitive to new trends and models. Martina knows this is an opportunity for her to make profits over and above the membership and hourly bookings. She started out with an inventory level costing about $15,000 (estimated retail value $35,000). This should adequately service about 400 members.

9. The company's year end is March 31.

Sarah Smith Sporting

Contributed by
Laura Simeoni
Sysim Consulting Limited, Director and Professional Development and Training
Consultant, Oakville, Ontario

Sarah Smith has been an avid sports enthusiast since her early days of playing soccer for her city team. Sarah continued to play soccer throughout high school and university. She recognized during those early years of soccer that staying fit was a critical ingredient in performing well in any sport and for staying healthy in general. So it was no surprise when Sarah announced that she would pursue her dream of opening a fitness facility. Three years ago, Sarah earned her degree in physical education. Sarah thought it would be useful to add to her skill set so she recently received a certificate in personal training. Once she completed the course she put all her energy into preparing a business plan and doing the ground work for her new business. Knowing Sarah's love for sports and fitness, her parents fully supported her business decision.

Sarah began to spread the news by "word of mouth" that she would soon open her own fitness and training facility. Sarah hired some high school students to deliver flyers that she designed and had printed at a local print shop. She paid the students a total of $500 to deliver the flyers to neighbourhoods within 10 km of her business location. Her dream came true on February 1, 2020. Sarah Smith Sporting (SSS) officially opened its doors to its first customers. The first 20 visitors received a one-year free membership. Sarah believed this would encourage the first 20 visitors to share their positive experience with their friends and encourage them to become new paid members.

Prior to opening on February 1, 2020. Sarah signed a five-year lease to rent the premises where she would conduct business. The premises had been previously used by a fitness club so all the necessary amenities, such as a reception area, showers, and fitness rooms, were ready for use. On January 2, 2020, she paid the landlord a $1,000 security deposit for any damages that may be caused by her business while renting the premises. The security deposit would be returned at the end of the lease minus any costs to repair damage from other than normal usage. In addition, Sarah paid for the first month's rent in the amount of $500. She also gave the landlord 11 cheques, one for each month in the coming year. To comply with the terms of the lease agreement Sarah arranged for property and personal insurance for the period February 1, 2020, to January 31, 2021.

Sarah also purchased equipments such as mats, balls, skipping ropes, and hand weights. She spent a total of $3,000 for these equipments. Sarah is hoping that the equipment will last more than one year as this will help to preserve cash in the company. She also purchased a computer and an "off-the-shelf" software package commonly used for businesses such as SSS.

In addition to the flyers that cost her $400 to design and print, Sarah advertised in a local newspaper. The advertising was going to run for four weeks starting February 14, 2020.

After studying various pricing structures at other fitness and training facilities, Sarah decided to offer the following pricing structure:

1. One-year membership—paid in full on the date of joining: $500 per membership

2. One-year membership—paid in two equal installments: $600 per membership paid one-half on the date of signing the membership contract and one-half six months later

3. One-year membership—paid in 12 equal installments: $720, the first one paid on the date of signing the membership contract. Monthly payments of $60 per month paid every 30 days from the first payment date.

The membership allows full use of the fitness facilities during all hours of operation.

Sarah plans to work at the club 7 days a week for 10 hours a day. Knowing that she cannot operate the club alone, she hired one full-time trainer and one part-time trainer. In order to entice these two well-known trainers, she offered them each a signing bonus: $1,000 for the full-time trainer and $500 for the part-time trainer. In addition to their competitive salary, she offered them a 5% bonus based on annual membership revenues. Sarah hopes that this will encourage the trainers to promote the business and bring in new members.

Sarah soon realized that all these costs were adding up quickly. She decided to approach a local bank where she had been a customer for several years. She asked the bank manager if she could borrow $10,000 to get the business started. The bank reviewed her business plan and felt comfortable with lending her the money given that Sarah had personally invested $20,000 into the business. The terms of the loan required Sarah to maintain a positive working capital and to provide monthly unaudited statements within 10 days of month end plus annual financial statements reviewed by a public accountant.

Given these bank requirements and having only studied first-year accounting, she decided to seek some accounting advice. Sarah texted you, a former university roommate who is now preparing for the CPA examinations, to ask if you could meet. You agree to meet Sarah on February 25 at the fitness facility.

Sarah has several questions about how to account for the recent business transactions. Specifically, she needs to understand what revenues and expenses will be reported in the first month end's financial statements. She wants to understand the alternatives if any exist. In addition, she wants to understand what type of entity she should use for this business venture.

Required

Prepare the report for Sarah. You are not required to prepare the financial statements at this point in time. However, some general advice regarding the appropriate accounting standards to adopt and the ideal form of business structure to pursue would be useful.

Severn Logistics

Severn Logistics (SL) was privately incorporated in 1985 and services the Greater Toronto Area and the Highway 11 corridor in Ontario. SL is in the "less than load" business, making its money by filling the trucks with several smaller loads and delivering them to and from Toronto.

Recently, the financial controller for SL retired, leaving the owner, Sven Bower looking for a new one. After several months of interviews, Sven made an offer to you for the position and with a hefty pay raise and substantial benefits, you accepted. This is your first week on the job, it is now December 31, and you need to make all of the property, plant, and equipment journal entries today that haven't been done as of yet. SL's year end is December 31.

The following events require your attention:

- On July 1, SL purchased land south west of Toronto that has the potential to be another loading terminal. In addition to the land, the purchase also included two transport trailers and one cube van. The total purchase price was $5.6 million and was paid 40% in cash and the balance as a five-year loan. The loan carries an interest rate of prime plus 2% with equal annual principal payments (every July 1). Interest is also paid annually on July 1. Appraisers have valued the land at $6 million, the two transport trailers at $220,000 each, and the cube van at $110,000. Although the transaction has taken place and possession has transferred, no entry has been made. The expected useful life of the trailers and the van are estimated at six years each. SL depreciates its trailers on a straight-line basis. Residual value is estimated at $10,000 for each trailer and zero for the van.

- On August 1, SL sold one of its buildings in Northern Ontario for $600,000. The building originally cost SL $250,000 and had accumulated depreciation of $118,000 at the time of the sale. Depreciation of $15,000 that had accumulated up to August 1 had not been recorded in the books. The proceeds were received in cash.

- On January 1, the previous controller determined that trucks with a cost of $575,000 and accumulated depreciation of $115,000 would actually have an estimated useful life of eight more years with no residual. The previous estimated useful life had been 10 years, with two years having already passed (so the useful life of nine years is from January 1 and beyond).

- A customer list from MTC Transport was purchased by SL on September 1 for $75,000 cash. It is expected that the list will generate revenues for the next six years.

- SL has internally developed a strong customer list of its own. The owner, Sven, has stated that this list is worth about $220,000 if sold.

- A warehouse terminal and land in the Kawartha area was purchased on November 1 for $750,000 cash. The land is valued at $600,000 and the terminal at $150,000. SL depreciates terminals at 6% per year using the declining-balance method.

- SL has an administrative building just west of Ottawa that is recorded on its books at $800,000. The building was purchased five years ago and has been depreciated over 20 years. On December 31, it was determined that there was a major soil issue around the building, which will make it difficult to sell. It is estimated that the building's fair value and value in use is now 30% of its original cost, with an estimated $40,000 in costs to sell.

Additional information:

- SL records its depreciation to the nearest month. In other words, an asset purchased October 1 would have its depreciation prorated (3/12ths).
- No entries have been made to reflect any of the transactions above.
- Prime is currently at 2%.

Required

Prepare journal entries, with supporting documentation, for the issues above. State any assumptions that you make.

Stealth Sky Views

Stealth Sky Views (SSV) is a private company that operates tourist rides from St John's, Newfoundland. Tourists pay for a one-hour ride that takes them to Signal Hill and up the coast. Sam, the owner, has noticed a significant increase in his rider base and is now looking at expanding by purchasing a new plane. Sam is considering several finance options (Exhibit I) and would like you, his accountant, to assist him.

Required

Provide Sam with a report that calculates each of the three financing options he has laid out, along with journal entries where requested. He would ideally like to minimize the amount of cash that he is required to repay over the next three years in order to cover operating costs. He would also like you to comment on the advantages and disadvantages of the various options. You may assume that the receipt of any cash and the purchase of the plane take place on January 1 and that SSV has a December 31 year end.

Exhibit I — Seaplane Financing Options

The plane Sam wants to buy is expected to cost $500,000. The freight charges to deliver the plane will amount to $5,000 and the plane is expected to last 15 years with proper maintenance and will have a salvage value of $20,000. Sam depreciates his assets on a straight-line basis. Sam would like you to provide the initial recording of the asset. You may assume that payment will be some form of loan for this portion and that the $5,000 delivery will be paid in cash; in other words, it will not be part of the financing. Sam would also like you to prepare the journal entry to record depreciation for the first year.

Financing Option #1

Obtain a $500,000 loan from the Royal Bank of Ryan. The loan would be repayable in five equal principal payments plus interest on December 31 of each year. The loan would carry an interest rate of 6%. Sam would like to see the entry for the receipt of the loan and the recording of the journal entries on December 31.

Financing Option #2

Issue $500,000 of bonds. The bond issue would be developed with a stated rate of 6% and would be a 10-year bond with interest paid semi-annually on June 30 and December 31. The current market rate for a similar bond is 4%. Sam would like the journal entry for the bond issue and the journal entry for the first two interest payments. SSV would use the effective interest rate to amortize any bond discount or premium.

Financing Option #3

Issue 50,000 common shares at $10 per share to private investors. Sam currently has 100,000 common shares outstanding, with his wife holding half and Sam holding half. He also has 5,000 preferred shares outstanding. They are all owned by his father and are cumulative, paying a dividend of $4 per share. For the first time, no dividends were paid last year. It would be expected that a $100,000 dividend would be declared on November 1 of this year with a payment date of February 1. Sam would like the journal entry for the issuance of the shares and any dividend entries for this year under the assumption the dividend does get declared.

Tor's Party & Rentals

Tor's Party & Rentals (TPR) is a party and novelty store located just north of Windsor. TPR is a private company, and was founded in 2008 by Amanda Harkings. TPR sells all kinds of party needs, from balloons to loot bags, and from gift wrap to food items. TPR also sells party supplies for special holiday occasions and huge sporting events. TPR has a party room on location that can be booked for parties and other special events. TPR has a December 31 year end and operates by using a fairly simple accounting structure. Jessica Altooze has been the bookkeeper for TPR since it opened in 2008 and has been diligent in recording the journal entries and preparing the year-end financial statements. In November 2020, Jessica won the lottery and immediately retired from the bookkeeping business and moved to South Carolina. This left Amanda on her own and without any real skills in accounting. Amanda immediately asked her auditor for someone with an accounting background to help her and you were hired as a result.

TPR had one major creditor at the beginning of 2020. One of the major banks loaned TPR $500,000 for ongoing operating costs. The outstanding portion of the loan was $400,000 at the beginning of the year. The bank requires TPR to maintain a current ratio of 1.8:1 or the loan may become immediately repayable. It also requires TPR to have a debt to total asset ratio of no greater than 55%.

It is now early January 2021 and you have an unadjusted trial balance (Exhibit I). Not all 2020 year-end journal entries have been made yet, but any unrecorded adjusting journal entries can be found in Exhibit II.

Required

(a) Complete the adjusted trial balance and create the 2020 year-end financial statements, except the statement of cash flows, for Amanda.

(b) Prepare a short memo to Amanda that addresses any concerns you have, specifically with respect to the covenants attached to the loan.

Exhibit 1	Unadjusted Trial Balance

	Debit	Credit
Cash	$ 49,000	
Accounts receivable	2,300	
Merchandise inventory	312,000	
Prepaid insurance	2,200	
Prepaid advertising	1,000	
Cash register machines	8,300	
Accumulated depreciation—Cash register machines		$ 4,400
Equipment	324,000	
Accumulated depreciation—Equipment		88,000
Accounts payable		18,000
Salaries payable		
Accrued liabilities		0
Unearned revenue		1,100
Interest payable		
Dividend payable		0
Income taxes payable		
Loan payable—Balloon machine		30,000
Long-term loan—Building		385,000
Common shares		35,000
Retained earnings		42,300
Sales revenue		1,036,000
Room rental revenue		43,000
Cost of goods sold	502,000	
Hydroelectricity expense	83,000	
Telephone expense	23,000	
Interest expense	15,000	
Salary expense	318,000	
Insurance expense	10,500	
Supplies expense	8,300	
Advertising expense	3,200	
Depreciation expense (all assets)	0	
Miscellaneous expense	21,000	
Legal expense		
Income tax expense		
Dividends		
	$1,682,800	$1,682,800

Exhibit II | **Adjusting Journal Entries**

Information required for adjusting journal entries:

1. There is no interest accrual required for the mortgage loan on the building because payment was made on December 31. The loan for the balloon machine carries an interest rate of 5% and has been outstanding for 15 days.

2. Depreciation of $800 on the cash register machines and $15,000 on the other equipment has not yet been recorded.

3. A dividend of $2,000 was declared but has not been recorded. It will be paid in March 2021.

4. The monthly electricity bill of $2,000 was received in early January 2021. This bill is for the month of December 2020.

5. Income tax expense of $27,000 is estimated as the payable.

6. Only 40% of the prepaid insurance amount related to 2020.

7. The lawyer's invoice for $800 for services performed in December 2020 was received in early January 2021.

8. Salaries that related to December 31, 2020, and not paid by the year end amounted to $12,000.

Intermediate Accounting I Cases

Alexander Properties

Contributed by
Sara Wick
Assistant Professor, University of Guelph

On January 1, 2020, Alexander Properties (AP), a private enterprise, transitioned to IFRS from ASPE. Brian McParland, the company's Chief Financial Officer, was responsible for all financial reporting issues upon transition. As he read through the international standards, he often saw ASPE methods as an option for reporting under IFRS. In any instances where the ASPE method was still an option, he instructed the company's controller, Fran Bouchard, to take the strategy "if it isn't broken, don't fix it."

It is now January 5, 2021, and the management team at AP is excited for some big expansion plans that are set to start this fiscal year and continue for the next five years. In order to finance the large expansion plan, management has decided to take the company public within the next couple of years. As such, there is a significant focus on maintaining a strong net income and key financial ratios such as return on equity and return on assets.

When IFRS was adopted at the beginning of 2020, Brian did not see the benefit of recording the investment properties at their fair value. At that time, the main user of the financial statements was the bank. The bank was not concerned with the fair values of the properties. As the company contemplates the upcoming IPO, Brian is starting to wonder if it would make more sense for the company to use fair value accounting to account for its investment properties.

Founded in 1990, Alexander Properties is well known for owning and operating commercial real estate. The company owns and operates several properties in large metropolitan areas including downtown Toronto, Montreal, and Vancouver. AP is headquartered in Toronto. Most recently, the company acquired two premium properties in New York City.

Alexander Properties operates as a private company but decided to transition to IFRS from ASPE as it always viewed becoming a public company as a viable option for obtaining financing. Over the past five years, the company has experienced significant growth as a result of the purchase of seven new properties.

The company's accounting department is managed by the controller, Fran Bouchard. Fran has a great understanding of the business and the relevant accounting as she has been the controller for almost 15 years. In light of the decision to take the company public, it has become a priority of Fran's to evaluate the statement of financial position and look for areas that could be improved. The most significant asset on the statement of financial position of the company is its investment properties. The company currently follows the cost method to account for these properties. By following this method of accounting, the true value of the asset is not reflected on the statement of financial position. At this point, Fran is not sure if there are fair value options under IFRS with respect to investment property.

Earlier that week, Brian McParland had asked Fran to present a summary of her findings to the management team in a meeting at the end of the month. Brian was responsible for the notion "if it isn't broken, don't fix it." He stressed that if she thought a method of accounting should be changed, he wanted a detailed explanation of why the change makes sense for Alexander Properties. His concern was focused on the long-term impact of any accounting change. Specifically, Brian wants to know what the impact would be on the current year net income, return on equity, and return on assets if any new accounting policies were adopted. He wants to know what the differences are between the revaluation model and the fair value model. The 2020 financial statements can be found in Exhibit I. Although Brian is concerned about these issues, he said to Fran "if worse comes to worse, we can just try out the fair value model, and if we don't like it, will just switch back."

As the economy weakened during 2008 and 2009, AP was able to show modest growth. AP is built on a strong foundation and therefore did not endure significant losses during this time. Since the company's inception in 1990, fostering long-term relationships with tenants has been a priority. When the financial crisis was at its peak, 70% of AP's tenants were occupying office space for five or more years. In order to foster these long-term tenant relationships, AP provides competitive prices in premium locations of the city. The companies AP serves have a desire and a need to be in the heart of the city.

At the end of 2009, AP purchased two premium properties in New York City at a discounted price. Although the properties required a significant amount of upgrading, AP was able to get them up and running in a very short period of time. Currently, both locations have a combined vacancy of 15%. When AP purchased the properties, management had forecasted both locations would remain 40% vacant until at least the end of 2015. As the two properties in New York City have been very successful, AP is planning on expanding further into the United States.

The company owns and operates 10 properties. In December 2020, the company had a real estate company value the properties to comply with the new IFRS standards. The fair values of the 10 properties can be found in the investment property analysis from the accompanying notes to the financial statements in Exhibit II.

Required

Prepare a report for Brian to assess whether it is optimal for the company to use fair value accounting to account for AP's investment properties.

Exhibit I | Simplified Financial Statements

Alexander Properties
Statement of Income
December 31, 2020
In Thousands of Dollars

	2017
Rental revenue	$ 31,711
Other property revenue	2,114
Total revenue	33,825
Property operating costs	10,809
Gross margin	23,016
Other expenses	1,350
Net income	**$21,666**

Note: Depreciation expense for the year totaled $6,000

Alexander Properties
Statement of Financial Position
December 31, 2020
In Thousands of Dollars

Assets		Liabilities	
Noncurrent assets		*Noncurrent liabilities*	
Investment property	$ 12,980	Mortgages and loans	$ 1,222
Loan receivable	1,407	Deferred tax liability	222
Investments	7,600	**Total noncurrent liabilities**	1,444
Total noncurrent assets	**21,987**	*Current liabilities*	
Current assets		Accounts payable	22,990
Deferred tax assets	850	Interest payable	500
Receivables	100,900	**Total current liabilities**	23,490
Cash and equivalents	110,980	**Total liabilities**	**$ 24,934**
Total current assets	**212,730**		
Total assets	**$234,717**	*Shareholders' equity*	
		Common shares	$ 120,000
		Retained earnings	89,783
		Total equity	**209,783**
		Total liabilities and equity	**$234,717**

Exhibit II	Investment Property Analysis

(In Thousands of Dollars)

Location	Purchase Date	Net Book Value	Fair Value December 31, 2017	Fair Value December 31, 2016
Toronto	February 10, 1990	$1,880	$2,940	$2,800
Toronto	February 10, 1990	$ 800	$1,281	$1,220
Vancouver	February 17, 1992	$1,560	$2,016	$1,920
Montreal	March 27, 1993	$ 520	$1,181	$1,125
Montreal	April 21, 1998	$1,580	$1,680	$1,600
Toronto	April 25, 1999	$2,000	$1,100	$1,000
Vancouver	November 23, 2003	$ 880	$1,947	$1,770
Montreal	December 17, 2003	$1,110	$2,200	$2,000
New York	December 15, 2009	$1,650	$1,815	$1,650
New York	December 15, 2009	$1,000	$1,199	$1,090

Better Health and Fitness

Better Health and Fitness (BHF) is a newly established business that offers yoga classes and yoga clothing and accessories. The BHF operates out of Saskatoon, Saskatchewan, and is owned by Carol Osborne a former yoga teacher for a large gym franchise. Carol decided to start her own yoga centre in order to provide a larger variety of customized yoga classes to small groups, including beginner, intermediate, and advanced classes. The BHF also has a small storefront that is used to sell yoga clothing, along with other accessories, such as headbands, water bottles, and yoga mats.

In order to help finance operations, BHF obtained a working capital loan from the small business department of a local credit union. The loan is a revolving line of credit that is secured by the company's inventory and accounts receivable. The loan is not to exceed a maximum of 50% of inventory and 75% of accounts receivable as at the company's year end (March 31, 2020). The BHF must present reviewed financial statements, prepared in accordance with ASPE, to the credit union within 60 days of its year end.

It is now February 2020, and Carol is starting to get nervous about the preparation of the financial statements. Carol has minimal exposure to accounting duties; therefore, she hired a local bookkeeper to help her select an appropriate fiscal year end, set up an accounting software package, and design processes and documents to be used in day-to-day functions.

Carol has contacted Lebeau and Liang LLP in regards to conducting a review of the BHF's financial statements. You are the senior accountant in charge of the review, and recently sat down with Carol to discuss the engagement.

Carol feels confident that all of her routine transactions have been posted correctly, but is unsure of some of the more complicated issues that arose during the year. Carol discusses with you the following unresolved issues:

1. BHF was able to obtain a large corporate client, Haschuk and Roney, Barristers and Solicitors, LLP. On July 1, 2019, BHF and the law firm agreed that the employees of the law firm would have unlimited access to the yoga classes for a yearly fee of $50,000, with 50% payable upfront. The fee is nonrefundable, noncancelable, and not dependent on the number of classes actually participated in by the law firm employees. Carol credited revenue for $50,000 when the contract was signed, and debited both cash and accounts receivable for $25,000 each. This large contract helped with cash flows, and is a major reason why BHF has a current cash balance of $10,000.

2. Mid-way through the year, BHF began selling energy bars and drinks in its storefront. BHF reached an exclusive agreement to be the sole distributor of Excel Energy Plus bars in Saskatoon. BHF was required to purchase 5,000 bars at the onset of the contract, at a cost of $2.50 per bar. On March 15, an ingredient included in the bars was allegedly linked to various illnesses. Currently, the Food and Drug Administration in the United States is investigating the allegations, and the outcome is uncertain. Canadian officials have not yet commented on the situation. BHF sold 1,340 bars during the year.

3. The aged accounts receivable balance is as follows:

		Balance	Current	30–60 days	61–90 days	over 90 days
1	Haschuk and Roney, LLP	25,000				25,000
2	Yvette Seguin	200		200		
3	Jane Collie	45	45			
4	Nurses' association	4,125	4,125			
5	Arthur Smith	75			75	
6	Ian Waruszynski	150				150
7	Fresh Grocery Ltd.	850		850		
8	Timber Forest Products	1,650			1,650	
9	BioMed Ltd.	950		950		
10	Precious Metal Miners	1,275			1,275	
		34,320	4,170	2,000	3,000	25,150

BHF reached an agreement with a local nurses' association to provide 55 pairs of yoga pants and shirts for an upcoming walk-a-thon in May 2019. The shirt and pants were customized with an embroidery of each nurse's name. BHF charged the nurses' association a special promotion price of $75 per combo and delivered the goods mid-March. In late March, the nurses' association contacted BHF stating that the goods received are not the same as the goods ordered. The nurses' association has asked for a 40% discount on the goods, or else it plans to return goods and cancel its order.

Receivables 7 to 10 are a result of a promotion held by BHF in order to attract more corporate clients. Based on her experience with a larger gym franchise, Carol states that 10% of receivables past 60 days are typically uncollectible. However, she is very confident that the receivable from Haschuk and Roney, LLP will be collected.

Even though a violation of the covenant can result in the credit facility becoming canceled with the outstanding balance due immediately, Carol states that she is not too concerned because her accounts receivable and inventory are $34,320 and $96,550, respectively, while her loan is only $65,000. However, she would like you to prepare a report, to go along with the review engagement, that discusses the appropriate accounting treatment of the above noted accounting issues.

Required

It is now March 30, 2020, prepare the report for Carol, and provide any other recommendations relevant to the bank loan.

Chaser Industries

Chaser Industries (CI) was established in 1983 as a manufacturer of outdoor furniture. It has quickly become a respected company and well known for its creation of highly durable, eco-friendly patio furniture. In 1993, CI went public and is following IFRS for financial reporting purposes and has a December 31 year end. Ted Madunic, CI's controller, has been with them for 10 years and oversees the financial functions and the year-end audit functions. CI's auditors, Bomanji, Dagwood LLP (BD), have completed the audited financial statements for the last eight years. CI has typically had a very good rapport with the firm. You, CPA, are a newly minted senior staff accountant and this is your first time on the audit engagement and your first time as a senior on an audit.

During the past fiscal year, CI has undertaken some innovative approaches to its business. This has been spearheaded by CI's founder and major shareholder, Patrick Pilek. While outdoor barbecues and patios remain a popular part of a Canadian summer, the current economic recession has resulted in some customers delaying replacement of their seasonal furniture. As a result, Patrick has looked at new ways to lower costs and this has led to some accounting events that are not a normal occurrence for CI.

In is now January 3 and in anticipation of the upcoming audit, Ted has asked your firm to provide some alternatives and recommendations on how to deal with some of the year's events. CI has always prided itself on providing the most transparent financial presentation possible while maximizing net income.

Exhibit I summarizes the accounting issues that CI is requesting guidance on. Your partner would like you to provide a draft report to Ted and Patrick that fully analyzes the alternatives available.

Required

Provide the report.

Exhibit I	Summary of CI's Accounting Issues

- CI's furniture is manufactured with layers of composite wood and resin. Patrick researched ways of reducing the cost of manufacturing through the use of an advanced, computerized machine. The machine was created, on paper, by Patrick, and built by a company that designs and manufactures specialized equipment for businesses. The machine was built for a cost of $1,665,000 with installation costs totaling $25,000. Installation occurred in November. It is expected to last 10 years and substantially reduce operating costs. It is not clear yet if this new machine will reduce the number of employees at CI as the highly computerized equipment may replace some of the work currently being done. It will improve the quality of the furniture even further and create a competitive advantage within the marketplace.

- In order to help finance the cost of the new equipment, Ted researched and applied for a number of government grants that were put in place to stimulate the economy. While he didn't expect to necessarily receive all of the grants, he was pleasantly surprised that CI was awarded two different grants. A summary of each follows:

  - Grant #1: The Government of Canada provided CI with a $600,000 capital grant to offset the cost of the new equipment. The terms of the grant called for the construction of new equipment that would allow Canadian companies to continue to be competitive throughout the world. Payment would be made upon completion and installation of the equipment. The government required proof via invoices and a letter from the manufacturer of the equipment. CI has completed all the documents and mailed the information on December 15. CI was told to expect 8–12 weeks for payment.

  - Grant #2: The Government of Quebec agreed to provide a $150,000 grant to offset labour costs for medium-sized manufacturing firms. The terms of the grant were that CI would maintain a labour force of a minimum of 25 employees as calculated on a monthly weighted average throughout each of the next three years. The entire $150,000 (assume to be divided equally between the three years) was received on December 1. Should CI not achieve the labour targets in any given year, it will be required to repay that year's portion only. According to

labour data received by Ted, the required minimum of 25 employees was achieved this year.

- In addition to grants received this year, Ted informs you that there were some issues with a $60,000 grant received three years ago. The grant was to offset the hiring of recent university graduates under a federal government hiring program. The grant required CI to maintain a university graduate in its employment for each of three years with $20,000 each year being used to offset labour costs. Should the university graduate leave the employment of CI at any time within the three-year period, the entire amount would be repayable to the government. The entire $60,000 was received in cash and initially recorded as deferred revenue; $20,000 was recognized in year 1 as revenue and a further $20,000 recognized in year 2. When you examine the audit file, you note that the partner agreed with this accounting as there was strong evidence that the graduate would remain within CI's employment for substantially longer than three years. This year, however, the graduate decided to leave CI in order to sail around the world. The government has sent notification that it will be seeking repayment of the $60,000 as a result of this.

- Right near the end of December, the new federal Liberal government announced and funded a special "Green Canada Initiative" (GCI). As a part of a newly formed environmental accord with other countries around the world, the Government of Canada has pledged the reduction of carbon emissions in the future. To kick start this immediately, the government sent a total of $9 billion to Canadian companies under the GCI program. As a result, CI received $350,000 on December 28. The terms of the GCI program require companies to use the money to reduce environmental emissions. Companies must track and produce invoices and other supporting documentation in order to keep the money. A maximum of 25% of the money can be used for what the government calls educational awareness training. If a company runs an employee training program that creates awareness of environmental issues, it can have that training, meals, and any other related costs covered, to the 25% maximum. Any unspent funds or unsupported funds will have to be sent back to the government in five years. Ted does not know at this stage how, or if, he can actually spend the money.

Fantasyfootball.net

Fantasyfootball.net (FFN) is a company whose primary activities are hosting a real-time, online fantasy football website and writing and publishing an annual magazine that discusses fantasy football strategies, predictions, and articles. FFN has an August 31 year end. This year end was selected as the main football season begins in September.

FFN is a privately held company, owned by Danny Chen and Manny Schwaid, two friends who started the business to build on their affinity of fantasy football and capture a portion of the $800-million industry. Danny holds a computer science degree, and Manny holds an Honours Bachelor of Commerce degree and is a professional accountant. By providing faster service, along with more statistics, projections, and game play options, Danny and Manny felt that they could offer a unique service that differentiates their website from all of the competitors. In addition, FFN is seeking to expand its services by offering fantasy coverage of American college and Canadian professional football, to go along with American professional football.

Given the significant growth in the industry, FFN has recently received many offers to sell the business. Danny and Manny are unsure about selling their business as they enjoy their jobs, and believe that there will be much room for future business growth. However, the owners also know that fantasy football could be just another fad that is currently at its peak. In addition, the rate of change in the online gaming industry could lead to a possible alternative platform. Therefore, the owners feel it is prudent to at least consider the offers to sell.

A general review of the purchase offers suggests that fantasy football companies generally sell for an average of two times revenues and four times net earnings. The owners review the internal financial statements for 2020, which report revenues of $975,000 and earnings of $536,250. Danny quickly determines that FFN could be sold for $2,047,500 or just over $1 million for each owner. This is a considerable sum of money given that they have invested only five years with FFN. However, Manny states that the internal financial statements are only draft at this stage because he has yet to consider the impact of the following events:

1. FFN writes an annual fantasy football magazine. The magazine goes on sale in July, and is sold through the company's website and through various retailers. This year, FFN secured a large contract with Books, a large book and magazine retailer in Canada. The contract allows Books to return any unsold magazines at the end of October (history suggests that annual magazines no longer sell after October as they become outdated and lose their relevance). A total of 40,000 magazines were shipped to Books in July. Books will be required to pay FFN $3 per magazine if all 40,000 are sold, $3.50 per magazine if less than 40,000 but more than 20,000 magazines are sold, and $4 per magazine if less than 20,000 are sold. The magazines have a retail price of $6.99.

    The cost to develop the content and publish the magazine was incurred in the months of April to July. Accordingly, Manny recorded $120,000 in revenue when the magazines were shipped. Historically, FFN has sold 70% of its stock prior to August. Danny and Manny believe that the amount of foot traffic at Books should increase the percentage of magazines sold.

2. FFN revised the layout, graphics, and content of the annual magazine this year. The redesign resulted in an additional $45,000 in expenses in the current year, relative to the past three years, whereby the magazine maintained the same format as in prior years. Magazines normally go through a redesign phase every three to four years in order to provide readers with a fresh and current magazine. Manny has capitalized the $45,000 as an intangible asset (magazine design). The finite life asset will be amortized over its useful life.

3. FFN earns the majority of its revenue from fees charged to use its website to host a fantasy football league. FFN charges users $20 per season (seasons run from September to January). This year FFN offered two new promotions:

    (a) Early Bird Registration: Users who register and pay for a season prior to August 31 would be eligible for a reduced $15 fee. The fee is nonrefundable and must be used for the upcoming fantasy football season. A total of 5,000 users took advantage of the early bird price for the upcoming season. Revenue was recorded as users registered.

    (b) Three-Year Membership Fee Reduction: Users can register and pay for the next three seasons for a total price of $30. The fee is nonrefundable and must be used for the upcoming three fantasy football seasons. A total of 7,000 users registered for the three-year membership fee. Revenue was recorded as users registered for the three-year seasons' package.

4. In addition to redesigning the annual magazine, FFN also redesigned its website. The redesign resulted in some general changes, along with significant upgrades to the functionality of the website. The total cost of the website redesign was $95,000, of which $57,000 was a result of programming costs for the upgrades and advertising. Manny has capitalized all $95,000 in costs to the website intangible asset.

Given the nature of the company's operations, the vast majority of all costs are fixed overhead costs related to staff support, server maintenance, hardware maintenance, and website design. Any variable costs are immaterial.

Required

It is now September 2, 2020, assume the role of Manny and determine the revised revenue and net earnings amounts in accordance with ASPE.

Forestry Limited

Contributed by
Irene Wiecek
Senior Lecturer in Accounting, University of Toronto
Director, CPA Rotman Centre for Innovation in Accounting Education
Associate Director, Master of Management & Professional Accounting,
University of Toronto, Mississauga

Forestry Limited (FL) is a private company incorporated in Canada. Its head office is in Toronto but its primary operations are in China and include owning and managing tree plantations, sales of trees and logs, and manufacturing of wood products. In addition to the above, the company also holds tree-cutting rights for several large areas of government-owned forest. The company is currently at the centre of a major media debate. Another company has accused them of grossly overstating their estimated land and forest holdings. FL is denying all charges and maintains that it had qualified consultants estimate the value of the holdings. Due to an economic recession, sales are down this year.

In order to maximize the quality and quantity of trees harvested from the plantations, the company must manage the forest, including feeding the trees, using herbicides where necessary, managing water supply to trees, and thinning out trees so that the remaining trees have sufficient light and space to grow. In order to manage the water supply, the company builds terraces on the land on which the trees are standing. This helps hold the water but is very labour intensive and costly as it must be done by hand. All the materials needed must be trucked in and then carried to the worksite for installation. The trees are less susceptible to damage from bugs and/or other insects when they are well watered. It has been a very dry year and 25% of the forests are suffering from drought and insect infestation. FL is hopeful that with additional care, it can reverse any potential damage from this so that the value of the wood is not affected.

FL has just purchased the rights to cut down trees in a large forest in Northern China. The agreement allows it to harvest the trees for a five-year period. Although not written in the contract, it is understood that it will replant the area when finished. In order to access the trees, the company has had to build a major road into the forest. After the harvest is completed, the road will not be used by FL but the government has indicated that it would like to consider buying the road. The acquisition was financed by the issuance of noninterest-bearing convertible debt to an institutional investor. Under the terms of the debt, FL must maintain a debt to equity ratio of no greater than 2:1.

On December 31 (year end), the company signed an agreement to buy a plantation in New Zealand for $20 million from NZL. Immediately thereafter, FL agreed to sell the property to Gray Trees Limited (GL) for $22 million. GL had been unsuccessful in acquiring the plantation directly and had enlisted FL to negotiate on its behalf. In the December 31 financial statements, FL has booked the transaction as two separate transactions: a purchase and a sale (resulting in revenues for the current year showing a significant increase). The deal with GL closes on January 1 and GL will pay cash of $22 million to FL at that time. The $20-million payment to NZL is due January 1. GL is an established company that deals with FL all the time. GL is very profitable.

On December 15, FL signed an agreement with Logs Limited (LL) under which FL will harvest timber from a forest owned by LL and "sell" the logs back to LL. The agreement is worded such that FL "buys" the cutting rights for $7 million and then sells the cut logs for $14 million (market price). No money will change hands until the job is done, at which point, LL will pay FL the net amount of $7 million upon delivery of the logs. The harvesting was completed by year end and FL booked $14 million as revenues.

FL is not sure whether it should follow IFRS or ASPE.

Required

Adopt the role of the company's auditors and discuss the financial reporting issues.

Frosty Frozen Treats

Frosty Frozen Treats (FFT) was established in 1995, in Nanaimo, BC, by Partha Mashraw to produce natural ice creams using only milk, sugar, chocolate, and fruits. The company prides itself on its wide selection of varieties and the fact that it uses no preservatives or stabilizers.

Partha is planning to take the company public within the next few years; however, he is having doubts given the recent turbulence in the equity markets as a result of the global economic slowdown. The IPO market has become much more competitive as investors are hesitant to take on the risks associated with small cap companies. Only companies with a strong financial position and earnings growth have been greeted positively by the equity markets.

The controller of FFT is preparing the year-end financial statements and external audit working paper file. The controller is reviewing the following transactions that took place during the year (all figures are in '000s):

1. The company agreed to sell a large order of ice cream to a retailer in exchange for $10,000 cash and a note receivable for $50,000 at 3%. The note is repayable at the end of a two-year period. Interest must be paid at the end of each year. The retailer's normal borrowing rate is prime plus 3%. At the time of the sale, prime was 3%. FFT recorded revenues of $60,000.

2. Given the recent volatility in the market, FFT decided to enter into a futures contract to lock in the price of milk on April 1. The contract is traded on the Chicago Mercantile Exchange, under the symbol DC, and is for the standard contract size of 200,000 lbs. The contract was entered into at a price of $21.22 per hundredweight. As at year end, milk was trading at $19.54 per hundredweight. FFT has not recognized this futures contract in the accounts.

3. On July 1, the company received a $150,000 patent infringement settlement regarding a competitor's use of FFT's special recipe. The funds are going to be used to reinvest in the business's capital assets and expand operations within the next two years. Because the expansion is not taking place until next year, management decided to invest funds into an exchange traded fund that invests in a mixture of short and long-term bonds. The bond fund was trading at $12.50 per share on July 1, and at $13.38 on December 31. This bond fund is being carried at its historical cost.

4. On January 1, the company purchased for $150,000 a newly issued, five-year bond that was yielding 6%, when the market rate was 6%. Interest is paid annually. As of year end, global economic turmoil resulted in a flight to safety, pushing market yields down. The market rate for this bond is now 5%. Management plans to use the funds from the bonds to help finance the future expansion plans. The bond is currently being measured at amortized cost.

5. During the prior year, FFT purchased 10% of the common shares of Crispy Cones (CC), a producer of waffle ice cream cones, for $200,000. The shares of CC are not publicly traded, and the purchase price was established as five times net income of $40,000. The past fiscal year has proved to be a challenge for CC due to increased competition, commodity price inflation, and an inability to raise prices due to limits on consumer discretionary spending. CC's most recent financial statements report reveals net income of $27,500.

Prior to the above-noted transactions, pretax net income was $225,000. The management team is happy about the current year results as they will obtain a bonus of $11,250, or 5% of net income. The company has a December 31 year end.

Required

Assume the role of the controller and prepare a report that discusses the recognition and measurement of the financial instruments noted above. The company uses IFRS.

Kentuckyville Slugger

Kentuckyville Slugger (KS) is a manufacturer of baseball and softball accessories. The company was established by Sammy Sousa in 1913, and produced only wooden baseball bats. KS has evolved over the past hundred years to offer a wide variety of products, including aluminum bats, batting gloves, cleats, and fielding gloves. KS's products are sold in Canada, the United States, and Mexico. Since inception, the company has continued to be a family-run, closely held business with its manufacturing plant located in Red Deer, Alberta.

Recently, the company has been finding it difficult to compete in the global marketplace due to the fluctuating Canadian dollar, the lower wage costs in Asia, and a general decrease in consumer discretionary spending following the global credit crisis. The recent competitive pressures have made it difficult for KS to reinvest in its capital assets in order to become more efficient.

The current CEO, Michael Sousa, does not want to relocate as the company is a long-standing member of the Red Deer community, providing many citizens with well-paying jobs. However, the competitive landscape is making it difficult to continue the status quo.

Michael has recently come across a new government grant program that is part of an initiative to improve the productivity of Canadian companies and promote employment. The program provides eligible manufacturing companies with the opportunity to receive a forgivable loan to upgrade their capital assets in the interest of efficiency. The following criteria are used to assess eligibility:

- The grant must be used to invest in capital assets that will improve productivity, as measured by output per employee hour.
- The grant must promote employment in the manufacturing sector in Canada.
- The company must display a financial need for the application.

If obtained, the grant would allow KS to continue to operate in Red Deer with the same workforce and increase its output by at least 20%. Audited financial statements must be included with the grant application.

Brandon Sousa, CPA, is the controller of KS. Recently, Brandon has begun preparing the December 31, 2020 year-end financial statements to provide to the external auditors. Brandon recently met with Michael in order to discuss certain transactions that have yet to be recorded in the books of account. Michael would like Brandon to prepare a report that discusses the appropriate accounting treatment of these transactions. The notes from the meeting can be found in Exhibit I.

Required

Assume the role of Brandon and prepare the report. The financial statements are prepared in accordance with ASPE.

Exhibit I Notes from Meeting with Michael

- KS entered into a sales agreement with the Canadian Hardball Association (CHA) to provide 5,000 hardball bats (at a price of $50 per bat) for an upcoming international baseball tournament that will be held in Canada. The bats were shipped to the CHA during the month of November 2020. Per the agreement, the CHA has until February 2021 to inspect the bats in order to determine if they meet international safety and performance standards.

- KS has manufactured bats for similar tournaments in the past and has never had an issue meeting the safety and performance standards. Michael suggests not recording any revenue in the current year because the CHA has the right to accept or reject the quality of the bat.

- KS delivered 2,500 soft-spike cleats to The Shoe Store for $100,000 in December. The cleats were sold during the holiday season. The cleats can be returned to KS within one year of the purchase date in the case of a manufacturer defect. Past history suggests that 5% of the cleats are returned within the one-year return period. Michael suggests that the revenue should be recorded once the right of return period lapses.

- During the year, KS entered into a sales agreement with SportStore (SS) whereby KS designed and manufactured an aluminum bat that is to be sold exclusively through SS's retail stores across Canada. The exclusive agreement is for a two-year period, at which point the bat can be sold through other retailers. During the agreement period, SS must purchase a minimum of 100,000 bats from KS at a price of $55 per bat. During the year, SS purchased 45,000 bats.

- KS incurred $155,000 in design and development costs during the year in developing the bat. KS incurs $25 in costs to manufacture the bat. Michael suggests that the $155,000 design costs be expensed in the current year.

- KS sold on credit 2,500 KSX baseball gloves for $50,000 to Q-Mart in November 2020. Q-Mart is a large public company, with retail stores across Canada and the United States. Around year end, analysts have begun reporting that Q-Mart is having serious financial difficulties and may file for bankruptcy if its lenders do not restructure its debt. Q-Mart's share price has plummeted in recent weeks. Michael suggests writing off the $50,000 account receivable.

- During the year, KS acquired a new storage warehouse in Red Deer. The warehouse was purchased for $250,000. KS then incurred $10,000 in costs to install an HVAC system and $7,500 to replace the roof shingles. Michael suggests expensing the additional costs ($17,500) as repairs and maintenance.

Mandrake Pharmaceutical Ltd.

Mandrake Pharmaceutical Ltd. (MPL) is a biotech company that is involved in research and commercialization of products to treat a variety of human diseases and to boost human health. The company issued an IPO in the current year, and is traded on the Toronto Stock Exchange under the ticker MPL. The company also has bonds issued in the public market, which are currently yielding 8%.

Given the recent market volatility and global economic conditions, the share price of MPL has been under significant pressure. During its first year on the TSX, MPL's stock price has performed as follows:

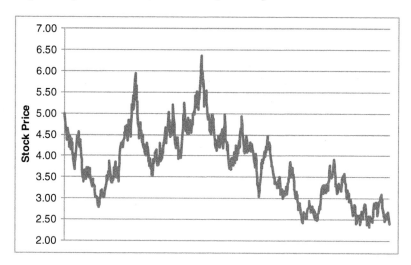

The stock price peaked at around $6.50 per share but has steadily declined since the company announced second-quarter earnings that missed analysts' expectations. Third-quarter earnings met analysts' expectations; however, this did not prove to be a catalyst for share price appreciation.

Shareholders were upset with the weak IPO issuing and are again becoming restless with the slumping share price. Shareholders are looking for management to generate shareholder wealth and there have been rumblings that a shareholder activist group is looking to change top management at the upcoming annual meeting. The low share price has also led to speculation that MPL will be taken over by a larger biotech company through a hostile bid.

The CFO is now preparing the annual financial statements for the year ended December 31, 2020, and considering the following transactions during the most recent quarter:

- MPL recently attracted two new researchers to the company. The researchers were paid an upfront signing bonus of $350,000 each. The researchers come from a larger company and have a proven track record of developing profitable products. For example, the researchers recently developed (in their previous employment) a highly profitable testing procedure that detects early stages of prostate cancer. The procedure is estimated to generate in excess of $5 million in discounted cash flows. The researchers must work for MPL for a minimum of three years, or else the bonus must be repaid.

- MPL purchased a patented pharmaceutical drug for $3.4 million from a smaller company that does not have the resources to commercialize the product. The product treats kidney disease and is named BlockXs. Generally, drug patents last for 20 years. However, the patent was applied for three years ago when clinical trials began.

The product has been recently approved by both Health Canada and the U.S. Food and Drug Administration (FDA), and will be available to the market next year. BlockXs is expected to earn the following net cash flows:

- Fiscal 2021—$1,250,000
- Fiscal 2020—$750,000
- Fiscal 2023—$750,000
- Fiscal 2023—$750,000

- Fiscal 2025—$750,000
- Fiscal 2026—$750,000
- Fiscal 2027—$750,000
- Fiscal 2028—$750,000

- During the most recent quarter, MPL had a breakthrough in its research and development of a new protein supplement called Protein². Protein² successfully merges the benefits of whey and casein proteins in an ultra absorptive formula. The following costs were incurred on the project during the past quarter:

Protein²—Costs Incurred

• Costs incurred in order to obtain government approvals and patents:	$ 33,000
• Purchase of equipment to be used to manufacture the protein supplement:	550,000
• Materials and services consumed in development of formula:	345,000
• Payroll and consulting expenses incurred in the design of a logo and packaging:	37,800
• Marketing of the product in fitness magazines:	34,750
• Cost of efforts to refine, improve, and enhance the formula:	177,500
• Materials used in preproduction pilot testing:	88,000
	$1,266,050

Management is excited to launch this product as the protein supplement industry is large, and growing. Both Health Canada and the U.S. FDA have approved the product, and a patent for the formula has been filed and approved. Protien² is expected to generate net cash flows of $450,000 per year over the next five years.

- MPL purchased a nontransferable right to distribute its products through a direct-to-doctor sales company. The company visits doctors and hospitals and directly promotes the benefits of the products in order to sell the product. MPL paid $1.2 million to acquire the distribution rights for a four-year period, and must pay a royalty of 2% of all products sold through this outlet.

Management expects that there is a 55% chance that this new distribution arrangement will increase total sales by 5%. Total revenue in the current fiscal year is $5,150,000. However, there is a 25% probability that sales could increase by as much as 10%, and a 20% probability that sales could increase by as little as 2%.

Required

You have been hired as part of the accounting group. The CFO has asked you to prepare a report that discusses the appropriate accounting treatment of the transactions noted above. The CFO would like you to not only address recognition and initial measurement but also subsequent measurement.

Meltdown Incorporated

Co-authored with
Stephanie McGarry
Laurentian University

Meltdown Incorporated (MI) recycles plastic and then sells it to manufacturing companies to produce toys, household items (such as coffee makers), and so on. MI was founded in 1998 by Samuel Abdesselam. Sam has maintained full ownership of MI, deciding not to take it public when so many other recycling companies were going public. While Sam is the only shareholder, MI does have a substantial bank loan and the bank requires an annual audit of MI's financial statements and MI follows ASPE. Sam has a background in operations, but is also very strong in accounting.

It is now early 2021 and you are the controller for MI, having been hired just days before the December 31, 2020, year end. In October 2020, Sam decided to step away from the business and spend more time at his second home in Florida. In order to ensure there was someone at the MI facility to oversee production and day-to-day operations, Sam hired a chief operating officer, Fred Finklestein. Fred's background is sales and operations and he has limited knowledge of accounting. Fred tried to run the accounting side of MI when he was hired, but determined that it wasn't his area of strength. He received Sam's permission to hire you to help him with accounting for some of the activities in preparation for year end, and to help him understand the accounting function better.

Required

Sam has some very specific activities for you and has provided you with the information he requires in Exhibit I. Prepare a report to Sam that answers his questions and be sure to provide him with all the necessary backup and calculations to support your discussion.

Exhibit I ‖ **Meltdown Information**

- It is MI's policy to prorate depreciation in the year of acquisition and year of disposal (based on the month acquired or disposed). Depreciation is only calculated and recorded once per year, at year end, unless an asset is sold.

- On March 1, 2020, MM purchased a new delivery truck with a cost of $54,000, a residual value of $3,000, and a useful life of eight years. The truck is being depreciated on a straight-line basis. Fred would like you to calculate and prepare the journal entry to record the depreciation on the truck for the December 31, 2020, year end.

- Fred is also considering selling the truck on March 1, 2021. He expects to be able to get $45,000 cash for it and would like to know what the accounting implication would be if this happened. He feels that he would understand it better if you provided a journal entry with supporting calculations.

- During 2020, MI purchased a parcel of land with a building on it across the street from its current location. The purchase price was $450,000 for the land and the building. MI intends to build a new production warehouse on the land and demolished the old building on it. The cost of demolishing the building was $20,000 and MI was able to recoup $8,000 of these costs by selling the scrap to a recycler. Fred is unsure of how this should be accounted for and has asked you to provide the journal entry with support.

- MI also purchased new equipment on November 1, 2020. The equipment cost $125,000. In addition, MI had to pay $5,000 in shipping fees to have the equipment delivered and $8,000 to have a cement pad poured for the installation of equipment. Fred believes there was $15,000 of labour downtime as a result of the installation. The equipment has an expected salvage value of $8,000 and it is standard MI practice to depreciate equipment using a declining balance rate of 20%. Fred has asked you to set up the equipment on the books at the total cost of $153,000 and record the depreciation for the year end.

- Fred came to you and wanted to know why the land across the street that was purchased in 2020 could not be recorded at the estimated fair value of $800,000. "Since we purchased that land, prices have skyrocketed in the area. Just yesterday, I had a call from a casino developer asking if they could buy it for $780,000. I think we could easily get $800,000 for it, but Sam doesn't want to sell it. I think we should record it at what we could get for it. What do you think?"

- During 2020, Fred worked hard to attract new business. In November, he managed to sign a contract with Simcoe Toys (ST) that would see MI selling 500,000 kg of recycled plastic to ST over the next two years at a price of $2 per kilogram. Fred is quite excited about the contract and the fact that ST paid $200,000 in advance of the start of production. The amount was received December 1, 2020. As of December 31, 2020, MI had produced and delivered 50,000 kg of recycled plastic to ST. You noted to Fred that it appears that the $200,000 deposit was recorded as revenue. Fred has asked you if there is anything wrong with that entry. If there is, he would like to know why and for you to make any correcting entry that you feel is appropriate.

- MI sells to many customers on credit. MI employs a credit manager who reviews a client's financial history prior to allowing them to buy on credit. It is MI's policy to use the allowance for doubtful accounts method based upon the aging of receivables. The balance is adjusted yearly after taking into account any adjustments for customers' accounts written off.

  A snapshot of MI's current accounts receivable balance at year end shows that it has a balance of $529,200 with an allowance for doubtful accounts debit balance of $6,000. (Note that this is prior to any adjusting journal entries that you would make.) A more detailed breakdown of the accounts receivable balance shows the following amounts aged:

0–30 days:	$280,000
31–60 days:	$155,000
61–90 days:	$ 75,600
Greater than 90 days:	$ 18,600

  You note that included in the above aged balances is an amount of $30,000 from a customer, Cutthroat Kitchens. This customer went bankrupt in November 2020, and there is no possibility of receiving payment from it. Fred doesn't know what to do with this amount but knows that you will.

  It is standard MI policy that 2% of receivables from 0 to 30 days will ultimately be uncollectible, 4% for 31–60 days, 20% for 61–90 days, and 80% greater than 90 days will be uncollectible. This policy is implemented after adjusting for any amounts at year end that will definitely not be collected.

- In January, MI decided to stop using a significant piece of manufacturing equipment. The equipment, purchased in 2018, is still quite useful because it can be retrofitted to produce many different items, but it no longer fits within MI's strategic plan. Details of the disposal are as follows:

Year	2018	2019	2020
Cost	$750,000	$750,000	$750,000
Accumulated depreciation	(25,000)	(50,000)	(75,000)
Net book value	$725,000	$700,000	$675,000

  According to the board of directors' meeting minutes, while management of MI intends to sell the machinery because it is only three years old and still has considerable life, the company may continue to use it to produce some units until a buyer is found.

  Management is responsible for these asset disposal decisions. Assets can be ready within 30 days' notice, and the marketing department has begun advertising on local websites in order to sell the equipment.

  Based on the area in which MI is located, there are many manufacturers and a sale should occur in the short term. When it was advertised for sale in January 2020, MI posted an asking price of $450,000 for the equipment.

Exhibit I | **Meltdown Information (Continued)**

MI predicts that it will take approximately one month to disassemble the equipment. MI has had a number of interested buyers but one in particular has expressed some strong interest. A new company wanting to produce outdoor resin furniture is interested, but is unable to purchase the equipment immediately because it won't be opening up until February 2021. The potential buyer is, however, willing to place a 25% deposit on the equipment immediately.

- As a means of cutting costs, Fred is considering revising the presentation of the financial statements to show just revenues and expenses instead of the current presentation of showing a full cost of goods sold statement. Fred is questioning the purpose of presenting such detail in the financial statements. "You and I know what is going on in these books, why do we need to show all this stuff?" He has also asked you to include in your report reasons why financial statements are prepared annually.

Munich IT Solutions

Munich IT Solutions (MITS) is a fast-growing, medium-sized business that primarily provides integrated server solutions that manage the storage, organization, and retrieval of information. MITS provides IT solutions by offering both server hardware and database management software.

MITS's CEO, CFO, and COO are compensated based on a 10% bonus of pretax net income if revenues exceed $4 million. The net income and revenue measures are based on the financial statements prepared in accordance with IFRS. The board of directors implemented such a bonus structure in order to help align the goals of top management and shareholders, and also ensure that executives do not cut discretionary spending in order to reach a net income bonus threshold.

MITS's top management team is excited about the current year's results because the draft financial statements reveal revenues in excess of the $4-million threshold and a bonus of $156,390 will be payable. The draft financial statements are to be reviewed by the internal audit department, in anticipation of the external auditor's field work next week.

You have just been hired as an internal auditor, reporting directly to the internal audit manager. The manager has called you into her office to discuss your first engagement:

MANAGER: "Welcome to the team. We are very happy that you decided to accept our offer of employment."

YOU: "Thank you. I am very excited to be here, and look forward to being a part of the team."

MANAGER: "Excellent. Well, your first engagement is a very important task. I would like you to review our draft income statement prior to the external audit next week. Specifically, I would like to you focus on the revenue line item. Please prepare a report that outlines any concerns that you have, and addresses any accounting issues."

YOU: "Okay, sounds interesting. How can I start?"

MANAGER: "Well, here is a copy of the draft income statement (Exhibit I). In addition, I have prepared the following notes of the current year's operations for your review (Exhibit II). This should be enough to get you started on your report. We can meet again once you have prepared your report."

YOU: "Sounds good. I'll get started right away."

Required

Prepare the report.

Exhibit I	Draft Income Statement

For the year ended December 31 (unaudited)

Sales

Mainframe server sales	$2,200,000	
Small business solution sales	2,625,000	
		$4,825,000

Cost of sales

Mainframe server	1,200,000	
Small business solutions	1,350,000	
		2,550,000
Gross profit		$2,275,000

Expenses

Advertising and promotion	$ 187,950
Amortization	98,000
Insurance	16,540
Interest	19,560
Legal and accounting	8,900
Lease expense	44,500
Office and general expenses	25,000
Repairs and maintenance	17,000
Utilities	34,000
Wages and benefits	272,000
	723,450

Operating income	$1,551,550
Other service income	12,350
Income before taxes and bonus	1,563,900
Bonus (10%)	156,390
Income before taxes	1,407,510
Current taxes (30%)	422,253
Net income	$ 985,257

| Exhibit II | Information Regarding the Current Year's Operations |

1. Mainframe Servers: MITS sells large mainframe servers for $550,000. The cost of the server is $300,000. MITS delivers and installs the server at the customer's site. The customer signs off on an acceptance form once the server is instaled and tested. MITS has never had a customer reject the installation of a mainframe server.

   In order to help promote sales, MITS began to offer a two-year warranty with all mainframe servers. The warranty is expected to cost an average of $45,000 per server to service the warranty over the two-year period. Industry competitors that offer similar warranties set the warranty price as two times expected cost.

   MITS has received orders for four mainframe servers during the current year, of which all four have been delivered and instaled and three have been accepted by the customer. During the current year, the periods of the warranties for the servers covered by MITS totaled 13 months.

2. Small Business Solutions: MITS's typical small business solution customer is a growing business without a designated information technology department that purchases server hardware. MITS sells a small business solution of $175,000, with payment in advance to allow MITS to order the servers. The small business servers cost $90,000.

   Included with the purchase of a server is one year of database management services. If a customer does not want the database management services, MITS provides a discount of $25,000 from the mainframe purchase price. All customers wanted the services in the current fiscal year and MITS provided a total of 47 months of DMS services as a result of these sales.

3. Database Management Services (DMS): MITS recently began marketing its DMS on a stand-alone basis for $3,500 per month, which is consistent with competitor prices. As of year end, the company has not received any orders for only DMS; however, management expects orders to begin to pick up shortly.

4. The gross margin percentage on the small business server and mainframe server is expected to be the same.

5. Small business solutions server revenue is recorded when the cash is received.

North Shore Car Dealers

North Shore Car Dealers (NSCD) is a holding company that owns two car dealerships in Ontario. One dealership services the city of Barrie, while the other dealership operates out of Orillia. Both dealerships sell new and used vehicles and have a full mechanic and body shop. The corporate structure is as follows:

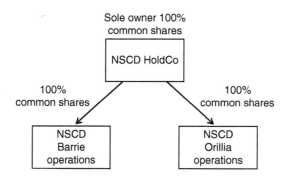

The owner of NSCD is planning to retire in the near future, and is looking to sell the NSCD Barrie dealership. Preliminary negotiations suggest that the dealership will be sold for tangible net worth plus two times net earnings, calculated in accordance with ASPE.

The financial statements of all three corporations have never been audited, as they have been prepared with a Notice to Reader report (compilation). Recently, a dispute has emerged between the owner of NSCD and the potential purchaser regarding the treatment of certain related-party and nonmonetary transactions. Accordingly, the owner of NSCD has approached your accounting firm seeking assistance with the proper accounting treatment of the following transactions:

1. On June 30, 2020, NSCD Orillia sold a building to NSCD Barrie for $600,000 cash. This amount has not been supported by an independent appraisal. NSCD Orillia had purchased the building for $1 million on January 1, 2010. NSCD Orillia used straight-line depreciation over the estimated 20-year life of the building. NSCD Orillia's contributed surplus account contains a credit balance of $100,000 from previous related-party transactions. NSCD Barrie does not have a balance in its contributed surplus account.

2. During the year, NSCD Orillia traded three used cars with a cost of $35,000 and a blue book value of $44,000 to NSCD Barrie for two used trucks with a cost of $33,000 and a blue book value of $43,000.

3. The controller's duties for both dealerships are performed by a single employee, who is paid from the Orillia operations. The controller is paid an annual salary of $75,000. The wage expense is included in only NCSD Orillia, although she spends her time equally between the Orillia and Barrie operations.

4. NSCD Orillia has guaranteed a long-term mortgage of $450,000 taken by NSCD Barrie. The Barrie dealership is experiencing some financial difficulties; however, it is difficult to predict if there is any risk of loan default.

Required

Prepare the report that discusses the appropriate accounting treatment of the above-noted transactions.

Northern Forestry Resources Ltd.

Northern Forestry Resources Ltd. (NFP) is an integrated pulp and paper company, with operations in Canada. NFP operates in the pulp, paper, and wood product market and has sales offices in Canada, China, and the United States. NFP's four operating segments are as follows:

- Pulp mills: The pulp mills convert wood chips (plant fiber source) into a thick fiber board (pulp). The pulp is then shipped to paper mills for further processing. Some pulp is transferred internally, while some pulp is sold to external customers.

- Newsprint and paper mill: The paper mills convert wood, pulp, and other fibers or ingredients into paper by using a Fourdrinier machine. The newsprint is sold to major newspaper companies, while the paper is sold through various outlets.

- Sawmills: The sawmills' main operation is to turn logs into boards. The boards are dried, dyed, and smoothed. The finished products are shipped to the lumber market.

- Coated and specialty paper: The coated and specialty paper mills are essentially the same as the newsprint and paper mills, except that the finishing equipment is enhanced in order to create coated and specialty papers. The coated and specialty paper division had an impairment loss two years ago when market conditions were much worse. The market conditions have reversed and are now more favorable.

The pulp and paper industry in Canada has come under significant pressure in recent years due to increased competition from global markets, a fluctuating Canadian dollar, and more scarce and distant sources of fibre supply.

The following are the quarterly earnings reported by NFP over the past two years:

| ('000s) | Current Year | | | | Prior Year | | | |
Quarter	4th	3rd	2nd	1st	4th	3rd	2nd	1st
Revenue	2,355	2,877	2,756	2,987	2,765	3,987	3,359	3,456
Earnings	(277)	(199)	(165)	177	212	388	375	455

Based on internal and external indicators, the auditors plan to conduct a comprehensive impairment test on the operating assets. The auditors know that the bank relies upon the financial statements in order to assess compliance with various loan covenants, including a tangible net worth test.

In order to assist with the impairment testing, the CFO has compiled detailed information regarding the cost bases of the capital and intangible assets (Exhibit I), future cash flow information (Exhibit II), and liquidating values for the capital assets (Exhibit III).

Required

Assume the role of the senior auditor in charge of the NFP year-end audit, and prepare a report that discusses the asset impairment tests of the operating assets under both ASPE and IFRS. Assume that an appropriate discount rate for the company is 7%.

| Exhibit I | Information Regarding Capital and Intangible Assets Cost Bases |

- The breakdown of the capital and intangible assets is as follows:

('000s)	Cost	Accumulated Depreciation	Net Book Value
Land	$ 1,235	$ 0	$1,235
Production buildings and equipment			
Pulp mills	7,655	3,455	4,200
Newsprint and paper mills	2,870	1,780	1,090
Sawmills	2,360	1,245	1,115
Coated and specialty papers	2,755	1,275	1,480
Roads and timber holdings	765	550	215
Other buildings and equipment	1,243	780	463
	$18,883	$9,085	$9,798

('000s)	Cost	Accumulated Depreciation	Net Book Value
Water rights	$ 300	$108	$ 192
Power purchase agreements	1,780	641	1,139
Forest Stewardship Council (FSC) and other licensing	350	126	224
Supplier agreements	275	99	176
	$2,705	$974	$1,731

- The combined NBV of the capital and intangible assets is $11,529.

- The following is a breakdown of the pulp mills' net book value:

Pulp mills selling to external customers	Net Book Value
Thunder Bay, Ontario, Mill	$ 965
St. Andrews, Quebec, Mill	855
Terrace Bay, Ontario, Mill	775
Pulp mills transferring internally	
Vancouver Island, B.C., Mill	730
Pine Falls, Manitoba, Mill	875
	$4,200

The Vancouver Island mill ships solely to the newsprint paper mills, while the Pine Falls mill ships only to the coated and specialty paper mills.

- The roads and timber holdings, the other building and equipment, power purchase agreement, and FSC/licensing asset classes are used equally by the four operating segments. (Note, 25% is used by the pulp mills that sell externally, while the internally transferring pulp mills' percentage is included with their respective division.)

- The supplier agreements are used exclusively by the specialty papers segment.

- The water rights are used exclusively by the sawmills.

- The land is used throughout all four operating segments. The net book value of the land is broken out as follows:

Pulp mills	
Thunder Bay, Ontario, Mill	$ 175
St. Andrews, Quebec, Mill	155
Terrace Bay, Ontario, Mill	120
Vancouver Island, B.C., Mill	95
Pine Falls, Manitoba, Mill	105
Newsprint and paper mills	225
Sawmills	195
Coated and specialty papers	165
	$1,235

- The Thunder Bay, St. Andrews, and Terrace Bay mills use the road and timber holdings, other building and equipment, power purchase agreements, and FSC/licences equally.

| Exhibit II | Cash Flow Information Regarding Capital and Intangible Assets |

- The cash flows from the pulp mills that sell to external customers are expected to be as follows:

Combined unit	$600 annually for the next 10 years
Thunder Bay Mill	$150 annually for the next 10 years
St. Andrews Mill	$250 annually for the next 10 years
Terrace Bay Mill	$200 annually for the next 10 years

- The cash flows from the newsprint and paper mills are expected to be as follows:

	Years Out:						
	1	2	3	4	5	6	7
Incremental Cash Flows	450	550	655	600	500	375	150

- The cash flows from the sawmills are expected to be as follows:

	Years Out:				
	1	2	3	4	5
Incremental Cash Flows	350	300	250	200	150

- The cash flows from the coated and specialty papers are expected to be as follows:

	Years Out:									
	1	2	3	4	5	6	7	8	9	10
Incremental Cash Flows	550	600	600	650	650	700	600	550	500	250

| Exhibit III | Liquidating Values of Capital Assets |

- The liquidating values of the segments are estimated to be as follows:

• Combined unit	$2,500
Thunder Bay Mill	$ 550
St. Andrews Mill	$1,000
Terrace Bay Mill	$ 950
• Newsprint and paper mills	$2,250
• Sawmills	$1,500
• Coated and specialty papers	$2,500

Pinnacle Properties Corp.

Construction Phase

Pinnacle Properties Corp. is a young company, established with the intent of earning rental income from apartment complexes. The company is owned by Bahram Habib. During the most recent year, the company built a 24-unit apartment complex. The construction commenced on March 1 and was completed by December 31, 2020 (year end).

The following is a detailed breakdown of the construction costs incurred (it is safe to assume that the costs were incurred evenly throughout the year):

	Cost	Useful Life (Years)
Appliances	$ 10,749	8
Asphalt driveway	9,249	8
Building permit fees	12,792	40
Cabinets and countertops	37,332	10
Drywall	33,996	40
Electrical wiring	24,927	20
Excavation, foundation, and backfill	47,634	40
Exterior doors	5,790	15
Framing and trusses	104,415	40
Gutter and downspouts	2,847	15
HVAC	26,580	10
Insulation	9,996	20
Interior doors and hardware	10,068	15
Landscaping and sod	21,264	8
Lighting and fixtures	7,116	15
Other	57,255	40
Other fees and inspections	9,495	40
Painting	22,914	8
Plumbing	35,259	20
Roof shingles	25,416	8
Sheathing	11,607	40
Siding	38,574	8
Stairs	5,028	40
Steel	4,911	40
Tiles and carpet	34,308	15
Trim material	22,182	15
Water and sewer inspection	11,283	40
Windows	18,708	10
Wood deck	5,844	20
Total	$667,539	

On March 1, 2020, the company issued a $500,000 bond payable at a rate of 10% to finance a significant portion of the construction costs. Details of other interest-bearing debt outstanding during the year are as follows:

8% 15-year bonds, issued September 1, 2009	350,000
6% 5-year bonds, issued July 1, 2015	175,000

Given the recent expansion with the company, Bahram has hired you as a controller. The company has adopted the cost model for its investment properties.

Required

Bahram has asked you to determine the cost-basis of the apartment complex and prepare an estimate of the annual depreciation. The company reports under IFRS.

Pinnacle Properties Corp.

Operating Phase

Seven years have transpired since the construction of the 24-unit apartment complex. Currently, the 24 units are fully rented, and operations are running smoothly. The company is getting ready to prepare the 2027 year-end financial statements. Again, Bahram has asked for your assistance with certain transactions related to the apartment building. Specifically, the following transactions must be accounted for:

1. During the year, the following repairs and maintenance took place:

   (a) On April 1, 2027, the roof and shingles were removed and replaced with a new and improved shingle design. The total cost of the new shingles was $26,500. The new shingles are expected to have a useful life of eight years.

   (b) On October 1, 2027, the entire apartment was repainted for a cost of $18,000. At the same time, the landscaping was redone, including laying new sod, for a total of $29,000. Both the painting and the landscaping are expected to have a useful life of eight years.

   (c) Prior to these transactions, no repairs or maintenance were required on the building.

2. At December 31, 2027, 24 new alarm systems were instaled, one in each unit. The total cost of the new alarm system was $35,000. The building did not include an alarm system prior to this installation.

In addition to the above transactions, Bahram is contemplating the use of either the fair value model (FVM) under IAS 40 or the revaluation model (RVM) under IAS 16. He is wondering how the financial statements would be impacted if the either of the FVM or RVM was implemented since inception (ignore any retroactive adjustments). Based on various valuation reports and industry standards, Bahram estimates the following fair values:

- 2020 $850,000
- 2021 $665,000
- 2022 $750,000
- 2023 $835,000
- 2024 $900,000
- 2025 $900,000

The sharp declines in 2021 and 2022 are a result of a global economic recession, with a rebound in 2023.

Required

Prepare a report that addresses Bahram's concerns.

Riverside Nursery

Jenny Kinnear just completed a university degree in natural resource sciences. Given the tough economic times, it has been difficult to find any form of meaningful employment. Prior to moving to Montreal in order to attend university, Jenny lived with her parents in a small farming community. Accordingly, Jenny has been thinking about acquiring some farm land on the outskirts of Montreal and establishing a farm and nursery. Farm land can now be obtained for a reduced price. Jenny has discussed the idea with her retired parents, and they suggested they would move to Montreal if she decides to pursue the business in order to assist her to get the business up and running.

On January 1, 2019, Jenny decided to go into business by incorporating Riverside Nursery (RN). RN immediately purchased a plot of farm land from a family of retiring farmers. The land was obtained for the bargain price of $1 million. A bank loan, with an interest rate of 5%, was obtained in order to help finance the land acquisition cost.

Jenny and her parents decided to segregate the farm land in order to be able to grow seasonal produce (strawberries, beans, peas, corn, etc.), Christmas trees, and raise chicken and cattle. A storefront is also included on the land. A map of the land can be found in Exhibit I.

It is now December 2020, and Jenny is beginning to worry about RN's financial statements. She knows that the bank loan requires RN to file audited annual financial statements. RN has engaged Abdillahi and Blouin LLP to perform the audit. In order to prepare for the upcoming audit, Jenny has hired you, CPA, for a special consulting contract. Specifically, Jenny provides you with the terms of the consulting project:

> "I feel that the nature of RN's business is fairly straightforward, except for inventory. Therefore, I would like you
> to prepare a report that discusses all theoretically possible measurement bases of inventory, along with the result-
> ing impact of each measure on revenue recognition. Based on your theoretical discussion, I would like your report
> to focus in on the actual accounting standards. Because the bank will accept either ASPE or IFRS financial state-
> ments, I would like you to discuss how my inventory should be accounted for under both standards."

Jenny provides you with some additional information regarding the operations of RN (Exhibit II), along with some financial information related to the inventory (Exhibit III).

Required

Prepare the report for Jenny.

| Exhibit I | Map of Farmland |

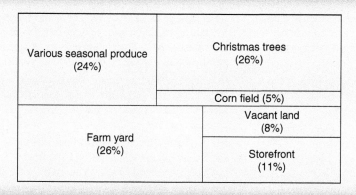

| Exhibit II | Information from RN's Operations |

Year end
- Jenny selected the fiscal year to run from January 1 to December 31 in order to capture a full season of the seasonal produce and corn field activities.

Seasonal produce
- RN grows a variety of seasonal produce, including peas, strawberries, cucumbers, and peppers.
- At the end of the season, RN sells produce through various means: (1) in bundles through their storefront; (2) through local retailers that promote local produce; (3) through farmer's markets; and (4) by allowing customers to pick their own basket of produce on site.
- The corn field is a component of the seasonal produce. The corn is grown and then sold through the same outlets as the rest of the seasonal produce. During the month of October, the corn field is turned into a Halloween corn field, whereby customers walk through for $10. The Halloween corn field was a huge success this year, and a great source of supplemental income. Jenny paid $7,500 to design the layout of the corn field, and to purchase the required accessories.

Christmas trees
- The Christmas tree market can be classified as pure competition. There is an abundant supply of trees, such that any individual supplier cannot impact the price. In addition, there are an abundant number of purchasers, such that any single purchaser cannot impact the price. Finally, the product is considered to be homogenous as well, aside from the type of tree (e.g., Douglas fir, white pine). Although trees may come in different shapes and colours, the value of a tree is based solely on its height (the shape can be altered through pruning while colour can be adjusted through dyes).
- A Christmas tree is priced similar to any commodity that trades in a market. The market price of a Christmas tree is determined

based on its equivalent of a commodity spot price. The following are the current Christmas tree prices for white pine:

3 Feet:	$30		7 Feet:	$45	Note: estimated selling costs are 10% of the sales price.
4 Feet:	$35		8 Feet:	$47	
5 Feet:	$38		9 Feet:	$55	
6 Feet:	$40				

- Generally, white pine trees are not grown to exceed 9 feet as their retail commercial value disappears at this level.
- Trees are scrapped as soon as it becomes apparent that they no longer have any value. Aside from any weather calamities or insect infestation outbreaks, the scrappage rate is fairly consistent from year to year.
- The growth rate for white pine depends a lot on whether trees are free to grow or are suppressed under a canopy. Average height growth for young suppressed white pine is often less than 6 inches per year. However, with free-to-grow trees on the better sites, height growth is normally 2–3 feet per year.

Farm yard
- During the past year, RN set up a chicken pen. The chickens are used to produce eggs, which are sold through retailers and at farmers' markets. Eventually, the chickens will be sold as poultry.
- A hen's reproduction cycle is set by the length of the day. During the summer months, a hen usually produces one egg per day. A hen will lay fewer eggs as the day shortens, eventually skipping days between laying eggs. Many hens stop laying eggs all together until the spring arrives because winter is a bad time to raise chicks given that cold weather decreases a chick's chance of survival.
- RN is planning to purchase cattle next year, and offer dairy products as well (milk, cheese, etc.). No expenses have been incurred in this regard for the current year.

| *Exhibit III* | Financial Information Related to inventory |

- During the year, RN started its Christmas tree farm by purchasing 8,000 white pine seedlings for $8 each. The seedlings are just below one foot tall when planted this year. Approximately 3% of all seedlings do not survive their first year.

- RN purchased and installed a sprinkler system that covers farm land area (seasonal and Christmas trees) for a total of $175,000. The system has an expected useful life of 8 years.

- RN consumed $55,000 in water directly related to the use of the sprinkler system.

- RN hired two student employees to work directly to maintain (prune, weed, water, etc.) the seasonal produce and Christmas trees. The two employees earned $35,000 in total over the course of the summer months.

- RN incurred costs of $13,000 for seeds related to the seasonal produce items.

- RN utilized fertilizers during the past year in order to aid with the growth process. Super Grow fertilizer was used for both the seasonal produce and trees, and cost $29,000. In addition, a total of $17,500 worth of Tree Booster was purchased during the year. A total of $2,500 worth of the product remained at year end.

- An organic pesticide was used during the year as well. A total of $27,000 and $34,000 was spent on Tree Bug Zapper and Pest Be Gone, respectively. The ending balance of Tree Bug Zapper and Pest Be Gone was $3,500 and $2,500, respectively.

- In order to help aerate the soil, RN purchased a land cultivator for $55,000. The equipment is expected to have a useful life of six years, and was used for the land around both the seasonal produce and trees.

- RN purchased 100 chickens (87 hens able to lay eggs, 10 chicks, and 3 roosters) for a total cost of $950 from a local farm. The hens are expected to be able to lay eggs for the next five years, at which point the hens will be sold for $8 each to a local grocery store.

- RN purchased $6,500 of chicken feed during the year. The year-end inventory of chicken feed is $2,250. In addition, RN purchased a cage for $2,500, which is expected to last 12 years.

- A dozen eggs are sold for $4, which reflects a premium as they are sold as organic eggs.

- Hens can be sold in the open market for $8 per hen.

Rosetta Inc.

Rosetta Inc. (RI) is a new corporation that just acquired the assets of an unincorporated technology business on September 1, 2019, from Jess Stone. Extracts from the purchase and sale agreement entered into by RI and Jess Stone are provided in Exhibit I. RI is owned by three shareholders: Carlos Guevara, the CEO of RI, who owns 20% of the shares of RI; and two investors, who each own 40% of the shares. Jess Stone is not a shareholder of RI.

Jess Stone developed new touch screen technology but lacked the financial resources necessary to benefit commercially from this technology. The touch screen technology is far superior to the current technology and has many potential uses, ranging from mobile devices, computer screens, and laptops.

RI put the technology it purchased to work immediately by entering into a licensing agreement with Mica Inc. (Exhibit II). In addition, RI has developed a new PC computer monitor with the touch screen and entered into an agreement with Ferrous Inc. to distribute the technology.

You, CPA, have been recently employed by RI as the special assistant to Carlos Guevara. On July 3, 2020, Carlos calls you into his office and says he has an assignment for you:

> "The financial statements of RI for the fiscal year ending August 31, 2020, are required to be audited. I want you to address the significant financial accounting issues pertaining to the preparation of RI's financial statements for its first fiscal year ending August 31, 2020, and provide your recommendations on the accounting treatments to be used."

As you leave Carlos's office, he provides you with a file that includes some additional information about the operations of RI (Exhibit III).

Required

Prepare a report that addresses the requests of Carlos Guevara.

| *Exhibit I* | Extracts from the Purchase and Sale Agreement Between RI and Jess Stone |

Purchase and Sale of the Business Assets of Jess Stone
- RI will purchase the technology and the research findings of Jess Stone as at September 1, 2019
- RI agrees to purchase the equipment owned by Jess Stone as at September 1, 2019
- Jess Stone agrees to be responsible for all liabilities as at September 1, 2019

Purchase and Sale Price
- RI will pay to Jess Stone an amount of $3.5 million for the technology and the research findings
- RI agrees to pay to Jess Stone the appraised value of $420,000 for the equipment

Contingent Consideration
- RI agrees to pay to Jess Stone an amount equal to 50% of net income (determined in accordance with generally accepted accounting principles) in excess of $500,000 for the fiscal year ending August 31, 2020

Employment Contract with Jess Stone
- RI and Jess Stone agree to enter into a two-year employment contract, and RI agrees to pay to Jess Stone an annual salary of $200,000
- Jess Stone agrees that all research findings during the employment are the property of RI

| *Exhibit II* | Extracts from the Licensing Agreement Between RI and MICA Inc. |

Licensing Arrangement
- RI agrees to provide to Mica the exclusive right to use the touch screen technology referred to as FeldsparX for a term of three years commencing on December 1, 2019
- RI agrees to deliver the technology to Mica on December 1, 2019
- Mica agrees to pay to RI a licensing fee in the amount of $900,000, with the first payment of $300,000 due on December 1, 2019; and agrees to make payments in the amount of $300,000 plus interest of $36,000 on December 1, 2020, and $300,000 plus interest of $18,000 on December 1, 2021

Royalty
- Mica agrees to pay to RI a royalty fee in the amount of 15% of the gross margin (determined in accordance with generally accepted accounting principles) realized by Mica from sales of goods that use the FeldsparX technology
- Mica agrees to provide to RI a quarterly statement of gross margin realized by Mica that is subject to the royalty payable to RI
- RI, or its representative, has the right of access to the records and information of Mica necessary to audit the gross margin reported by Mica to RI

Exhibit III | Information Obtained About the Operations of RI

Licensing Arrangement with Mica
- Revenue in the amount of $300,000 has been recognized in the accounting records
- Royalty revenue in the amount of $135,000 has been recognized in the accounting records based on a gross margin of $900,000 reported by Mica for the six months from December 1, 2019, to May 31, 2020
- Mica is a financially sound entity

Research and Development
RI acquired the following technology and research findings from Jess Stone:

Project Technology/ Assigned Name	Fair Value	Current Status
FeldsparX	$ 700,000	licensed to Mica for three years (see Note 1)
QuartZ	1,500,000	used in the commercial production of goods (see Note 2)
BasalT	900,000	used in the commercial production of goods (see Note 3)
Grandiorite	400,000	testing use in a possible product
	$3,500,000	

Note 1—FeldsparX Technology: Management of RI decided to license use of the FeldsparX technology rather than to produce goods using this technology itself. Management expects that this technology will have a useful life of three years.

Note 2—QuartZ Technology: Management of RI estimates that the QuartZ technology will generate total revenue in the amount of $7.5 million over a four-year period commencing December 1, 2019.

Note 3—BasalT Technology: Management estimates that the BasalT technology will generate total revenue in the amount of $2.7 million over a three-year period commencing March 1, 2020.

Jess Stone has started work on a new project, Kryptonite, after becoming an employee of RI and this project is presently in the conceptual formulation state of a possible product that uses the technology.

A research and development asset in the amount of $3.5 million is reported on RI's statement of financial position as at May 31, 2020. All research and development costs incurred by RI have been expensed in the accounting records.

Sales Arrangement with Ferrous Inc.
Ferrous Inc. has placed a large order for PC touch screen monitors produced by RI that uses the QuartZ technology. The sales agreement requires RI to have the goods available for delivery to Ferrous by August 31, 2020 and to make deliveries to Ferrous as requested during September and October 2020. Ferrous will be holding a special sales event during these months. Ferrous has requested that the goods are not to be delivered until September and October as they do not have the warehouse space to store all of the items for the special sale. Revenue pertaining to this agreement is $2,500,000 and the related direct production costs are estimated to total $1,350,000. These goods will be covered by RI's inventory insurance.

Ferrous made the nonrefundable fee payment of $1,250,000 required by this agreement on June 1, 2020. This amount has been recognized as sales revenue. The final $1,250,000 is to be paid by Ferrous on October 31, 2020. Ferrous is a financially sound entity.

Sales Arrangement with Mega Mart Ltd.
RI entered into an agreement with Mega Mart Ltd., a large global retailer, to distribute a lower-end touch screen for price-sensitive customers. This touch screen makes use of the BasalT technology. The sales agreement requires RI to deliver units of the touch screen to Mega Mart. Mega Mart will display the screens in a prime location and retain 20% of the per-unit sales price ($50 per unit), with the remaining 80% of the sales price to be sent to RI. Any unsold touch screens that are not sold by Mega Mart will be returned to RI. In addition, Mega Mart will provide RI an upfront payment of $250,000 in order to help offset working capital requirements.

According to the sales agreement, RI shipped 30,000 units to Mega Mart Ltd. in April 2020. At the time of delivery, RI recorded revenue of $1.2 million, debited cash for $250,000, and set up an accounts receivable for the remaining $950,000.

Tammy's Toy Shop

It's December 31, 2020, and you're sitting at your desk looking out the window watching the snowflakes fall. Your friends have the day off and have just left to go skiing. You are required to stay at work as the report that you are preparing for the most influential partner in your accounting firm is due tomorrow.

Your firm is doing some special work for Tammy Bai and her company Tammy's Toy Shop (TTS). Tammy has been approached by Eduardo Santiago, sole shareholder of Santiago Enterprises, with a proposal that would have TTS purchasing 45% of the outstanding shares of Santiago Enterprises (SE). Eduardo has told Tammy that the injection of funds (the cash received by SE when TTS purchases the shares) will be used to create leading-edge toys for children and young adults.

Tammy would like to ensure that the information provided by Eduardo to her is accurate as she doesn't want her own retirement income to melt away due to a bad investment, nor does she want to spend too much. Tammy has given your partner all the information that she has with respect to SE. Your partner has delegated this task to you and is providing you with very specific instructions on how to write the report to her.

Tammy is interested in SE and states that it looks like a good investment. She noted that the financial statements are showing a large profit and Tammy is interested in a steady stream of income to help her ease into semi-retirement in the summer months. Still, she does not fully trust Eduardo, so she has asked your firm to look at the information about SE (Exhibit I) and let her know of any discrepancies that you may find. Note that SE has never been audited before.

Your partner has asked that your report begin with an overview that addresses TTS's investment objectives and then discusses Eduardo and SE. This overview should include a discussion of the users of the information, their objectives, and the reporting implications. You should ensure you make specific reference to the conceptual framework where applicable. Tammy has asked for some clarification of some accounting terms she found in the excerpts (Exhibit I). Within the report to your partner, prepare notes to help Tammy understand these terms. Your discussion should include detailed calculations of accounting issues when asked to do so or deemed appropriate. You should split your discussion between those issues affecting the investment in SE and those specific to TTS.

Both companies are private companies. TTS is interested in going public in the future and Tammy has asked you for some IFRS explanations regarding her own financial information, so read Exhibit I carefully.

Required

Prepare the report to your partner.

Exhibit I — Information About Santiago Enterprises

- SE has been around for a number of years. In the past 10 years, SE has had reduced profits, which Eduardo has attributed to a decline in retail purchases by consumers.

- The past two years have shown resurgence within SE and record profits have been recorded. According to Eduardo, this turnaround is due to the increased marketing to kids and teenagers through various social media websites. Santiago's unadjusted net income for the year ended December 26, 2020, was $1,340,000.

- During 2020, SE purchased a group of assets for $1.1 million. The assets included land with an appraised value of $800,000, equipment with an appraised value of $150,000, and a building with an appraised value of $600,000. SE recorded this transaction by debiting land for $800,000, equipment for $100,000, and building for $200,000. The equipment is being depreciated over seven years and the building over 20 years.

- SE owns 19% of the outstanding shares of Acme Toys and Games Inc. (ATG). SE is a major customer of ATG as it purchases many of its toy components from them. SE has three members on ATG's board, with another seven members from other organizations. During the year ended December 28, 2020 (you have ATG's financial statements), ATG incurred a loss of $322,000 and paid dividends of $110,000. SE has recorded dividend revenue of $8,500.

- TTS is contemplating going public around 2020 and would like an example of what the impact would be on the financial statements. Disregarding any other information for the moment, Tammy provides you with a scenario where she has a $500,000 bond payable and equity investments with a cost of $340,000 and a year-end market value of $380,000. She would like to know how these would be recorded and presented under IFRS.

- No dividends have been paid on the SE shares in the last 50 years.

- During the year, SE decided to exchange a computer tablet-manufacturing machine that had cost $822,000 and had accumulated depreciation of $420,000 with another tablet-making machine with another company. This machine had a cost of $960,000 and had accumulated depreciation of $444,000. The fair value of SE's machine was $480,000 at the time. SE has recorded a gain of $78,000. The exchange was done because Eduardo preferred the fact that the acquired machine allowed you to work from both the right and the left side.

- In January 2020, SE changed its estimated percentage of bad debts from 4% of sales to 3% of sales. A note from the controller of SE states that "although historically we have found that our bad debts are running at approximately 4.5% of sales, we feel that our increased profits this year will result in our customers wanting to pay us back on a timely basis."

- Sales this year amounted to $20,200,300.

- Due to the decline in popularity of the DVD players, SE has stopped making its top-of-the-line supercharged DVD player in fire engine red. The DVD-making machine is currently on the books at a cost of $550,000 and has accumulated depreciation totaling $200,000. The fair value of the machine is estimated at $50,000. SE has not made any entry this year regarding this machine.

- On December 1, 2020, SE signed a contract with DIY Depot to supply it with toys for the next five years beginning January 2021. Under the terms of the contract, SE would produce and deliver toys to DIY Depot and DIY Depot would pay SE a fixed amount of $1 million for the five-year contract. SE requested that DIY Depot pay 50% of this amount upfront to help defray the costs of producing the toys. SE has recorded this $500,000 as revenues in 2020.

- Tammy is somewhat confused about the difference between depreciation and valuation. She would like you to explain this to her. She is also unsure of how you go about choosing the number of years to depreciate. She wonders if it is prescribed somewhere.

- TTS has depreciable assets on its books with a cost of $5.4 million and a fair value of $8.8 million. TTS has heard that under IFRS you may be able to value your depreciable assets at fair value instead of maintaining them at cost. Tammy would like you to explain to her, using the above information, how her statements would look if she were to follow IFRS.

- In addition to the investment in SE, TTS is considering investing in Madison Manufacturing (MM). TTS is contemplating purchasing 30% of MM, which would result in a purchase price of $450,000 cash for the investment. Currently, MM is reporting assets of $4,550,000 and liabilities of $3,300,000. Asset values reflect fair market values, except for capital assets, which have a net book value of $630,000 and a fair market value of $825,000, and inventory, which has a fair value that is $20,000 less than book value. The capital assets have a remaining useful life of six years.

- Madison is actively traded with a fairly consistent 2020 share price of $14.

- Tammy would like to know how this would be recorded by her company assuming she maintains her current ASPE reporting framework.

Vision Security Enterprises

Vision Security Enterprises (VSE) is a home and commercial security company. The company was established in 1968 by Luigi Bruce, its sole shareholder, to provide security services in Halifax. Since its inception, VSE has grown to provide its services across all major cities in Atlantic Canada.

In order to continue growing the company, Luigi has decided to expand into Ontario and Quebec. In order to facilitate the expansion, VSE is planning to become a franchiser whereby local entrepreneurs can purchase an exclusive right to be the Vision Security provider in their community. This is a significant change in strategy as VSE currently owns and operates all of the locations in Atlantic Canada.

In order to help facilitate the strategic shift, Luigi hired Jason Armand early in the fiscal year as the new manager of the Ontario and Quebec region. Jason is familiar with the franchisee–franchisor relationship as he was formerly employed at a large pizza restaurant chain.

Luigi is very happy with the performance of Jason thus far as 15 franchises have been opened throughout Ontario and Quebec during the year, along with five locations opened and operated by VSE. Luigi will have no problem signing Jason's bonus cheque, which is calculated as 10% of the operating income generated from the Ontario and Quebec markets.

You are the controller of VSE and recently began preparing for the December 31, 2020, year-end audit. The year-end audit will require more work this year because of the company's expansion, specifically the new franchisor transactions. As you prepare for the audit, you review the preliminary income statement, as prepared by Jason, for the Ontario and Quebec segments (Exhibit I), along with information regarding various transactions that occurred during the year (Exhibit II). VSE prepares its financial statements in accordance with ASPE.

Required

Prepare a report that discusses the appropriate accounting treatments for the Ontario and Quebec markets. As the report will be used as part of Luigi's evaluation of Jason's performance, be sure to discuss various alternative accounting treatments.

Exhibit I	Segmented Income Statement

	Ontario	Quebec	Total
Revenues			
Initial franchise fee—promotional rate	$ 225,000	$ 450,000	$ 675,000
Initial franchise fee—regular rate	1,350,000	1,350,000	2,700,000
Continuing franchise fee	20,000	20,000	40,000
Security services	165,000	137,500	302,500
	1,760,000	1,957,500	3,717,500
Expenses			
Advertising and promotion	113,500	128,750	242,250
General and administrative	98,700	101,240	199,940
Office expense	97,750	106,790	204,540
Professional fees	37,620	38,980	76,600
Supplies and material	97,890	102,810	200,700
Wages and benefits	394,550	425,780	820,330
	840,010	904,350	1,744,360
Income from operations, pretax	$ 919,990	$1,053,150	$1,973,140
Bonus	$ 91,999	$ 105,315	$ 197,314

Exhibit II	Additional Information Regarding the Ontario and Quebec Operations

- Before the franchise agreement is signed, there is a period of discussion whereby the general feasibility of the new location is assessed. Market research is conducted and the prospective franchisee's financial strength is examined. VSE incurs all of the costs during this stage. During the year, VSE, franchised seven locations in Ontario and eight locations in Quebec. The franchise agreements were signed during the following months:

	Jan.	Feb.	Mar.	Apr.	May	June	July	Aug.	Sep.	Oct.	Nov.	Dec.	Total
Ontario	0	0	0	0	1	1	2	1	2	0	0	0	7
Quebec	0	0	0	1	1	1	2	1	1	1	0	0	8

- As is standard in the franchisee industry, VSE developed a policy to charge an initial franchise fee and a continuing franchise fee. The initial fee of $225,000 is paid through the following, nonrefundable payments:

  - The franchisee must pay a down payment of $25,000 when the franchise agreement is signed. Once signed, VSE will provide significant assistance to help the franchisee commence operations (e.g., help select an appropriate location, train employees, develop policies and procedures, provide legal and management assistance); however, the franchise is responsible to pay for all of the direct costs of establishing the new location.
  - A second payment of $50,000 is due once the franchisee commences operations. It takes approximately four to five months from signing the franchise agreement to commencing operations. VSE's involvement with the franchisee largely ends

when the new location commences operations. Five of the seven locations Ontario are open and six of the eight locations in Quebec are open.
  - The final payment of $150,000 is due within one year of operations commencing. VSE does not have any experience to assess the likelihood of a franchisee surviving its first year.
  - Each franchisee is required to pay $2,500 per month in a continuing franchise fee for VSE. The continuing franchise fee covers various shared costs, such as regional advertising, software and hardware upgrades, and ad hoc support.

- Jason encouraged initial growth by providing a promotional agreement with the first three franchisers. These franchisers were charged an initial franchise fee of $225,000, due upon opening, with no continuing fee for the first three years. All three franchises are open and paid their initial fee. These franchises have been opened for a combined 10 months during the fiscal year.

- The following are number of months the franchisees were required to pay monthly franchise fees:

	Jan.	Feb.	Mar.	Apr.	May	June	July	Aug.	Sep.	Oct.	Nov.	Dec.	Total
Ontario	0	0	0	0	0	0	0	0	0	1	3	4	8
Quebec	0	0	0	0	0	0	0	0	0	1	3	4	8

No continuing franchise fees were collected from the franchises that signed an agreement in April and May.

- During the year, VSE opened and operates two stores in Ontario (Toronto and Ottawa), and one store in Quebec (Montreal). The locations were opened late in the fiscal year but were still able to generate sales during November and December. The Ontario locations sold 30 security systems, while the Quebec locations sold 25 security systems.

The security systems during the year were sold for the promotional price of $5,500, which includes the hardware, installation, and a two-year monitoring contract. The promotional price was issued with the hopes of attracting new business as VSE penetrates into the new markets. The normal retail price of the hardware alone is $6,000, with an additional $500 for installation. Customers can opt out of the two-year monitoring contract, which will reduce the price by $750. In addition, customers who already have the hardware can purchase the monitoring services for $1,250. All systems have been instaled as of the year end.

- Jason undertook a large marketing campaign in November and December 2020 with the intention of attracting new franchises and increasing awareness of VSE's service offering. The advertising blitz is going to run into January 2021. Jason believes that the benefits of the marketing program will be realized in the next year. Accordingly, he capitalized $250,000 in marketing costs as at year end in order to match the costs to sales in future periods.

Intermediate Accounting II Cases

Alpha Classic Car Restorations

John Wallace is an automotive enthusiast. He has over 25 years of experience as a mechanic for the dealership of a large car manufacturer in Oakville. John also gained experience doing minor body work and painting.

Recently, John decided to retire from the car dealership and pursue his interest of restoring classic American muscle cars. Accordingly, John started Alpha Classic Cars Restoration (ACCR). John leased an industrial building and converted it into a repair and body shop. The building's land has a small parking lot that is used to showcase the restored vehicles that are for sale.

Generally, John selects the classic muscle cars that ACCR will restore and then places them for sale to the general public in the lot. John also posts his vehicles to various Internet sales sites, frequents car shows, and uses the classifieds of local newspapers to market his inventory. ACCR also takes custom jobs, whereby an individual can request the car to be restored.

ACCR has a December 31, 2020, year end, and just completed its first year of operations. John had a friend help him compile financial statements for the year end (draft financial statements can be found in Exhibit I). ACCR's bank requires the preparation of annual audited financial statements in accordance with IFRS (details of the loan agreement can be found in Exhibit II), and the auditors are scheduled to commence year-end work on January 18.

Realizing that ACCR needs accounting assistance, John has hired you, CPA, as a consultant on December 24, 2020. Your first task is to review the draft financial statements and provide any recommendations to comply with IFRS. In addition, John required some assistance preparing a statement of cash flow. John has provided you with a file for review, which outlines all of the significant transactions that have taken place during the year (Exhibit III).

Aside from the year-end statements, John would also like to know whether he will be able to pay any dividends in the current year. He has drawn a minimal salary, and is hoping to supplement his income by paying a $35,000 dividend with the current cash balance.

Finally, John has asked you to provide some advice regarding the additional controls or procedures that could be implemented to improve the day-to-day operations of the company.

Required

John has asked you to prepare a report that discusses all of the material accounting issues (i.e., identify the issues, discuss the implications, offer alternative treatments, and provide a recommendation). Revised financial statements should be included in the report. The report should also address John's other concerns. Provide journal entries, where appropriate.

| Exhibit I | Draft Financial Statements |

Statement of Financial Position

As at December 31 (unaudited)	2020
Assets	
Current	
Cash	$ 35,449
Accounts receivable	45,000
Inventory	95,775
Prepaid insurance	1,775
	177,999
Capital assets	287,250
	$465,249
Liabilities and shareholders' equity	
Current	
Accounts payable and accruals	$ 8,455
Income taxes payable	17,334
	25,789
Long-term bank loan	277,240
Common shares	74,500
Retained earnings	87,721
	162,220
	$465,249

Income Statement

For the year ended December 31 (unaudited)	2020
Sales	$ 320,000
Cost of sales	128,000
Gross profit	192,000
Expenses	
Advertising and promotion	2,000
Bad debt	0
Depreciation	22,750
Insurance	1,500
Interest	16,920
Legal and accounting	2,500
Lease expense	30,000
Office and general expenses	2,775
Repairs and maintenance	750
Utilities	11,000
Wages and benefits	22,500
	112,695
Operating income	79,305
Other service income	25,750
Income before taxes	105,055
Provision for income taxes (16.5%)	17,334
Net income	87,721
Opening balance—retained earnings	0
Net income	87,721
Dividends	0
Closing balance—retained earnings	$ 87,721

Exhibit II	Bank Loan Agreement

The Bank of Toronto has provided a $300,000 loan to help finance working capital and capital assets. The following are the terms and conditions of the loan.

- **Security:** The bank secures its loan with a first claim against inventory and accounts receivable.

- **Repayment:** The loan is to be repaid over a 10-year period, with blended monthly payments.

- **Interest rate:** The rate of interest is 6%, effective annual rate (EAR).

- **Covenants:** ACCR must comply with the following covenants:
  - The current ratio must not be below 2:1.
  - The debt to equity ratio must not exceed 3:1. Debt is defined as both current and long-term liabilities.

  A violation of either covenant will result in the loan becoming payable upon demand.

- **Financial statements:** Audited financial statements are to be presented no later than 60 days after year end. Financial statements can be prepared with ASPE.

Exhibit III

Notes of Significant Transactions

- During the first year of operations, ACCR made the following sales:

1. 1972 Chevy Camaro, Z28	$45,000
2. 1978 Chevy Corvette Coupe, 25th Anniversary	$33,000
3. 1969 Pontiac GTO	$38,000
4. 1967 Ford Shelby Mustang	$55,000
5. 1974 Dodge Dart	$33,000
6. 1970 Buick GSX	$40,000
7. 1970 Chevelle 454 SS	$37,000
8. 1970 Plymouth Hemi	$39,000

- ACCR is so confident in its workmanship that it offers a 10-year bumper-to-bumper warranty with all car sales. The warranty covers all defects and breakdowns that are not directly related to regular wear and tear. John is unsure of how much the warranty will cost to service, but is confident that his vehicles will stand the test of time. Based on his experience, John estimates the probability of a vehicle making a warranty claim during the 10 years of coverage are as follows:

Year 1	2	3	4	5	6	7	8	9	10
1%	2%	2%	5%	5%	10%	12%	15%	18%	20%

The average retail value per claim is $1,250. The average cost of parts and service at ACCR is about 60% of that of a dealership.

- ACCR sold the 1972 Chevy Camaro to a wealthy telecom CEO during the year. Shortly after delivery of the vehicle, John found out that the CEO resigned from the company due to various accounting irregularities and restatements. John has been in contact with the customer and knows that he is happy with the car, and fully intends to pay once things settle down.

- ACCR entered into a lease agreement on January 1 for the land and building that is used as the repair and body shop. ACCR is required to make monthly payments of $2,500, commencing January 31, for a 10-year period (at which point, John expects to be fully retired and live off of his pension). The following additional information is available regarding the lease:

  - The rate implicit in the lease is 7%.

- The building and land have fair values of $170,000 and $56,667, respectively.
- The building has a useful life of approximately 13 years.
- The lease payments were set to provide the lessor with a return of 60% related to the building and 40% related to the land.
- There is no bargain purchase option, or renewal option, at the end of the lease.
- The capital asset breakdown is as follows:

Capital Assets	Cost	Accumulated Depreciation	Net Book Value
Machinery and equipment	$250,000	$15,500	$234,500
Leasehold improvements	10,000	1,000	9,000
Office equipment	25,000	3,125	21,875
Vehicles	25,000	3,125	21,875
	$310,000	$22,750	$287,250

The leasehold improvements include changes to the building and land (e.g., paving). The machinery and equipment is expected to have a residual value of $95,000 after their 10-year useful life. Both the office equipment and vehicle are expected to have useful lives of eight years, with no residual values.

- The income taxes presented in the financial statements are based on the pre-tax income times the tax rate of 16.5%. No adjustments have been made to calculate taxes in accordance with the Income Tax Act even though the deferred taxes method has been adopted. The following are the CCA rates relevant to the capital assets of ACCR:

  1. Machinery and equipment: 30%
  2. Leasehold improvements: 10 years, straight-line
  3. Office equipment: 20%
  4. Vehicles: 30%

- The inventory balance includes a 1971 Corvette Coupe. The car was a custom order for a doctor. Due to financial problems, the doctor was unable to purchase the vehicle, at which point ACCR repossessed the vehicle. The vehicle is included in inventory at its cost of $35,000. The vehicle will require minor moderations, costing up to $5,000, to make it ready for resale at a price of $35,000.

Appexia Corporation

Contributed by
Allan Foerster and Bruce J. McConomy
Lazaridis School of Business & Economics, Wilfrid Laurier University

Janice Snow, CPA has recently left the public accounting firm of Jordan & Co. for a position with a client firm, Appexia Corporation a publicly accountable entity that specializes in producing equipment for use by other manufacturers in their assembly lines. For several weeks, she had been looking forward to her first day as Director of Financial Reporting, and today she has her first official meeting with Andreas Magnuson, CPA who is the Vice-President of Finance.

Andreas greeted Janice at the door to his office. "Come on in and welcome to Appexia. We are thrilled to have you join our team. I have set up a number of meetings with key members of the management team to orient you to the new initiatives we have undertaken this year. During these meetings, you will be provided with a data sheet for various significant initiatives started in the current year. Here is an unaudited copy of our preliminary financial statements for the year ended December 31, 2020 (Exhibit I). As you can see, we are starting to get squeezed regarding our debt. The maximum debt to equity ratio allowed by our bond holders is 1.7:1 resulting from our recent bond issue, and there is only a small cushion. You should also know that we are planning an issue of Common Shares sometime in the first six months of 2021, so meeting the analysts' consensus estimate of $1.45 per share (EPS) is critical to ensure that we receive a good price for our new shares."

As you leave Andreas' office, you hear his final comment. "After you meet with the team, please send me a report on your thoughts on any issues you encounter, especially any adjustments you think may be necessary to the draft financial statements. Don't worry about income tax expense or deferred taxes, the estimated taxes on the draft financial statements are fine for now."

Meeting One: David Sloane, Vice-President Sales and Marketing

"Janice, welcome to the Appexia team. I know you have a busy day ahead of you so I have summarized a couple of our new initiatives in my area."

"We have never had a customer incentive plan; however, to launch our new Apex-10 Advanced Grinding Machine we decided to provide an incentive to our customers. I have summarized the program for your future reference" (see Exhibit II-A).

In conjunction with the launch of the Apex-10, we are now offering an optional two-year warranty that our customers can purchase at the time of acquiring the Apex-10. The optional warranty covers potential product issues not covered in the standard warranty. The program is summarized on this data sheet (see Exhibit II-B). This has sure provided a nice boost to our revenue in 2020."

As you leave the office, David suggests "let me know if you need any further information."

Meeting Two: Sophie Kershaw, Treasurer

"Good morning Janice. I don't mean to be rude however I am a little pressed for time. I am meeting with the underwriters, TRW Capital, to plan our equity offering for Q1 in 2021. Andreas asked me to put together several documents for you. The first outlines our $5.0 million convertible bond (Exhibit III). We were very fortunate to raise this amount of capital to support our plant expansion without impacting our EPS. The second data sheet (Exhibit IV) summarizes our first grant of stock options approved by the Board of Directors at the January 2, 2020 meeting. No impact on our 2020 financial statements as none of the options have vested yet, but we believe this will align the goals of the Appexia management team with interests of our shareholders. The underwriters have also asked us to provide a draft statement to cash flows to go along with the other draft financial statements that we have provided them. We use the indirect method."

"It was nice to meet you. Please feel free to drop by anytime."

Meeting Three: Rebekka Johannsen, Vice-President Operations

"Hey there Janice come on in. We have been in need of someone with your expertise with all of the recent accounting standard changes. If you have met with David Sloane, you have no doubt heard about our plant modernization. My part of that project was to upgrade our equipment for manufacturing the Apex-10. We were able to acquire the equipment on a lease instead of purchasing the equipment to avoid any impact on our Balance Sheet. We have never leased before but it may make it easier for me to continue our upgrade program over the next few years. This data sheet will give you an idea of the details of the lease" (see Exhibit V).

"Thanks again for dropping by. Nice to have another woman on the management team."

Required

You gather all your notes and return to your office to draft your report to Andreas Magnuson.

Exhibit 1-A	Appexia Corp.

Balance Sheet as at December 31, 2020 (DRAFT)

	2020	2019
Current assets		
Cash	$ 818,258	$ 849,080
Accounts receivable	2,508,960	1,273,620
Inventory	4,417,920	2,122,700
Total current assets	7,745,138	4,245,400
Noncurrent assets		
Land	1,400,000	-
Building	3,200,000	-
Equipment	2,270,900	1,384,200
	6,870,900	1,384,200
Less: Accumulated depreciation	386,900	200,000
	6,484,000	1,184,200
Intangible assets	480,000	620,000
Total noncurrent assets	6,964,000	1,804,200
Total assets	$14,709,138	$6,049,600
Current liabilities		
Bank indebtedness	$ 473,943	$ 752,500
Accounts payable	1,674,000	884,600
Income taxes payable	1,023,800	652,500
Total current liabilities	3,171,743	2,289,600
Convertible bond	5,000,000	
Total liabilities	8,171,743	2,289,600
Shareholders' equity		
Share capital	1,880,000	1,880,000
Retained earnings	4,657,395	1,880,000
Total shareholders' equity	6,537,395	3,760,000
Total liabilities and shareholders' equity	$14,709,138	$6,049,600

Exhibit 1-B | **Appexia Corp.**

Statement of Comprehensive Income (Draft)
For the year ended December 31, 2020

	2020	2019
Revenue	$18,336,280	$13,116,900
Cost of sales	8,400,000	5,291,250
Gross profit	9,936,280	7,825,650
Depreciation expense	186,900	138,420
Amortization expense	140,000	140,000
Other operating expenses	4,629,600	3,191,030
Operating income	4,979,780	4,356,200
Finance expense	350,790	92,650
Income before taxes	4,628,990	4,263,550
Income tax expense	1,851,595	1,705,420
Net income which is Comprehensive Income	$ 2,777,395	$ 2,558,130
Earnings per share	$ 1.90	$ 1.50
Weighted average shares	1,461,787	1,461,787*

*(Note: No common share transactions have occurred since 2018).

Exhibit II-A | **APEX-10 Customer Incentive Data Sheet**

- Starting on January 1, 2020, for each Apex-10 machine purchased, the customer receives a coupon for $3,000 to be applied to a future purchase of another Apex-10 machine. The coupons expire on December 31, 2022.

- During 2020, sold 75 machines at a selling price of $60,000 each (included in 2020 revenue)

- At the end of 2020, no coupons had been redeemed. However, since the sales were made to long-standing customers, the company was anticipating a 100% redemption rate in coming years.

Exhibit II-B | **APEX-10 Warranty Data Sheet**

- In addition to the one-year warranty included with the transaction price, customers were given the option to purchase a special two-year warranty that covers product failures not covered in the standard warranty. When purchased, the special warranty becomes effective on the first day of the subsequent quarter (e.g., warranties purchased in February become effective on April 1st and the special warranty continues for the next 8 quarters).

- The warranty was sold at the time the machine was sold at a price of $5,000

- During 2020 purchasers of 60 Apex-10 machines also purchased the optional warranty (included in revenue for the year). The 60 machines were purchased evenly over the year (5 per month).

- Expectations are that costs for coverage relating to the special warranty will be $3,000 per machine with most of the costs incurred in the second of the two years.

- In 2020, the company incurred warranty costs of $36,000 relating to the special warranty. It also incurred costs of $100 per month, per machine, for its regular warranty.

Exhibit III	Convertible Bond Data Sheet

- The Convertible Bond was issued on January 2, 2020, with a face value of $5,000,000, a term of 10 years, and it pays interest each June 30 and December 31 at an annual rate of 4%. The company received $4,600,000 cash; the cash was later used to acquire land and buildings on July 1, 2020, valued at $1,400,000 and $3,200,000, respectively. The remaining $400,000 of convertible bonds was also issued on January 2, 2020, in exchange for equipment valued at $4c00,000. All other equipment additions recorded on the balance sheet were paid for with cash. There were no disposals of equipment during the year.

- The company turned down an option to issue debt without the conversion feature at a rate of 6%.

- Each convertible bond debenture can be converted into common shares on the basis of 20 common shares for each $1,000 of the bond's face value, until the date of maturity (December 31, 2029).

- No bonds were converted in 2020.

Exhibit IV	Stock Option Plan Data Sheet

- Approved at the January 2020 Board meeting.

- About 500,000 options granted to Appexia's senior executives, the options may be converted into 500,000 common shares after they vest.

- Fair value of $1,250,000 determined by an options pricing model.

- Exercise price set at $12.50 per share (market price at the grant date $12.50) three-year vesting period, starting January 1, 2020 (the options are then exercisable for two years—January 1, 2023, to December 31, 2024).

- The fair value of $1.25 million includes an estimate that over the service period approximately 10% of option holders would leave the company before the options vested (3.33% per year).

- Average market price of common shares during 2020 was $14.00.

Exhibit V	Equipment Lease Data Sheet

- Total package of equipment leased has a fair market value of $4,800,000

- Lessor management stated that they used a rate of return of 6% for their calculations, based on an eight-year term and a guaranteed minimum value for the equipment at the termination of the lease of $600,000

- First payment of $672,030 was paid on July 2 when the lease was signed, with subsequent payments due on July 1st each year.

- Lease payments are included in operating expenses by Appexia as they are paid.

- Appexia management believes that, at a minimum, at the termination of the lease the equipment could be sold for an expected value of $440,000. Appexia uses the straight-line method of depreciation for its property, plant, and equipment.

Better World Storage Corporation

You are an accountant working at Robi & Co. George Maranzan, a partner in your firm, leaves you the following voicemail message:

"The scheduling manager tells me you have some time available. We have recently been advised that management of Better World Storage Corporation (BWSC) has received an offer from Ventura Capital Partners to sell 100% of all issued and outstanding common shares. I have a meeting with management in two weeks regarding this issue, and I haven't had much time to think about this engagement.

I have prepared some background information on the company for you to review, including background information on the client (Exhibit I), the company's most recent internal financial statements (Exhibit II), and the proposed share purchase agreement (Exhibit III). I also met with BWSC management earlier this month and made some notes from that meeting (Exhibit IV). They should all be in your inbox by now.

Can you please prepare a report that I can use for the upcoming meeting?

I am glad that you have some time available!"

Required

Prepare the report for George.

Exhibit I	Background Information

Better World Storage Corporation (BWSC) duplicates, DVDs, MP3s, and all forms of electronic files from master copies provided by its clients. The company started operations in 2000 in the basement of the home of part-owner, Samantha Arthurs. Sales increased quickly, and within one year of starting operations the company moved into a rented space in downtown Toronto. The market that BWSC currently serves is mainly large companies that require training programs, corporate messages, and so on.

The company is owned equally by Samantha Arthurs, Grant MacArthur, and Ashley Carvalho. Samantha started the venture and

has always managed the sales function. In order to keep the company growing, she brought in Grant and Ashley as equal shareholders. Grant and Ashley each paid $30,000 for one-third of Samantha's shares.

Grant is a good administrator and handles the accounting functions for the company. Samantha's skills are mainly in sales. Ashley looks after the production end and stays abreast of changes in technology.

BWSC has an October 31 fiscal year end.

Exhibit II | Internal Financial Statements

Statement of Financial Position

As at October 31 (unaudited)	2020	2019
Assets		
Current		
Cash	$ 151,764	$ 160,502
Accounts receivable	334,894	411,760
Inventory	86,800	124,200
Prepaid insurance	4,720	2,060
	578,178	698,522
Capital assets (note 1)	661,897	417,158
Future income tax asset (note 2)	35,000	35,000
Long-term note receivable	20,000	0
	$1,295,075	$1,150,680
Liabilities and shareholders' equity		
Current		
Accounts payable	$ 158,318	$ 130,176
Bank loan—current portion	41,998	72,000
Income taxes payable	44,609	92,720
	244,925	295,096
Long-term bank loan (note 3)	35,334	77,334
Due to shareholders	58,100	53,100
Common shares	1,200	1,200
Preferred shares	20,000	20,000
Contributed surplus	4,000	0
Retained earnings	931,516	703,950
	956,716	725,150
	$1,295,075	$1,150,880

Exhibit II	Internal Financial Statements (Continued)

Statement of Income

For the years ended October 31 (unaudited)	2020	2019
Sales	$2,531,760	$2,221,720
Cost of sales		
Opening inventory	124,400	26,860
Purchases —materials	1,018,972	959,138
—wages	289,663	219,416
Total	1,433,035	1,205,414
Closing inventory	(86,800)	(124,400)
	1,346,235	1,081,014
Gross profit	$1,185,525	$1,140,706
Expenses		
Commissions	$199,372	$ 174,957
Depreciation	127,684	104,796
Management salaries and benefits	110,448	110,040
Management fees	109,600	112,600
Rent	75,840	74,020
Office and general expenses	48,723	46,877
Advertising and promotion	37,585	31,284
Repairs and maintenance	27,173	24,686
Automobile and travel	26,326	22,782
Bad debt	15,596	21,188
Interest	16,864	39,320
Computer system installation	13,760	0
Telephone	13,458	10,510
Insurance	10,864	10,214
Legal and accounting	8,083	3,414
Lease expense	18,143	0
	$859,519	$ 786,688
Operating income	326,006	354,018
Gain on sale of equipment	4,560	0
Income before taxes	330,566	354,018
Provision for income taxes	99,000	112,000
Net income	231,566	242,018
Opening balance—retained earnings	703,950	465,932
Dividend on preferred shares	(4,000)	(4,000)
Closing balance—retained earnings	$ 931,516	$ 703,950

Exhibit II   **Internal Financial Statements (Continued)**

Notes to the Financial Statements

1. Capital assets

	Cost	Accumulated Depreciation	2020 Net Book Value	2019 Net Book Value
Furniture and fixtures	$ 23,434	$ 12,418	$ 11,016	$ 13,770
Computer equipment	50,842	12,835	38,007	18,421
Leasehold improvements	19,404	19,404	0	2,842
Vehicle	40,352	27,985	12,367	17,667
Production equipment	931,074	330,567	600,507	364,458
	$1,065,106	$403,209	$661,897	$417,158

2. Future income tax asset

A future tax asset has been recorded for noncapital losses carryforward. The losses were incurred during a bad year in fiscal 2018. BWSC expects strong future profits to be able to generate taxable income to fully utilize the tax losses. The owners decided not to use the tax losses in the 2020 or 2019 fiscal years because they expect their marginal tax rate to increase significantly in the near future due to significant growth in income.

3. Bank loan

A small business bank loan and line of credit for $200,000 (presently unused) are secured by a general security agreement, a registered general assignment of book debts, and chattel mortgages on duplication equipment. Principal repayments on the small business loan are due as follows during the years ended October 31:

2021	$41,998
2022	20,034
2023	11,700
2024	3,600

Interest on the small business bank loan is paid at 12% on the outstanding monthly balances. Interest on the line of credit is calculated at prime plus 1.5% on outstanding monthly balances.

Exhibit III   **Share Purchase Agreement**

Purchase Price Calculation

The final purchase price is to be determined based on an adjusted book value approach, whereby all assets and liabilities are adjusted to their fair values to determine the fair value of the equity. In addition, a premium for goodwill will be calculated based on a multiple of net income for the most recent fiscal year.

Therefore, the purchase price is calculated as follows:

• Purchase Price = Adjusted Equity Value + (Net Income × Earnings Multiple)

Earnings Multiple

A goodwill multiple of between 1 and 2 is common for similar companies.

Net Income

Net income must be determined based on generally accepted accounting principles (IFRS).

Adjusted Book Value

All assets, liabilities, and equities must be recognized and measured in accordance with generally accepted accounting principles (IFRS).

Exhibit IV | Notes From George's Meeting with Grant Macarthur

New lease agreement

BWSC signed an agreement on November 1, 2019, to lease equipment from Sultan Leasing. The following information relates to the agreement:

1. The term of the noncancellable lease is five years, at which time the asset is expected to have a residual value of $7,000, which is not guaranteed.

2. The asset's fair value, at November 1, 2019, is $80,000, with an economic life of seven years.

3. The asset will revert to Sultan at the end of the lease term, at which time the asset is expected to have a residual value of $7,000, which is not guaranteed.

4. Sultan leasing assumes direct responsibility for the executory costs.

5. The agreement requires equal annual rental payments of $18,143, beginning on November 1, 2019.

6. The lessor's implicit rate is 10% and is known to BWSC.

Grant has recorded this as an operating lease and expensed the annual payment during the fiscal year.

Provision for income taxes

The provision for income taxes included in the financial statements is recorded based on the taxes payable in the current period (that is, the amount payable based on taxable income). Management has prepared the calculation by focusing only on the undepreciated capital cost (UCC) and depreciation difference because they are unsure of any other differences.

A review of Schedule 8 of the Corporate T2 reveals UCC balances of the following:

	Cost	UCC
Furniture and fixtures	$23,434	$10,518
Computer equipment	50,842	6,835
Leasehold improvements	19,404	19,404
Vehicle	40,352	29,985
Production equipment	931,074	289,567

The total capital cost allowance taken in 2020 was $140,545. The average tax rate for BWSC is 31.16% on the current year's income.

Preferred shares

On November 1, 2019, BWSC issued 2,000 redeemable and retractable preferred shares at a value of $10 per share. The shares are redeemable by BWSC at any time after January 2021. The shares are retractable for the original $10 per share at the discretion of the holder at any time up to January 2021, after which the retractable feature expires. The preferred shares require the payment of a mandatory $2 per share during the retraction period, after which the dividends become noncumulative and are paid at the discretion of the board only.

Long-term note receivable

On July 1, 2020, BWSC provided certain services to a preferred customer in exchange for a long-term note receivable. BWSC provided its services in exchange for five payments of $4,000. BWSC provided its preferred customer with this offer to help stimulate the sale given the recent financial crisis. The first payment is due July 1, 2021.

Loyalty program points

During the most recent board meeting, it was decided that BWSC will begin offering points under a loyalty program. BWSC will provide its customers with 1 point for every $100 spent. The points can then be redeemed for a discount on future services. A total of 100 points will result in a $500 discount.

Postretirement benefits

BWSC has just implemented and sponsored a defined benefit plan for its employees in fiscal 2020. No past service benefits have been granted.

The following additional information was obtained from an actuarial report that has been prepared as at the year end:

Service cost for 2020:	$95,000
Discount or settlement rate:	8%
Actual return on plan assets for 2020:	8%
Contribution (plan funding) in 2020:	$87,000
Expected rate of return for 2020:	8%

The initial contribution of $87,000 was made on August 1, 2020. Currently, BWSC has expensed the contribution as part of the management salaries and benefits (on the income statement).

Car Toons Audio Inc.

Car Toons Audio Inc. (CTAI) is a young company that recently completed its initial public offering. The company designs and develops leading-edge car stereo equipment, including MP4 compatible decks, speakers, amplifiers, and subwoofers.

The company is investing heavily in research and development. In order to reduce strain on cash, the management team is compensated mostly through share-based compensation in the current year. In addition, the company has raised cash through the issuance of common shares in the open market and by offering various complex financial instruments. Management believes that all cash should be diverted toward the research and development process in order for the company to become the leader in automotive stereo equipment.

In addition to the stock options, management receives a bonus of 5% of net income if diluted EPS is greater than $0.10. The bonus is the only cash compensation that management receives at this stage of the company's life cycle. Management is excited because this year's draft income statement (Exhibit I) shows diluted EPS in excess of $0.10, and therefore, a bonus will be paid.

Lebeau and Liang LLP has been the auditor of CTAI since the company's inception. You are a senior accountant with the firm and have been assigned the year-end audit for CTAI. The partner, Sharmila Chaudary, has just met with the company's management and discussed various accounting issues. She has asked you to prepare a report to be provided to the client that addresses all of the accounting issues, along with any other issues that you feel are important. Sharmila's notes from the meeting can be found in Exhibit II. In addition, the company's current and future tax expenses must be calculated. Tax-related details can be found in Exhibit III.

Required

Prepare a report for Sharmila. IFRS is the appropriate accounting standards for CTAI.

Exhibit I	Draft Income Statement

Car Toons Audio Inc.
As at December 31, 2020

REVENUE	$44,500,740
Cost of goods sold	23,540,891
Gross margin	20,959,849
EXPENSES	
Accounting and consulting fees	$ 175,000
Advertising and promotion	1,575,000
Amortization	1,276,758
Bad debt	87,500
Insurance	85,000
Interest on convertible bonds	80,000
Legal fees	225,500
Office and general expenses	750,850
Rent	325,000
Repairs and maintenance	450,755
Research and development	11,345,000
Travel	133,750
Utilities	333,565
Wages and benefits	325,000
	$17,168,678
Earnings for the year before income taxes	$ 3,791,170
Income tax expense	1,137,351
Earnings for the year	$ 2,653,819
Earnings per share—basic	$ 0.13
Earnings per share—diluted	$ 0.11
Weighted average shares outstanding—basic	20,550,750*
Weighted average shares outstanding—diluted	25,880,750*

*Note that these values have been calculated and verified by the manager on the file and are deemed to be correct.

| Exhibit II | Notes from the Partner's Meeting with CTAI's Management |

1. At the beginning of the year, the board of directors approved a compensatory stock option plan that grants options to the company's four executives to purchase 100,000 shares each of the company's common shares. The board expects that the period of benefit/service for these options is two years. The options can be exercised at a strike price of $1 per share any time over a three-year period commencing after the initial two-year service period ends. The fair value of the options, as determined using an option pricing model, is $1,550,000.

2. The company issued 500,000 preferred shares for $4 per share to an investment bank in June 2020. Each preferred share is convertible for a fixed number of common shares (six common shares), and has a mandatory 7% annual dividend that must be paid on December 31 of each fiscal year. The shares must be redeemed by the company for cash if the market price of the common shares exceeds $4 per share. Currently, the common shares are in a trading range around $1.25 per share. The board declared and paid the mandatory cash dividend on December 31.

3. At the beginning of the current year, the company issued $2.5 million convertible bonds, of which $2 million was correctly allocated to debt. The bonds' market yield is 4% annually, pays interest semi-annually, matures in five years, and can be converted into common shares at the ratio of 1,500 shares per $1,000 bond.

4. Given the volatility of commodity prices, CTAI entered into a forward contract with the Bank of Vancouver. On July 1, CTAI locked the price of 5 million kg of aluminum at $1.25/kg. Aluminum is important to the company's operation because it is used to create a cabinet that houses all of the components in the CD player deck. Upon its inception, CTAI did not have to put forth any cash. All cash transfers will take place on settlements in two years. As at December 31, the price of aluminum is trading on the Chicago Board of Trade at $1.15/kg.

| Exhibit III | Tax-Related Details |

5. The company's tax rate is 30%. The income statement tax expense is calculated with the taxes payable method.

6. The office and general expense account contains $85,000 in meals and entertainment.

7. There are $175,000 in nondeductible expenses included in the accounting and consulting fees line item on the income statement.

8. The net book value (NBV) and undepreciated capital cost (UCC) for the capital assets are as follows:

| | NBV | | UCC | |
	2020	2019	2020	2019
Land	$ 1,250,000	$ 1,250,000	n/a	n/a
Buildings	4,500,750	4,650,775	$ 2,767,211	$ 3,255,543
Furniture and fixtures	650,000	693,333	412,533	485,333
Machinery and equipment	12,567,000	13,404,800	7,975,856	9,383,360
Leasehold improvements	2,456,000	2,701,600	1,607,452	1,891,120
	$21,423,750	$22,700,508	$12,763,052	$15,015,356

9. There were no capital asset additions or dispositions during the year.

Custom Auto Parts

Today is November 1, 2020. You, CPA, have just been hired by Custom Auto Parts (CAP) as an accountant to provide financial expertise during its current expansion. CAP was founded in 1995 by Jerome Blackman (sole shareholder), and CAP has remained a private corporation ever since. From its humble beginnings, CAP has grown substantially. CAP's operations focus on the production of both standard and unique car parts. CAP always strives to use modern technology to produce quality car parts. When CAP commenced, it produced car parts for Canadian automotive companies that were seeking to outsource their production. Soon after, as word spread on the quality of its parts, CAP's products were being sought after by companies outside of Canada. In addition, CAP began selling its products to individuals who were looking for unique car parts to restore older cars.

As a car buff, you are very excited about the position as it allows you to apply your accounting knowledge in an industry that interests you. On your first day, you met with CAP's CFO, Robert Ryder. Robert begins by explaining how excited he is that you have joined CAP's team and he looks forward to the expertise that you will bring to CAP's accounting department.

Robert continues by explaining that as CAP has grown, so has its dependency on external financing. Just this year, CAP had purchased additional equipment to handle its recent growth. CAP has had a long-standing relationship with its bank. However, given the recent credit crisis, the bank has changed its policies on all loans. Robert has provided you with a copy of CAP's statement of financial position (see Exhibit I) as at October 31, 2020, which is CAP's fiscal year-end date.

After the meeting, Robert asks you to analyze the new accounting issues surrounding CAP and to provide recommendations on their resolution. He concludes by reminding you that the bank is eager to see the year-end financial statements. As you make your way back to your desk, you begin by reviewing a file outlining important transactions undertaken by CAP. You note the following issues:

1. On November 1, 2019 (the beginning of the fiscal year), CAP acquired a portion of its equipment through a lease agreement with Lessor Corp. The lease contract has the following terms and conditions:

   - CAP agrees to lease equipment from Lessor Corp. with a fair market value of $900,000.
   - The term of the lease is for seven years, with annual rental payments of $145,000 due at the beginning of each year. CAP knows the implicit interest rate on the lease agreement is 5%. CAP knows that it could borrow at an incremental rate of 6%.
   - There is no residual value.
   - CAP will cover the executory costs associated with the lease. The executor costs will be approximately $10,000 per annum and are included as part of the $145,000 rental payment.
   - The lease offers a bargain purchase option to purchase the equipment for $50,000 at the end of the seventh year. At the end of year seven, the fair market value of the asset is expected to be $70,000.
   - The first payment was made on November 1, 2019, with annual payments thereafter.

   You remember from auditing a client in the past that equipment such as this usually has an economic life of nine years. CAP has classified this lease as an operating lease. You remember from your discussion with Robert that he was unsure of the benefits of leasing versus buying an asset. This information is important for Robert for any future capital budgeting decisions.

2. After reviewing the statement of financial position, you notice that there are preferred shares valued at $100,000, which equals a total of 1,000 shares outstanding. The preferred shares are redeemable and have a 5% annual dividend. The dividend will double every three years up to a maximum 20% dividend yield. The preferred shares become convertible into common shares if CAP does not pay the specified dividend on the preferred shares.

3. The file also contained a letter from CAP's lawyer (Stonechild, Pilla, and Partners). The letter from the lawyers explained a current lawsuit undertaken against CAP. Apparently, a customer had asked for 50,000 parts to be produced and delivered no later than July 15, 2020. However, due to major downtime in July, CAP could not produce the parts as scheduled. In turn, the customer was late in delivering its vehicles to its distributors and had to pay a penalty equivalent of $600,000. This customer is now suing CAP for retribution for these costs. The letter goes on to state that retribution will be inevitable; however, it is believed that a settlement between $350,000 to $550,000 can be reached.

4. On November 1, 2019, an additional $500,000 of long-term loan was taken out to help finance the purchase of certain manufacturing equipment for $600,000. (Note: the additional $100,000 was paid for with cash.) Given this new loan and CAP's revised debt load, CAP must now maintain a maximum debt to equity ratio of 3:1 and its financial statements must comply with ASPE. If CAP breaches the covenant, the bank has the ability to call for the loan in full.

   The manufacturing equipment that was purchased during the year will be depreciated over 10 years. It is classified as class 39 and has a CCA rate of 25%. CAP is taxed at the highest possible rate of 45%, and the half-year rule applies. Robert explained that CAP has not taken any consideration for potential tax consequences on the equipment purchase. (Note: for simplicity, assume that all other future tax considerations have been properly addressed.)

After reviewing this information, you realize that you have much to contemplate as to how these issues should be dealt with.

Required

Provide a report to Robert outlining your recommendation on the accounting issues and note other important issues.

Exhibit 1	CAP's Financial Position

Custom Auto Parts
Statement of Financial Position
as at October 31

Assets

Current assets

		2020	2019
Cash		$ 35,000	$ 20,000
Accounts receivable		13,000	10,000
Inventory		20,000	12,000
Prepaids		3,000	3,000
	Total current assets	71,000	45,000
Property, plant, and equipment (net)		2,800,000	2,200,000
Total assets		**2,871,000**	**2,245,000**
Liabilities			
Current liabilities			
Accounts payable		25,000	20,000
Notes payable		13,000	25,000
Current portion of long-term debt		150,000	50,000
		188,000	95,000
Long-term debt		1,800,000	1,450,000
Total liabilities		**1,988,000**	**1,545,000**
Shareholders' equity			
Share capital		100	100
Preferred shares		100,000	100,000
Retained earnings		782,900	599,900
Total equity		**883,000**	**700,000**
Total liabilities and shareholders' equity		**$2,871,000**	**$2,245,000**
	Debt to equity	2.67	2.21

Dorion Fresh Water

Dorion Fresh Water (DFW) sells bottled water that comes from a freshwater spring in the town of Dorion, Ontario. DFW owns the land, and much of the surrounding area, where the freshwater spring is located. In addition, DFW has all of the equipment needed to extract the water from the spring and place it into bottles.

As a young, newly qualified professional accountant, you are looking to get out of public practice and become an active owner/manager of a small business. An opportunity has arisen to purchase all of the common shares of DFW, and you are contemplating this acquisition.

The significant competition in the bottled water market, combined with the relatively small operation of DFW and lack of brand equity, suggest that there is currently no significant goodwill associated with DFW's earnings. Accordingly, the purchase price will be based on DFW's net book value, calculated in accordance with ASPE, with an adjustment for only the fair value of capital assets. Your intention is to use your business network, and social media marketing skills, to expand DFW's operations and increase profitability.

As part of your due diligence, you discovered the following information:

1. The long-term debt is payable to a local credit union. No payments must be made until the end of 10 years, at which point the principal and all accrued interest are due in full. DFW received $250,000 four years ago to this day, and interest accrues at 6% annually.

2. DFW implemented a new rewards program at the beginning of this year. DFW included a liner under the bottom of each cap. The liner includes the text: (1) free bottle of water or (2) please try again. One in 10 bottles includes a free bottle of water. The promotion was a success. A total of 105,455 bottles were sold during the year, and 4,556 free bottle liners were redeemed. The cost of a bottle of water is $0.75 and the retail value is $1.50.

3. Capital assets are appraised at $485,000 by an independent, qualified third party.

4. The capital stock includes common shares and preferred shares. There are 500 preferred shares with a cost and redemption value of $10 and $12 per share, respectively, and a 6% mandatory, cumulative dividend yield. These shares will be retained by the current owners of DFW.

A copy of DFW's most recent internal statement of financial position is presented in Exhibit I. DFW has never had an audit or review.

Required

Based on your review of the financial statements and the information obtained during due diligence, prepare your estimate of the purchase price. Be sure to fully discuss any proposed changes to the financial statements required to comply with ASPE.

| Exhibit I | Internal Financial Statements |

Statement of Financial Position

As at Year End (unaudited)

Assets

Current

Cash	$ 17,555
Accounts receivable	55,780
Inventory	234,575
Prepaid insurance	2,335
	310,245
Capital assets	455,775
	$766,020

Liabilities and shareholders' equity

Current

Accounts payable and accruals	$256,775
Income taxes payable	33,455
	290,230
Long-term debt	$250,000
Capital stock	$ 55,000
Retained earnings	170,790
	225,790
	$766,020

Notes to Internal Statement of Financial Position

Inventory

Inventory is carried at the lower of cost and net realizable value.

Guarantee/Commitment

DFW has provided a guarantee on $50,000 of debt for a related company, Thunder Bay Springs (TBS). TBS has been experiencing financial difficulties, and there is a 10% chance that it may be insolvent within the next six months. TBS is currently working with its bank to refinance its debt and avoid bankruptcy.

Contingencies

1. DFW is being sued by a former employee for wrongful dismissal. The employee is suing DFW for $40,000, and the case is currently in mediation. Legal counsel suggests that it is unlikely that $40,000 will be paid out, but there is a 50% chance of paying $20,000 and a 50% chance of paying $10,000. The case will likely settle at the end of next year.

2. DFW is suing a competitor for infringement regarding the use of its trademarked logo. Legal counsel suggests that it is very likely that DFW will be awarded a settlement of $25,000.

Eastjet Airlines

Eastjet Airlines (EJA) is a regional airline that services most cities in the Maritimes and Eastern Canada. The company began in 2007 when three friends felt that the Maritimes was an underserviced market. Joe, Jack, and Jamal each own one third of all the issued common shares and exercise equal control over the company.

After their start-up phase, management began to expand its routes. Currently, EJA offers only short-haul flights to and from Halifax, Moncton, and Sydney. However, EJA has planned an expansion of operations into Ontario as it received approval to fly into both Toronto's Pearson Airport, and the Thunder Bay International Airport. EJA plans to offer its first flights into Ontario in early 2022.

In order to service the new routes into Ontario, EJA purchased a new airplane for $1 million. EJA obtained a 10-year mortgage from the Bank of Sydney in order to finance the acquisition of the planes. The terms and agreement of the mortgage can be found in Exhibit I.

Jack, who is responsible for the accounting functions, has always prepared the financial statements for internal reporting purposes. The statement of financial position, as at December 31, 2020, is included in Exhibit II.

As a result of the new bank loan, the financial statements must now be audited. As a result, EJA has hired Lebeau and Liang LLP (L&L), a Certified Professional Accountant firm, to complete the audit. You are the senior accountant at L&L, assigned to the audit.

You met with Jack as part of your auditing planning. Jack states "I understand that there is Part I (IFRS) and Part II (ASPE) GAAP in Canada. Currently, the bank has not disclosed which set of standards must be used to prepare the financial statements. Therefore, could you help me understand the significant differences between ASPE and IFRS, as they relate to our financial statements?" The notes from your meeting can be found in Exhibit III.

It is now January 10, 2021. The partner has asked you to prepare a report addressing the client's concerns, and to discuss the policy differences between ASPE and IFRS.

Required

Provide the report.

Exhibit I	Mortgage Agreement with the Bank of Sydney

Total balance:	$1,000,000
Term:	10-year amortization, blended annual payments due on December 31.
Commencement date:	January 1, 2020
First payment:	Due December 31, 2020
Interest rate:	8% fixed over the 10-year period
Covenant:	EJA shall maintain a debt to equity ratio that is no greater than 2:1.
Collateral:	Secured debt against the value of the aircrafts
Compliance:	Audited financial statements to be filed by January 31 of each year.

| Exhibit II | Internal Financial Statements |

Statement of Financial Position

As at December 31 (unaudited)	2020	2019
Assets		
Current		
Cash	$ 151,764	$ 160,502
Accounts receivable	334,894	411,760
Inventory	86,800	159,400
Prepaid insurance	4,720	2,060
	578,178	733,722
Capital	661,897	382,158
Future income tax asset	35,000	35,000
Long-term note receivable	20,000	0
	$1,295,075	$1,150,880
Liabilities and shareholders' equity		
Current		
Accounts payable	$ 158,318	$130,146
Bank loan—current portion	41,998	72,000
Income taxes payable	44,609	92,920
	244,925	295,066
Bank loan—FirstBank of Canada	93,434	130,664
Common shares	900	900
Preferred shares	20,300	20,300
Contributed surplus[1]	4,000	4,000
Retained earnings	931,516	699,950
	956,716	725,150
	$1,295,075	$1,150,880

Note to the Statement of Financial Position:

The statement of financial position does not include the impact of any of the issues related to:

(a) The new bank debt (mortgage with the Bank of Sydney) or the related aircraft

(b) Flight No. 877 [Exhibit III]

(c) Common share redemption

(d) The convertible bonds

[1] Related to preferred share redemptions in the past.

| *Exhibit III* | Notes fom your Discussion with EJA Management |

Purchase of Aircrafts and New Bank Debt

Jack informed you of the fact that the December 31, 2020, statement of financial position does not include the acquisition of the new aircraft, or the new bank debt. Jack did not even record the journal entry for the first payment made on December 31, 2020.

Bank Loan with the First Bank of Canada

The total outstanding balance of $93,434 is due in full on January 15, 2021. Jack has left the total balance as long-term as at the December 31 year end because on January 3, 2021, he was able to renegotiate the loan on a long-term basis. Jack has provided you with a copy of a non-cancellable agreement to refinance the debt as January 3, 2021.

Flight No. 877

On November 24, 2020, 26 passengers on Flight No. 877 were injured upon landing when the plane skidded off the runway. Fortunately, no one was injured seriously; however, personal injury suits were still filed on December 1, 2020, for damages totaling $50,000. Legal counsel has studied each suit and advised EJA management that it is probable (about a 60% chance) that they will lose the lawsuit. The loss could range anywhere between $20,000 and $50,000. If the lawsuit is lost, there is a 20% chance that EJA will have to pay $20,000, a 55% chance that it will have to pay $50,000, and a 25% chance that EJA will pay $35,000.

Cancellation of Common Shares

On September 15, the company reacquired and cancelled 9 shares (3 from each of Jack, Joe, and Jamal). The redemption price was $1,035 per share. Jack was unsure of how to account for this transaction, and therefore did not make any entries as at year end for the redemption. Prior to the reacquisition, there were 900 shares outstanding.

Convertible Bonds

In order to obtain additional capital to finance the expansion, EJA issued $500,000 in 8%, 10-year convertible bonds on January 1, 2020, for $500,000 cash. Each $1,000 bond includes the right to purchase 1 share for $750 during the life of the bond. The current market rate for similar nonconvertible bonds is 9%. The fair value of the option using an option pricing model is $49,760.

Full Speed Computer Services

Full Speed Computer Services (FSCS) is a company that services computer hardware and sells parts. The company operates in Nova Scotia and is owned by Charles Worthing. Charles is a successful businessperson and also a part owner of Full Speed Mobile Devices (FSMD), which is a mobile device sales and service company. The corporate structure is as follows:

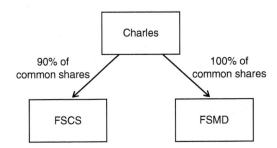

In January 2020, FSCS received a loan from a major bank to help finance an expansion of operations. The bank requires audited financial statements to be prepared and also prohibits the debt-to-equity ratio to exceed 2:1. Your firm has recently been engaged to complete the December 31, 2020, audit. As the audit senior, you recently met with Charles, who said that FSCS will adopt ASPE. You also discover the following information:

1. FSCS constructed a storage shed on land it leased for a five-year period on January 1, 2020. The company is required to remove the storage shed and restore the property to its original condition at the end of the lease term. The costs of removing the storage shed and restoring the property, at the end of the lease term, are estimated to be $200,000. FSCS's credit-adjusted risk-free rate is 8%.

2. FSCS completed construction of a new plant in Halifax in November 2020. The cost of the plant was $1.2 million. The federal government provided a grant of $200,000 to aid in construction costs. It also announced a forgivable loan of $400,000 to be paid in installments of $100,000 per year, to offset wages paid. The loan must be repaid in its entirety if the business is sold or wound up within four years. The first installment was received in January 2021, just a few days after the year end of December 31, 2020.

3. During the year, FSCS exchanged a parcel of land for a storage warehouse and $50,000 cash with FSMD. The parcel of land had a carrying value of $150,000, and a fair value of $250,000. The storage warehouse received by FSCS was being carried in FSMD's books of account at $75,000, and has a fair value of $200,000. FSCS has recorded a gain of $100,000 on the exchange.

4. On January 1, 2020, FSCS raised additional financing by issuing 10,000 preferred shares for $20. The preferred shares have a cumulative dividend of $1 per share and are redeemable by FSCS at any time for $22 per share. The preferred shares can be converted into a bond, at the option of the holder, repayable over a five-year period with a fixed interest rate of 7%.

Required

Prepare a report that discusses the accounting issues and provides recommended treatments. You have been asked to ignore any first-time audit adoption issues (e.g., opening balance issues with retained earnings) until later in the engagement; rather, you are expected to consider the implication of a covenant violation.

Gold Sparkle Auto Wash

Gold Sparkle Auto Wash (GSAW) is a car wash in a busy residential suburb of Halifax, NS. GSAW offers coin-operated, self-serve car wash, along with a full service car wash. Recently, the company obtained a bank loan in order to upgrade its equipment and spruce up the exterior of the building and signage. The bank loan includes a covenant stipulating that total debt (current and long-term) to equity is not to exceed 3:1.

The covenant has GSAW's owner, Samantha Williams, concerned about the company's total liabilities at year end. Specifically, Samantha is unsure about the impact on the bank covenant of the following:

- Samantha received a customer complaint regarding a recent full service car wash. The customer alleges that the washer scratched the car, causing damage of $2,000. The customer would like GSAW to incur the costs to repair the vehicle, or else he will proceed to small claims court. Samantha has experience with these situations. He estimates that, based on the terms and conditions of the cash wash agreement, there is only a 10% chance that the customer will receive a $2,000 reward. There is a 50% chance that the customer will be awarded $500.

- In the community, it is standard practice that all businesses donate $5,000 to a local community charity with the mandate of eliminating homelessness. GSAW has always donated in the past. The fundraising campaign was delayed in the current year and is scheduled to take place during the days just after the year end. During the current year, Samantha has pledged to contribute again this year.

- When decommissioning the car wash, the company will be required to incur various clean-up costs. Samantha expects that it may cost upwards of $10,000 to decommission the car wash, but he is unsure of an exact amount. The car wash is expected to last at least another 20 years.

- Although GSAW just completed an upgrade of the machinery, it is likely that some maintenance will be required on the equipment within the next three years. In addition, a major overhaul will be required in another eight years.

- GSAW implemented a loyalty program in order to help increase customer loyalty and boost earnings over the long run. Customers receive one "Gold Point" for every full service car wash. Ten Gold Points can be redeemed for a free car wash (retail value of $24.99).

  Financial records indicate that a total of 8,750 Gold Points have been issued since the inception of the program, with 545 free car washes provided. Industry statistics suggest that 10% to 20% of all loyalty points issued will not be redeemed. GSAW has never recorded the loyalty points in the financial statements in the past.

- GSAW sells nonrefundable gift certificates that can be used for full service car washes. The company's policy is to record all gift certificates as deferred revenue and write off all unused gift certificates after two years. The gift certificates do not expire. The following is a summary of the gift cards issued, used, and written off:

	Six Years Ago	Five Years Ago	Four Years Ago	Three Years Ago	Two Years Ago	Last Year	This Year
Amount issued	$3,650	$3,375	$2,675	$3,480	$2,870	$3,455	$2,980
Amount used	3,250	2,850	2,250	2,950	2,210	2,560	1,175
Written off	400	525	425	530	660	0	0

Currently, GSAW has a deferred revenue balance of $2,700. Given the capital-intensive nature of car washes, GSAW will incur little variable cost to provide the services to settle the gift certificates. Specifically, GSAW has a contribution margin of 70%.

Samantha has hired you, an independent professional accountant, to prepare a report that discusses alternative accounting treatments for the above-noted issues. The financial statements must be prepared in accordance with ASPE; however, Samantha would like you to discuss any differences that would arise if the statements were prepared in accordance with IFRS. Assume a 5% risk-free discount rate.

Required

Prepare the report for Samantha.

Maple Gold Corp.

Maple Gold Corp. (MGC) is a precious metal exploration and development company. MGC was established in 2019 by a management team and board of directors that has a successful history of creating shareholder value through the acquisition, exploration, financing, and development of gold projects. The company is traded on the Venture Exchange under the ticker MGC. The shares are trading at $0.20 per share, which is in excess of the book value per share, based on expectations that management can reproduce their past results.

MGC owns a small portfolio of prospective gold properties in Quebec and Ontario and is currently exploring in the Ring of Fire in Northern Ontario. The company is looking to expand its portfolio by purchasing various properties that span across Canada. Accordingly, management would like to display a strong financial position to assist in their search for new debt or equity capital.

The first year of operations was geared mostly toward establishing the business, closing deals on two properties, and beginning exploration activities. The 2020 fiscal year has been very hectic as MGC acquired an additional property and significantly ramped up exploration activities. Management has been too busy running the day-to-day operations that they have not been able to devote a significant amount of time to the accounting duties.

Accordingly, they have just hired you, CPA, as controller in order to help management focus more of their time on property acquisition and development. It is now January 4, 2021, and you have been asked to help prepare the draft 2020 financial statements and year-end audit file. The draft statement of financial position and income statement, along with excerpts from the notes to the financial statements, are found in Exhibit I. Exhibit II contains a summary of outstanding accounting issues from the current year-end file.

Required

Prepare a report that analyzes all of the accounting issues you have identified. Be sure to explore alternative accounting treatments, where appropriate, and to provide a reasoned conclusion. Management has specifically asked that you provide a general discussion of the deferred tax implications of the accounting issues that you identified and analyzed. A detailed analysis is not required at this stage because the tax specialists will be performing the detailed calculations.

Exhibit I **Financial Statements**

Maple Gold Corp.
(An Exploration Stage Company)
Statement of Financial Position
As At December 31, 2020, and 2019

	DRAFT 2020	AUDITED 2019
Assets		
Current assets		
Cash and cash equivalents	$ 548,669	$1,020,920
Receivables	48,595	55,785
Marketable securities	370,000	370,000
Exploration tax credit receivable	55,275	22,750
Due from related party	19,000	21,000
Prepaid expense and deposit	35,450	14,725
	1,076,989	1,505,180
Mineral properties (Note 1)	6,700,500	4,485,775
Property, plant, and equipment	14,070	16,780
	$7,791,559	$6,007,735
Liabilities and Shareholders' Equity		
Current liabilities		
Accounts payable and accrued liabilities	$ 78,950	$ 87,950
Due to related party	17,000	12,000
	95,950	99,950
Asset retirement obligation (Note 2)	84,700	79,900
Shareholders' equity		
Share capital (Note 3)	7,806,800	5,517,560
Contributed surplus (Note 3)	478,550	468,550
Deficit	(750,296)	(234,080)
Accumulated other comprehensive income	75,855	75,855
	7,610,909	5,827,885
	$7,791,559	$6,007,735

| Exhibit I | Financial Statements (Continued) |

Maple Gold Corp.
(An Exploration Stage Company)
Income Statement
As At December 31, 2020 and 2019

	DRAFT 2020	AUDITED 2019
Expenses		
Accretion of retirement liability	$ 4,800	$ 4,523
Administrative services	131,275	50,177
Depreciation	2,710	1,130
Consulting fees	105,000	43,750
Directors' fees	36,000	15,000
Investor relations and shareholder information	117,500	48,960
Office and miscellaneous	93,330	38,890
Professional fees	125,575	52,320
Property investigation	32,555	13,560
Property writedowns	0	1,000
Rent	41,850	17,440
Salaries and wages	145,000	60,420
Share-based compensation	0	0
Transfer agent and filing fees	11,450	4,770
Travel and promotion	13,450	3,960
	$ 860,495	$ 355,900
Other Income		
Interest income	215,225	51,540
Gain on sale of marketable security	0	11,760
	215,225	63,300
Loss for the year before income taxes	645,270	292,600
Future income tax recovery	(129,054)	(58,520)
Loss for the year	516,216	234,080
Deficit, beginning of the year	$(234,080)	0
Deficit, end of the year	$(750,296)	$(234,080)

Exhibit I — Financial Statements (Continued)

Excerpts from the Notes to the Financial Statements

1. Mining properties

The company is in the process of exploring its mineral properties and has not yet determined whether these properties contain ore reserves that are economically recoverable. Mineral exploration and development costs are capitalized on an individual prospect basis until such time as an economic ore body is defined or the prospect is sold, abandoned, or determined to be impaired. Costs for a producing prospect are depreciated on a unit-of-production method based on the estimated life of the ore reserves. Costs for prospects abandoned are written off.

The company reviews the carrying value of mineral properties and deferred exploration costs when there are events or changes in circumstances that may indicate impairment. Where estimates of fair value are available, an impairment charge is recorded if the fair value is less than the carrying amount. Reductions in the carrying value of properties are recorded to the extent the carrying value of the property exceeds the greater of: (1) the discounted value of future cash flows or (2) the net realizable value (proceeds less the costs to sell).

The following table shows the activity by property from January 1, 2020, to December 31, 2020:

Property	Dec. 31, 2019	Acquisitions	Explorations	Tax Credits	Writedowns	Dec. 31, 2020
Peter Lake	$2,275,855	0	$ 548,545	$(27,855)	0	$2,796,545
Wolf Gate	0	$975,855	137,095	0	0	1,112,950
Mink Landing	2,209,920	0	585,755	(4,670)	0	2,791,005
	$4,485,775	$975,855	$1,271,395	$(32,525)	0	$6,700,500

2. Asset retirement obligation

The company's obligations with respect to asset retirement relate to reclamation of the Peter Lake property site on which project operations are situated. The obligation is recognized in the period in which the obligation is created based on the estimated future reclamation costs using a long-term credit-adjusted risk-free rate of 6%. The total undiscounted future obligation is $135,000. The company estimates its obligations to be settled over approximately the next 10 years.

Balance—December 31, 2019	$79,900
Accretion expense	4,800
Balance—December 31, 2020	$84,700

Exhibit I	Financial Statements (Continued)

3. Share capital

Authorized: Unlimited common shares without par value

	Date	Number of Shares	Amount	Contributed Surplus
Balance, as at December 31, 2019		62,244,278	$5,517,560	$468,550
1) Shares issued for mineral properties	Jan. 31	30,000	6,000	
2) Shares issued for mineral properties	Jan. 31	200,000	40,000	
3) Shares issued for mineral properties	Mar. 31	50,000	7,500	
4) Shares issued for private placement	June 30	4,000,000	720,000	800
Share issuance costs			27,550	
5) Warrants exercised	June 30	115,000	17,250	9,200
6) Special shares issued for private placement	Nov. 30	6,000,000	600,000	
Share issuance costs			94,940	
7) Shares issued for mineral properties	Nov. 30	55,000	11,000	
8) Shares issued for private placement	Dec. 31	4,500,000	765,000	
		77,194,278	$7,806,800	$478,550

4. Related-party transactions

a) At December 31, 2020, the company owed $17,000 (December 31, 2019: $12,000) to companies with directors and officers in common. This obligation does not have any repayment terms or interest.

b) The following related-party transactions were in the normal course of operations and are measured at fair value being their exchange amounts:

	December 31, 2020	December 31, 2019
1) Directors' fees	$ 36,000	$ 15,000
2) Management salaries	145,000	60,420
3) Toronto Capital Partners Inc.—professional fees (company with a director in common)	25,000	15,000
4) Doug Clark—professional fees (legal firm with a partner and company director in common)	17,500	22,500
Total	$223,500	$112,920

Exhibit II | Notes of Outstanding Issues from the Year-end File

1. Recent geological reports suggest that the Peter Lake property may not have as large a gold deposit as original expected. Given this negative news, management hired an independent specialist to assess the ounces of gold that could be realistically mined from both the Peter Lake and Mink Landing properties. The following is a summary of the specialist's report:

Ounces	2021	2022	2023	2024	2025	2026	2027	2028	2029	2030
Peter Lake	0	130	265	400	425	535	535	475	475	265
Mink Landing	0	265	420	525	840	780	900	900	750	750

Current industry expectations are that the price of gold will average approximately $1,250 per ounce with expected extraction costs of $300 per ounce.

2. The Wolf Gate property was acquired by entering into a lease agreement with Geraldton Development Ltd. (GDL), a construction company. GDL owns the land, but has no intention of exploring and/or mining the property. Accordingly, a lease agreement was reached whereby MGC has the rights to explore and mine any gold deposits found over a 10-year period of time.

The lease agreement required MGC to pay an upfront fee of $975,855 to GDL. A royalty fee of 3% is payable for either: (1) the gross sales from mining any gold extracted from the land; or (2) the selling of the property in excess of $975,855 to a third party. The lease allows MGC to require GDL to sell the land to a third party if a gold deposit is found with 2,500 ounces or more.

If the land is not sold to a third party, MGC must restore the land to its original condition at the end of the 10-year period. Based on recent asset restorations of a similar size, it would cost MGC approximately $500,000 to bring the land back up to its original condition. Management of MGC feels that there is a 60% chance that they will find a gold deposit on the land in excess of 2,500, in which case, it will sell the land to a larger developer.

3. MGC owns the following marketable securities of publicly traded companies:

Company	Shares	Dec. 31, 2020 Market Value	Dec. 31, 2019 Market Value
Wolfsteed Resources Ltd.	450,000	$90,000	$83,000
Premier Silver Mines Ltd.	375,000	56,250	65,000
Western Gold Inc.	175,000	70,000	10,000
Kimberly Miners Ltd.	200,000	0	40,000
Atlantic Eastern Miners	175,000	87,500	76,500
South Boreal Resources Ltd.	550,750	110,150	95,500
		$413,900	$370,000

MGC has not made any adjustments to reflect the 2020 market values in the financial statements. During the year, MGC sold its 200,000 shares of Kimberly Miners Ltd. for $0.40 per share. The shares' cost basis was $0.10 and were trading at $0.20 at the end of 2019. This transaction has not been recorded.

Exhibit II | **Notes of Outstanding Issues from the Year-end File (Continued)**

4. MGC implemented a share-based compensation program during the current year as opposed to paying large cash salaries. The purpose of the compensation package is to allow management to take on more of the risk and reward of ownership, with the ability to receive greater compensation in the long run if the company is successful. In addition, cash flow would be saved during this crucial time of start-up and exploration.

The following combination of stock options and salary was awarded to the management team during the most recent year:

Name	Position	Salary	Director Fee	Stock Options
Brian Campbell, P. Eng., P. Geo.	President, CEO, and Director	$ 35,000	$ 6,000	500,000
Scott Vanek, P. Eng., MBA	VP Exploration and Director	25,000	6,000	400,000
Daniel Marleau	Chairman of the Board	10,000	6,000	400,000
Carla Grewal, CPA	Chief Financial Officer and Director	25,000	6,000	400,000
Mark Brooks, MBA	VP Corp. Development and Director	25,000	6,000	400,000
Jeffrey Scotts	Corporate Secretary and Director	25,000	6,000	400,000
		$145,000	$36,000	2,500,000

All of the options were issued on January 1, 2020, with a strike price of $0.35 per share when the shares were trading at $0.25 per share. The options could be exercised any time during the next five years and are expected to keep management motivated over the five-year period. Some additional information regarding the common shares of MGC and market rates is as follows:

- Volatility (σ), calculated over the past month: 15%
- Volatility (σ), calculated over the past 6 months: 30%
- Volatility (σ), calculated over the long run (> 1 year):   45%
- 30-day Government of Canada treasury bill rate: 2%
- 1-year Government of Canada bond yield: 4%
- 5-year Government of Canada bond yield: 6%

5. The EPS for the current year has yet to be calculated.

6. During November 2020, the company issued 6 million special common shares for $0.10 each. The common shares were issued to an investment bank in Toronto, and have the following characteristics:

a. The shares have a retraction privilege that is in effect if MGC's retained deficit balance exceeds $1 million. When the retained earnings are in a surplus position, the shares can be redeemed by the company for $0.35 per share, regardless of the market price.

b. The special common shares carry a 10%, non-cumulative dividend. In any given year, dividends must be paid on the special shares before any other dividend could be paid to the remaining common shares.

Mobile Updates

Mobile Updates ("MU") is a small Canadian company that designed and operates a sports app. The sports app strives to provide a unique user experience as its core competency.

The company is publicly traded on the TSX under the symbol MU. MU went public in 2014 after being a privately held company for over five years. The founders of MU (the MacDonia family) continue to hold a larger portion of the common shares and the preferred shares (see Exhibit II).

You, CPA, have been hired as an accounting analyst, reporting directly to the controller, Malcom Peterson. Your position has been newly created due to rapid growth since the initial public offering.

Your initial meeting with Malcom is summarized as follows:

MALCOM "*Hello CPA, welcome to the MU. We are very happy to have you here as we really need as much help as possible with the accounting duties. This has been a very busy year for us.*

As your first task, I would like for you to familiarize yourself with MU. Here is a binder with some key information, such as our corporate strategy (Exhibit I), our ownership structure (Exhibit II), our most recent financial statements (Exhibit III), and key metrics we use in our calculations (Exhibit IV)."

CPA "*Okay – thank you. I will review these once I head back to my office*"

MALCOM "*Great.*

After you familiarize yourself with MU' background, then, we will need you to help tackle some remaining accounting issues (Exhibit V). None of these issues have been reflected in our DRAFT 2020 financial statements

Our year-end audit is beginning next week and these are the remaining issues. Can you please address each issue, and provide a preliminary calculation of earnings per-share."

CPA "*I will do my best, and provide you with a memo within a few days.*"

MALCOM "*Sounds great – I am really excited that you decided to join our accounting group. I know that you will be able to add much value to our organization. Also, please do not focus on any of the impacts related to income taxes at this point. We will deal with the current and future taxes at a later date.*"

Required

Prepare a report for Malcom

Exhibit I   Company Strategy

Mission Statement

"Mobile Updates creates mobile-first sports experiences, connecting fans to a combination of real time news, scores, fantasy information and alerts while creating and curating content that is mobile optimized, comprehensive, customizable and shareable."

Porter's Five Forces

The app industry is highly competitive, with few barriers to entry (high threat of new entrants) and many substitute products (e.g., websites, television, etc.). Users hold all of the power, with supplier power not a major factor. Overall, Porter's Five Forces suggests that this is a very difficult industry to compete in.

Corporate Strategy

MU has two distinct sources of revenue: advertising on its digital media products and licensing of its mobile applications. The company's corporate strategy for revenue growth has focused around three pillars:

- Increased engagement in-app, via advanced statistics, customized user experiences, and graphic data displays, which should lead to more sessions and time of use.

- The addition of new and dynamic advertising units, including in-stream ads, rich-media and video units as well as custom and sponsored content in order to create better ways for brands to engage with sports fans on our platforms.

- The growth of both direct sales and programmatic advertising business, in order to forge stronger connections with major brands and agencies with increased mobile budgets industry-wide, demonstrating how ad dollars continue to move from legacy media to mobile.

Exhibit II   Ownership Structure

Corporate Structure

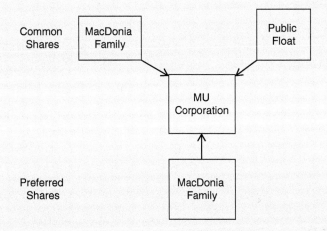

Share classes

Common shares: Voting common shares, with no par value, where each share represents one vote, dividends are paid at the discretion of the Board of Directors.

Preferred shares: Preferred shares with an annual cumulative dividend of $1 per share, three votes per share, and convertible into common shares at a ratio of 3 common shares per 1 preferred share.

Corporate Share Register

The shareholdings are summarized as follows:

- MacDonia Family

  ○ common shareholdings, 50,000,000 shares
  ○ Preferred shares, 555,000 shares

- Public Float
  ○ common shareholdings, 152,106,482 shares

Weighted-average number of shares outstanding

For purposes the 2020 EPS calculations, the following figures represent the weighted-average number of common shares outstanding:

- Basic: 215,504,000
- Diluted: Basic amount plus the impact of any dilutive instruments

Exhibit III **Draft Financial Statements**

Mobile Updates Inc.
Statement of Financial Position
(In Thousands of Canadian Dollars)
December 31, 2020, and 2019

	DRAFT	
ASSETS	2020	2019
Current assets:		
Cash and equivalents	25,472	17,090
Accounts receivable	2,701	1,178
Tax credits recoverable	3,822	1,648
Prepaid expenses	674	447
	32,669	20,363
Noncurrent assets:		
Property and equipment (note 1)	1,698	1,724
Intangible assets	5,889	3,967
Investments	1,727	4,196
	9,314	9,887
Total assets	41,983	30,250
LIABILITIES AND SHAREHOLDERS' EQUITY		
Current liabilities		
Accounts payable	3,649	2,424
Noncurrent liabilities		
Long-term debt	425	428
Shareholders' equity	37,909	27,398
Total liabilities and shareholders' equity	41,983	30,250

Note 1—Consists mostly of office equipment, leasehold improvements, and computer equipment.

Exhibit III | Draft Financial Statements (Continued)

Mobile Updates Inc.
Statement of Comprehensive Income
(In Thousands of Canadian Dollars, Except per Share Amounts)
December 31, 2020, and 2019

	DRAFT 2020	2019
Revenue	27,808	17,595
Operating expenses:		
Personnel	9,660	6,335
Content	1,121	972
Technology	1,646	999
Facilities, administrative and other	3,765	3,086
Marketing	2,230	1,547
Depreciation of property and equipment	442	422
Amortization of intangible assets	1,744	1,535
Acquisition costs	318	0
	20,926	14,896
Operating income	6,882	2,699
Interest expense	21	21
Income for the year	6,861	2,678
Earnings per share— basic	xxx	0.02
Earnings per share—diluted	**xxx**	**0.01**

Mobile Updates Inc.
Statement of Change in Shareholders' Equity
(In Thousands of Canadian Dollars, Except per Share Amounts)
December 31, 2020, and 2019

	Common shares		Preferred Shares		Contributed Surplus	Retained Earnings	Total Shareholders' Equity
	Amount	Number of Shares	Amount	Number of Shares			
Balances, December 31, 2019	33,262	202,106,482	1,665	555,000	−432	−7,097	27,398
Income for the year					0	6,861	6,861
Shares issued	3,650	33,715,735					3,650
Balances, December 31, 2020	36,912	235,822,217	1,665	555,000	−432	−236	37,909

Exhibit IV — Key Financial Metrics

US-CAD exchange rate	July 1, 2020—$1.30 CAD = $1US December 31, 2020 – $1.35 CAD = $1US
Risk-free rate	January 1, 2020—2% June 30, 2020—2.5% December 31, 2020—2.7%
Common share market value	January 1, 2020—$0.11 June 30, 2020—$0.09 December 31, 2020—$0.20
Common share volatility (historical, since IPO)	40%
Market rate for MU bonds	January 1, 2019—5% December 31, 2019—5.5% December 31, 2020—7%

Exhibit V — Outstanding Accounting Issues

Stock-Based Compensation

On January 1, 2020, management was issued a stock-based compensation plan. The stock-based compensation plan was discussed by the Board of Directors for many years, and was accepted in order to align management and shareholder interests with respect to increasing shareholder value. The Board adopted the stock-based compensation plan with the intent of motivating management over a three year period (i.e., the stocks are not exercisable for a three year period). Under the plan, management was issued 1,015,625 options to purchase the common shares of MU for $0.11 each. Any impacts of the stock options plan are not reflected in the DRAFT financial statements. Management would like you to estimate the value of the options using some publicly available Black–Scholes option pricing model/calculator as part of your analysis.

Forward Contract

On July 1, MU entered into a forward contract with FICI-Financial (FICIF) in order to reduce earnings volatility related to exchange rate movements. Under the terms of the contact, MU was to receive $1,000,000 U.S. Dollars (USD) in Exchange for $1,300,000 Canadian Dollars (CAD). MU could take all, or any portion, of the U.S. Dollars at any time during the period of July 1, 2020 to June 30, 2020. MU must take delivery of all $1,000,000 USD by the end of the contract term. Note that the contract is expected to be settled on a net basis. MU has not settled any portion of the contract at year end.

Lawsuit

During the year, MU was alleged to have copied a patented code related to programing advanced graphical displays. MU lawyers have estimated that there is a 25% that this litigation will result in a payment of $1,000,000, and a 75% chance that no payment will be required. MU's patent lawyers strongly believe that the code in question is unique and different from the patented code.

Statement of Cash Flows

We need a draft statement of cash flows prepared based on the information that is currently available. Management expects the direct method to be used in preparing the Operating Activities section of the Statement of Cash Flows.

Earnings-per-Share

We need to calculate the basic and diluted EPS to complete the Statement of Comprehensive Income.

Exhibit V   Outstanding Accounting Issues (Continued)

Long-term Debt

The long-term debt of $425,000 on the Statement of Financial Position represents 10-year bonds with a coupon rate of 6%, payable annually. The bonds were issued on January 1, 2019. Currently, the bond is being carried at amortized cost, as follows:

Year	Beg. Value	Coupon Payment	Interest	Amortization	End. Value
2019	$430,887[1]	$24,000	$21,544	$2,456	$428,431
2020	428,431	24,000	21,422	2,578	425,853
2021	425,853	24,000	21,293	2,707	423,145
2022	423,145	24,000	21,157	2,843	420,303
2023	420,303	24,000	21,015	2,985	417,318
2024	417,318	24,000	20,866	3,134	414,184
2025	414,184	24,000	20,709	3,291	410,893
2026	410,893	24,000	20,545	3,455	407,438
2027	407,438	24,000	20,372	3,628	403,810
2028	403,810	24,000	20,190	3,810	400,000

MU management wants to understand the implications of adopting fair value measurement as at December 31, 2020. At this point, they are unsure if they will proceed with this method of measurement management but would like to understand the impact on the financial statements. As a result, please analyze this issue separately from all other issues. Management expects you to estimate the fair value of the bond based on the information you have available as part of your analysis.

---

[1] Based on a market rate of 5% which was the market rate at the date of issuance.

Northern Nickel Explorers Ltd.

Northern Nickel Explorers Ltd. (NNEL) is a start-up company, closely held by a small group of successful business-people, geologists, and engineers. NNEL is a junior mining company that explores for gold and silver. During its first year of operations, the company focused on raising capital and purchasing assets.

Jack Gerikyan, the CFO, is preparing the financial statements for the December 31, 2020 year end. Jack is determining whether the company should adopt ASPE or IFRS. Management does not expect to go public anytime in the near future. However, management is working with a major financial institution in the hopes of securing long-term debt. Therefore, Jack would like to present a strong statement of financial position and favorable debt to equity ratio.

During the year, the company financed initial operations by issuing the following instruments:

1. At the beginning of the year, the company issued $500,000 10-year bonds at par. The holder of the bonds can convert $10,000 in bonds into cash based on the performance of the company. Specifically, each $10,000 bond can be converted into cash at the rate of 10% of net income. Draft financial statements reveal net income of $250,000.

2. On January 1, the company issued $2.5 million of six-year, zero-interest-bearing notes along with warrants to buy 1.25 million common shares for $10 per share. The company received $1.9 million for the notes and warrants. If offered alone, the notes would have been issued to yield 9% to the creditor. The warrants are valued at $550,000 with an option pricing model.

3. On January 1, the company issued $1.5 million of five-year, 6% convertible bonds at par value. Each $1,000 bond is convertible into 100 common shares. A similar bond (without conversion feature) would have been issued at a market yield of 9%. On December 31, $200,000 worth of bonds were converted to common shares.

4. On April 1, the company issued 15,000 8% noncumulative, retractable preferred shares for $100 per share. The shares are retractable by the holder on or after September 1 of the current year, and redeemable at the option of the company on or after September 2 of the current year. Commencing on September 2 the company is required to purchase 10% annually of the total outstanding preferred shares at $105 per share.

5. On March 1, the company issued 50,000 preferred shares with a 5% cumulative dividend for $10 per share. The preferred shares are redeemable, but not retractable. In addition, the preferred shares can be converted into common shares at any time, at a ratio of 1-to-1.

6. During the year, the company issued 200,000 common shares for $5 per share.

Required

Assume the role of Jack Gerikyan, and prepare a report to the board of directors that discusses the recognition, measurement, and presentation of the financial instruments issued.

Pyramid Holdings Limited

Contributed by
Jeffrey Botham and Bruce J. McConomy
Lazaridis School of Business & Economics, Wilfrid Laurier University

Pyramid Holdings Limited (PHL) is a private company based in Winnipeg, Manitoba, that offers storage solutions, such as shelving units and organizers, to a variety of business clients. Joan Chen has been the bookkeeper for PHL for several years, and prepared a preliminary trial balance for the fiscal year ended March 31, 2020 (Exhibit I). The company chose a March year end to coincide with its business cycle. The company's owner, James Steel, has been thinking of taking the company public in three or four years and would like to ensure the financial statements are attractive to potential investors.

When Joan Chen presented Jim with the preliminary trial balance for the 2020 fiscal year, a number of things struck him as being not quite right. Joan is not a CPA, so Jim prepared a list of items for follow-up with the auditor to make sure they are dealt with correctly (Exhibit II). During a heated discussion with Joan about several of the contentious issues on the list, Joan walked out of the meeting and quit before preparing PHL's final trial balance and financial statements.

You are the replacement bookkeeper assigned by the ABC temp agency to help PHL prepare financial information for the auditor. You are currently completing your business degree in the evenings, and hope to write your CPA examinations in a year or two. The auditor will be arriving in a week. Jim offered to hire you as a full-time replacement, once your two-week assignment as a temporary bookkeeper is up, as long as you can "make the numbers look good" for him and the company. He indicated that he expects that when the company goes public, he will be able to pay you a $6,000 bonus "if you can get the job done right." By coincidence, $6,000 is the exact amount you owe for your student loan, so it would come in quite handy!

You were able to call Joan, who provided you with some additional information (also in Exhibit II) before she left on a six-month trip to "parts unknown" where clearly, she does not want to be contacted again.

Required

PHL follows ASPE, and Jim has instructed you (and the auditors) to use the simplest methods allowed for PHL's financial statements. (Note: round all calculations to the nearest dollar.)

(a) Prepare all adjusting entries required for the March 31, 2020, financial statements and also include them in an adjusted trial balance work sheet.

(b) Jim would also like you to prepare a draft statement of financial position and draft income statement for discussion with the auditor. For purposes of calculating tax expense for the draft financial statements, you can do what Joan has done in prior years: ignore the impact of any timing differences and assume that accounting income equals taxable income. (The auditors will provide a more specific estimate in a few weeks.)

(c) Jim is also hoping that you can briefly summarize the requirements of "going public" for him, so that he will be prepared to discuss this with the auditors. (He specifically said you do not have to "run the numbers" for going public, he just wants to have an overview of the requirements of going public, including whether it will have any impact on PHL's accounting policies.) There is no need to do an extensive report on the impact of going public in a few years, because Jim is relying on the auditors to provide that analysis separately next year.

Exhibit I	Financial Statements

Pyramid Holdings
Preliminary Trial Balance
March 31, 2020

	Dr.	Cr.
Cash	$ 160,000	
Accounts receivable	180,000	
less allowance for doubtful accounts		$ 7,200
Inventory	181,000	
Inventory in Warehouse #2	50,000	
Property, plant, and equipment	240,000	
Accumulated depreciation—Property, plant, and equipment		21,000
Vehicles—Leased	4,000	
Vehicles	120,000	
Accumulated depreciation—Vehicles		25,000
Accounts payable		100,000
Accrued liabilities		55,000
Notes payable		50,000
Common shares		235,000
Retained earnings, April 1, 2019		185,000
Revenue		900,200
Cost of goods sold	290,000	
Salaries	200,000	
Payroll taxes	20,000	
Vehicle expenses	14,200	
Rent expense	65,000	
Rent expense—Warehouse #2	24,000	
Utilities	11,200	
Income tax expense	0	
Bad debt expense	3,600	
Depreciation and amortization	0	
Other expenses	15,400	
Total	**$1,578,400**	**$1,578,400**

Prepared by Joan Chen, Bookkeeper

Joan's Notes (see also Exhibit II)

- Remember to ask auditor about the shareholder loan and repayment.
- Professional fees for audit and going public?
- What to accrue for payroll that will be paid covering March 28–April 8, 2020, for $10,000? (The $10,000 covers all employees, and the standard work week is Monday–Friday, with paydays occurring every second Friday.)

Exhibit II # Items for Follow-Up with Auditor

The following is a list of items for follow-up with the auditor compiled by Jim. It includes information provided by Joan to you.

- PHL purchased a used delivery truck for $10,000 on July 1, 2019, and it was expensed as part of Vehicle Expenses.

- The lease payments for the company car, used mainly by the VP of sales for visiting clients, are incorrectly recorded under Vehicles—Leased. The monthly payments are $400 and began on May 1, 2019, for a three-year lease. (Note: only the first 10 months of payments had been made by March 31, 2020.) If PHL had purchased the car, it would have cost $30,000. The car has an expected useful life of six years.

- The company's heat, electric, water, and related utility bills had not been received when Joan prepared the financial statements, so she accrued a total amount of $1,000 for the three bills in the trial balance. When the final invoices arrived, the cost actually totaled $2,500, due to an extremely cold winter and repairs needed to a frozen water pipe. In addition, there was $10,000 damage (to carpets and so on) due to the flooding caused by the frozen pipe. Joan did not record the $10,000 amount disbursed because it should be covered by the company's insurance policy. There is an $800 deductible on the insurance claim that remains outstanding and will be deducted from the reimbursement from the insurance company.

- ATL Bank had loaned the company $20,000 during the first week of the 2019–20 fiscal year, and the company made a payment of $5,000 to the bank on November 1, 2019. Joan admitted she had not recorded the payment, and was going to speak with the auditor about it when they came in for the year-end audit. The bank charges 6% interest on the loan, but Joan did not record any interest because she did not consider it material. ATL charges its usual prime plus 1% (i.e., 6%) on the loan, with the interest due on the anniversary date each year. The $20,000 amount is included on the trial balance in Accounts Payable.

- The audit fee was estimated at $25,000. However, the audit firm has indicated that it will charge an additional $20,000 to help prepare an initial consulting report regarding factors to consider when Jim eventually takes the company public. The audit firm estimates that the consulting report and related work was "90% complete" on March 31, 2020. Neither of these items has been recorded in the trial balance.

- A shipment of inventory valued at $1,500 was shipped by a supplier on March 28, 2020, scheduled to arrive at PHL on March 30, 2020, but it arrived on April 3, 2020. It was delayed because it was shipped by truck and got caught in a snowstorm. The shipment was FOB shipping point. Joan records shipments based on the arrival date at the company's warehouse and therefore no entry had been made to include the inventory. Of course it was also not included in the physical count that took place on March 31, 2020, as it was not present for warehouse personnel to count.

- The company has not performed a detailed analysis of its allowance for doubtful accounts since the auditors were in last year; it was $5,600 at March 31, 2019 (before any accounts receivable were written off during the 2019–20 fiscal year). Joan booked a preliminary estimate of $3,600 of bad debts for fiscal 2019–20, because she did not know how the amount recorded in 2018–19 was calculated. Joan knows that the auditors like to see an aged accounts receivable schedule on the first day of their audit, so she has prepared one (Exhibit III).

- Joan took a week off between March 24 and March 31, and the invoices for new office furniture purchases that came in during that period totaled $15,000 and were recorded in inventory by her assistant. The office furniture had arrived at PHL on March 1, 2020, and is expected to last 10 years.

- Joan and her assistant attended the inventory count at the main warehouse. Similar to March 31, 2019, the owner assured her that there was "$50,000 of good inventory" at Warehouse #2, a warehouse in Brandon, Manitoba, that is rented from the owner (Jim's father) at a cost of $2,000 per month. Joan never verified the existence of the inventory, nor had she (or the auditors) even been to the warehouse. The cost of the goods purchased was "paid for" by the note payable that appears on the trial balance. The note is noninterest-bearing, so Jim says he is in no hurry to pay it. The $50,000 of inventory was originally purchased on December 31, 2017, according to Jim.

- PHL uses straight-line depreciation for all of its property, plant, and equipment other than vehicles (where double declining-balance depreciation is used). Aside from the items discussed above, there were no additions or disposals during the year. Property, plant, and equipment items are estimated to last for 10 years, and vehicles for five years. Joan had not recorded any depreciation expense for the 2019–20 year before she quit. However, depreciation charges prior to 2019–20 have been audited and were done correctly.

- Jim had arranged a special deal with one of his best customers (BCL) on October 1, 2019. The deal allowed the customer to purchase $22,000 (cost) of inventory for a price of $35,000. The "special" part of the deal was that BCL would not have to make any payments on the $35,000 outstanding amount for the goods until October 1, 2023. In addition, BCL would only be charged 2% interest on the amount outstanding to be paid each year on October 1. BCL was quite pleased with this deal because it has a bit of a cash flow problem, so BCL's bank charges it prime plus 3% (8% annually) instead of the 6% charged to PHL. Joan recorded the sale of $35,000 and the cost of goods sold of $22,000 in October 2019, but was unsure if other entries were needed.

- PHL pays tax at a 25% tax rate, and Joan had told Jim that based on her discussions with the auditors, "once again there are no permanent differences, so under ASPE taxes are pretty simple to calculate." Joan left before estimating the tax expense for fiscal 2019–20. However, she sent a cheque to the Canada Revenue Agency for $20,000 on March 15, 2020, because that was the tax expense from fiscal 2018–19 and so it was her best guess as to how much PHL will owe in taxes for fiscal 2019–20. However, she did not record the $20,000 payment before she left.

- When Joan provided Jim with the preliminary trial balance (Exhibit I), she included a few questions for the auditors at the bottom of the trial balance. You hope to be able to impress Jim by also dealing with these questions before the auditors arrive!

| Exhibit III | Aged Accounts Receivable |

Pyramid Holdings
Aged Accounts Receivable
March 31, 2020

Vendor	<30 days	31–60 days	61–90 days	>90 days	Total
Abacus International	$ 500	$ 500	$ 500	$ 500	$ 2,000
Beta Limited	1,000	750	250		2,000
BCL Limited				35,000	35,000
Charlie and Partners	15,000	15,000			30,000
Delta Inc.		20,000	24,000		44,000
Echo Limited			1,313	1,313	2,626
Foxtrot Corp.	2,424	2,424	2,424		7,272
Golf Unlimited				10,000	10,000
Aviation Partners			45,000		45,000
Acme Industries				2,102	2,102
Total	$18,924	$38,674	$73,487	$48,915	$180,000

Salmon Grill

Salmon Grill (SG) is a deli that sells fresh sandwiches, soups, and salads. Salmon Grill was founded by Jenny and Jason, who are brother and sister, and began as a small, local deli in Edmonton. Based on rave reviews of their salmon grilled sandwich, Jenny and Jason have decided to expand operations within Alberta. As part of the expansion plans, all of the assets were rolled over into a newly formed corporation that has a fiscal year end of December 31, 2020. The corporation issued 50,000 shares to each of Jenny and Jason for $3 per share. Upon incorporation, SG also received a 10-year, 9%, $250,000 loan with annual payments from the First Bank of Edmonton to help finance the expansion.

During their first year of operations, Jenny and Jason decided to hire Lebeau and Liang LLP (L&L) to help develop accounting policies that are consistent with ASPE for various new transactions. You, a senior accountant with L&L, have been assigned to the SG file and met with Jenny and Jason to discuss the various new issues. Jenny and Jason have provided you with the following information regarding the new issues:

1. SG implemented a customer loyalty program at the beginning of the year. Each customer receives one Grill Point for every large sandwich that they purchase. A customer receives a free large sandwich once they earn 10 Grill Points. A large sandwich sells for an average of $5 and costs an average of $3 to produce. As of year end, a total of 23,500 Grill Points were issued. Jenny and Jason did not know how to account for this program and stated that they will record the expense of the free sandwich when a customer redeems their points. Fixed costs are approximately 30% of gross margin.

2. To help finance their expansion across Alberta, SG issued 10,000 preferred shares to a group of private investors for $10 per share. The preferred shares carry a 10% annual, cumulative dividend yield and are redeemable by SG. The dividend rate was issued at such a high level because SG does not have access to any other sources of capital in the current year. In five years, the dividend is expected to double. Given that they are preferred shares and not retractable, Jenny and Jason recorded these shares as equity.

3. Given the volatility of commodity prices, SG has entered into a forward contract with the First Bank of Edmonton. On April 1, SG has locked the price of 100,000 kg of wheat at $0.75/kg. Upon its inception, SG did not have to put forth any cash. All cash transfers will take place on settlement. As at December 31, the price of wheat is trading on the Chicago Board of Trade at $0.87/kg. Jenny and Jason have made no entries at year end and will record the cost of goods sold with a wheat price of $0.75 in the next fiscal year.

4. On August 1, the company reacquired and cancelled 1,500 of Jenny's and 1,500 of Jason's shares at $4 per share. All 3,000 shares were re-issued to Khaled, a long-time friend, at a price of $5 per share. Jenny and Jason were unsure of how to account for these transactions.

5. On January 1, SG purchased a new grill. The purchase was financed through an "interest-free" five-year vendor loan, whereby SG is required to pay back $5,000 in each year. Jenny and Jason are excited about this financing promotion because they would have to pay 9% interest to borrow the money from the bank. Jason and Jenny recorded an asset and liability at $25,000. At year end, the $5,000 cash payment was recorded as a reduction of the long-term liability. SG uses the straight-line method to depreciate the asset, which has a seven-year useful life.

To protect its investment, the First Bank of Edmonton has included a restrictive covenant whereby SG cannot have a debt to equity ratio in excess of 1:1. Upon inception, the debt to equity ratio is 0.83:1. Both Jenny and Jason have expressed their pleasure with the debt to equity ratio.

The partner has asked that you prepare a report that helps Jason and Jenny understand the implications, if any, of the debt-to-equity covenant at year end. The partner reminds you that it may be ideal to start by first analyzing the accounting issues.

Required

Prepare the report.

Sensations Athletic Club

Sensations Athletic Club (SAC) is a new athletic facility, located in Saskatoon, Saskatchewan. SAC is owned and operated by Hulk Savage, a former Olympic gold medalist in weightlifting. Hulk decided to make his passion his business by opening open a local gym. SAC has the following mission statement:

"SAC provides the residents of Saskatoon the opportunity to live a healthier, happier, and longer life by providing affordable access to athletic equipment, aerobic classes, and specialized dieticians."

Hulk borrowed $10 million from the bank in order to finance the required start-up investments in working capital and capital assets. Hulk invested $2 million of his own money (that he earned through his career as a weightlifter and professional wrestler). The bank does not want the debt to equity ratio to exceed 5:1.

The first year of business has been a bit a rocky, as Hulk's expertise is in weight training, as opposed to running a business. However, SAC was able to attract 5,000 people to purchase full memberships.

It was difficult to attract new members during the first few months of operations. In order to attract more members, Hulk implemented the following creative marketing initiatives during the middle of the year:

- Savage Points—SAC offers its members 1 point per visit to the gym (maximum of 1 point per day). Savage Points can be redeemed for free passes for a guest or for a free protein drink.

- Initial Fee Return Guarantee—For three months, SAC provided new members with a guarantee period whereby their initial membership fee could be returned if they decide to discontinue their membership within the first year.

- Free Membership Challenge—Members are entered into a draw every time they access the gym, and provided with a chance to win free membership fees for life.

Hulk has come to you, Badami and Lusamba LLP, for assistance regarding the preparation of the December 31 year-end financial statements in accordance with ASPE. Hulk knows how much cash came in from memberships, but is unsure about how much revenue should be recognized. In addition, Hulk needs help understanding how the marketing initiatives impact the financial statement. Additional details on the marketing initiatives can be found in Exhibit I, which outlines your most recent discussion with Hulk.

Required

Prepare a report that addresses Hulk's concerns. The partner would like you to do a good job on this engagement as it may lead to more work, and the annual year-end audit. Therefore, the partner has asked you to prepare any journal entries to record your recommended accounting treatments.

Exhibit I	Discussion with Hulk Savage

- Memberships require a nonrefundable $500 initiation fee, followed by a monthly fee of $50. The monthly fee must be paid at the beginning of each month. The following is a monthly breakdown of the new memberships.

Jan	Feb	Mar	Apr	May	June	July	Aug	Sept	Oct	Nov	Dec
200	250	350	200	250	400	850	900	800	300	300	200

- SAC offered new members an initial fee return guarantee during the months of July, August, and September. The program was well received, and resulted in significant increases in membership. Hulk believes the program is so successful because it provides people with a risk-free opportunity to see what SAC has to offer. Hulk is confident that once a member has a chance to work out at the gym, and take advantage of all it has to offer, no one will discontinue their membership. As of December 31, not a single person has taken advantage of the initial fee return guarantee. Revenue has been recorded on a cash basis by Hulk.

- The Savage Points can be redeemed as follows:

  - A total of 10 Savage Points can be redeemed for a free pass for a guest. With a free pass, a member can bring a guest into the gym to use all of the facilities for free. The only condition is that a free-pass guest cannot partake in any aerobic classes if they are full (i.e., they cannot bump out a paying customer). Anyone can purchase a day pass to SAC for $5, which will entitle them to full access to the gym, including all classes.

  - A total of 15 Savage Points can be redeemed for a free protein shake. The shake can be purchased from SAC for $6.50. It costs SAC a total of $2.50, including all overhead allocations, to prepare the shake.

During the year, a total of 30,255 Savage Points were issued. Members took favorably to this promotion; the Points were redeemed for 60 free guest passes and 75 free protein shakes. Industry standards suggest that a total of 20% of all Points will not be redeemed. The only journal entries recorded in regards to the Savage Points was a debit to cost of goods sold and credit to inventory for the protein shakes.

- Every time a member swipes their membership card to access the gym, they are electronically entered into a random draw. The winner of the draw will then have a chance to win a free membership for life. In order to win the challenge, the member must do more push-ups than Hulk. The draw will take place on February 5 of the following fiscal year, and the push-up challenge will take place on February 25.

Stabilize It Ltd.

Stabilize It Ltd. (SIL) is the creator of a new technology that can be used in smart phones in order reduce distortion (blurriness) in motion pictures. The technology is currently being used by various companies across the globe. SIL also has a portfolio of other technologies and products that have been developed through its research initiatives. SIL's shares are currently being traded on the Toronto Stock Exchange, and the company is experiencing shareholder pressure to improve profitability.

You are the audit manager in charge of SIL's file for the December 31, 2020, year end. Your audit team is progressing well through the engagement, and you schedule a progress meeting with the senior auditor. The following dialogue takes place:

AUDIT MANAGER:	How is the audit coming along so far? Any issues or concerns?
SENIOR AUDITOR:	It's going well. I do have a few concerns. First, I have found some evidence that leads me to believe that the 2019 financial statements may have been misstated.
AUDIT MANAGER:	Wow—this can be serious. What is the issue?
SENIOR AUDITOR:	Well, as you know, a new inventory information system was installed during the 2020 year. This new system results in a new way to estimate inventory obsolescence. If this new system's method is applied to the previous year, our cost of goods sold will differ.
AUDIT MANAGER:	Okay. Let me look into this further and determine how to proceed. Any other challenges?
SENIOR AUDITOR:	Yes. As you are aware, SIL's voice-clarifying technology has been actively sought after by many companies. It appears that the division will be sold. I'm not sure how to deal with the impact of a potential sale on the financial statements. Also, it appears that management has changed the depreciation method for equipment and the amortization of the useful life of certain patents.
AUDIT MANAGER:	Okay, I will look into these issues further.

The senior auditor provides you with a copy of the most recent draft income statement (Exhibit I) and summary notes related to the above issues (Exhibit II).

Required

Assume the role of the audit manager and prepare a memo that will be included in the audit file.

| Exhibit 1 | Excerpts from the Financial Statements |

Stabilize It Limited
Statement of Income

For the year ended December 31 (audited)	2020	2019
Revenue and income	$4,875,200	$4,643,048
Cost of sales	1,243,176	1,137,547
Gross profit	$3,632,024	$3,505,501
Expenses		
Advertising and promotion	255,000	242,857
Depreciation—equipment	275,000	350,000
Amortization—intangibles	100,000	250,000
Insurance	22,500	21,430
Interest and bank charges	27,040	25,752
Legal and accounting	12,100	11,524
Lease expense	34,500	32,857
Office and general expenses	255,000	242,857
Repairs and maintenance	97,500	92,857
Utilities	112,575	107,214
Wages and benefits	625,000	595,238
	1,816,215	1,972,586
Operating income	1,815,809	1,532,915
Other income	275,790	262,657
Abnormal inventory write off	(200,000)	0
Government assistance	150,000	142,857
Earnings from continuing operations before taxes	2,041,599	1,938,430
Provision for income taxes (30%)	612,480	581,529
Net income	$1,429,119	$1,356,901
Retained earnings, beginning	$5,859,401	$4,502,500
Retained earnings, ending	$7,288,520	$5,859,401

Exhibit II ## Summary Notes

New Inventory System

During the year, a new system was installed by SIL. The controller and inventory manager were proponents of the new system as they both complained that the previous system was outdated and not sophisticated enough to provide information on the various items in inventory.

A new system was installed that provides management with more information at the individual item level regarding inventory turnover, discontinued products, and daily market prices. As a result, the controller and the inventory manager have new information by which to track inventory and to estimate inventory obsolescence. Accordingly, the inventory obsolescence policy was modified to reflect the more relevant and reliable information.

The inventory system was tested extensively as part of the interim audit, and the audit team is satisfied with the reasonableness and reliability of the information that comes from the new system. The amount of additional year-end inventory write off required under the new methods for 2020 is $500,000. Of this amount, management has estimated that $150,000 should have been written off in 2019 and $50,000 in 2018. Management has presented $300,000 of the write off as part of the cost of goods sold, and the remaining $200,000 as a separate line item.

Voice Stabilization Technology

Management is planning to sell SIL's voice stabilization technology. The technology has been successful; however, voice technology competencies vary from those related to video stabilization. Accordingly, management has decided to focus on SIL's core competencies, which are video-related technologies.

On October 1, 2019, the board of directors met and voted in favor of divesting the company of the voice stabilization technology. On October 15, management hired an investment banking firm in order to develop a divestiture plan and to identify a potential buyer. The divestiture plan was created and approved by the board on December 1, 2019. The investment banking firm is paid a fee of 10% of the sales price.

The investment banking firm did express some concerns about current market conditions and its impact on the sales price and the time required to close a deal. Merger and acquisition activity is down due to global economic activities; however, the investment bankers suggested that these assets could be sold for approximately $650,000 in current market conditions. The sales price could increase if there is a large number of purchasers and market conditions improve.

The tangible and intangible assets related to voice stabilization products are currently being carried at $765,000 (amortized cost). The voice stabilization operations generated sales of $750,000 in 2020 ($725,000 in 2019) and had total operating costs of $350,000 ($340,000 in 2019).

Change in Depreciation Policy

During 2020, management changed from straight-line to the double declining-balance method for depreciating certain equipment. The change was made because in today's business environment, machinery and technology changes rapidly, leading to more benefits being received when the equipment is still relatively new.

The following table presents the difference in depreciation under both methods over the years affected:

Year	Double Declining-Balance Depreciation	Straight-Line Depreciation	Difference
2018	$675,000	$350,000	$325,000
2019	475,000	350,000	$125,000
2020	275,000	350,000	$(75,000)

In addition, management changed the useful life of the patents being amortized from five years to eight years. The change was made because the technology is being adopted by more companies than expected and there are very few competitors doing research in this field.

The intangible assets were being amortized on a straight-line basis, have a historical cost of $1,250,000, and had an average useful life of five years beginning on January 1, 2017.

Tap 'n Pay

Tap 'n Pay Inc. (TNP) is a mid-sized company based in Halifax that has developed a new technology that allows for a faster and more secure debit or credit card tap payment. Tap payments can generally be done for transactions below $50 whereby a cardholder simply taps their card on the card reader to complete a transaction. TNP has also developed tap and pay technology for mobile devices. TNP generates revenue by licensing its technology to major financial institutions.

TNP had an initial public offering in 2019, but financial performance was not overwhelmingly strong, resulting in net income of $75,000. The company undertook a major expansion in 2020 in order to expand operations and further invest in research and development. Various financial instruments were issued at the beginning of fiscal 2020 in order to finance the expansion. Financial performance improved, with preliminary net income reaching $250,000 in 2020.

TNP's accounting department is beginning to prepare for the year-end audit. You decided to accept a position in TNP's accounting department. As you are a newly qualified Chartered Professional Accountant, the controller has asked you to help develop appropriate accounting treatments for various complex financial instruments. The controller provides some information on your first assignment:

> "We are very excited that you have decided to join our accounting department. We know that your strong technical accounting background will help us to properly account for the large number of newly issued financial instruments. The bank will certainly be looking at our financial statements in order to assess our debt to equity ratio. Our covenant requires us to maintain a ratio of no greater than 1.5:1.

> While the bank will be focusing on the debt to equity ratio, investors are expecting strong performance. Specifically, investors and analysts will be expecting that our EPS meets or exceeds the consensus estimate of $0.80 per share (diluted). I'm sure that our share price will experience a sharp decline if we miss expectations.

> At this point, I would like you to prepare a short memo that provides recommendations on the appropriate accounting treatment for all newly issued financial instruments. Note that the preliminary financial statements do not reflect journal entries for interest or dividends on any of these financial instruments. I would also like you to prepare a preliminary estimate of debt to equity ratio based on your recommendations, along with a calculation of the basic and diluted EPS. Assume that our marginal tax rate is 25%, but please disregard any issues with deferred taxes at this stage. We can deal with that later.

> Here are the preliminary estimates for debt and equity (Exhibit I) and here is some background information on the financial instruments (Exhibit II). Once your report is complete, we can sit down together to review your findings."

The controller hands you the files, and you return to your office to begin working on the report.

Required

Prepare the report for the controller.

| Exhibit I | Statement of Financial Position Summary |

TAP 'N PAY
Statement of Financial Position
For the Year Ended December 31, 2020

Liabilities

Current liabilities

Trade payables and other liabilities	$ 234,100
Other current liabilities	10,000
Total current liabilities	244,100
Employee stock options	75,000
Convertible bonds	1,000,000
Participating bonds—A Series	250,000
Participating bonds—B Series	250,000
Bank loan	275,000
Total liabilities	$2,094,100

Shareholders' Equity

Common share capital	$1,409,985
Restricted preferred shares	275,000
Convertible preferred shares—Class A	500,000
Convertible preferred shares—Class B	500,000
Retained earnings	357,800
Total shareholders' equity	3,042,785
Total liabilities and shareholders' equity	$5,136,885
Debt to Equity Ratio	**0.69:1**

Notes on Shares Issues

- Common share capital: 1,000,000 shares authorized; 156,665 outstanding
- Restricted preferred shares: unlimited shares authorized; 275,000 outstanding with a $1 par value
- Convertible preferred shares—Class A: 750,000 shares authorized; 100,000 outstanding
- Convertible preferred shares—Class B: 750,000 shares authorized; 50,000 outstanding

| Exhibit II | Notes on Financial Instrument Characteristics |

Convertible Bonds

- Bonds that can be converted into 50 common shares at a rate of $1,000 per bond per common shares. The bonds were issued with a yield to maturity of 5% when prevailing market rates on similar, nonconvertible bonds is 6%. The bonds carry a 5% coupon rate, pay interest annually, and mature in seven years.

Participating Bonds—A Series

- Bonds issued to a single holder (financial institution) at par with a six-year maturity. Interest is payable semi-annually at a rate of

5% of the previous year's net income for the entire bond issuance. If the company earns a net loss, interest is payable at a rate of 1% per annum.

- The bonds can be converted into the convertible preferred stock—Class A at a rate of 100 shares per $1,000 in par value of the bond.

- The bond maturity amount can be repaid in cash or in a variable number of common shares such that the amount of common shares issued on the date of maturity results in the bondholder holding shares with a fair value equal to the maturity value of the bond.

Exhibit II | Notes on Financial Instrument Characteristics (Continued)

Participating Bonds—B Series

- Bonds issued at par with a five-year maturity. Interest is payable semi-annually at a rate of 8% of the previous year's net income. No interest is payable if the company earns a net loss.
- The bond maturity amount can be repaid in cash or in a fixed number of common shares based on the ratio of 50 common shares per $1,000 in par value of the bond.

Restricted Preferred Shares

- Certain members of the management teams of acquired businesses have been granted restricted Class A junior preferred shares. These preferred shares are subject to mandatory repurchase by the company contingent on the respective employee's continued employment with the company during the requisite service period, which is normally three years from the issuance date.
- The preferred shares are recorded at their fair value, and amortized to compensation expense on a straight-line basis over the service period. The fair value is generally determined to be equal to the repurchase amount. The preferred shares are cancelled if the holder leaves the employ of the company prior to completing their service period.
- The preferred shares pay no dividends and are nonvoting.

Convertible Preferred Shares—Class A

- Preferred shares with a 3% cumulative dividend yield, convertible into common shares at a rate of 2 preferred shares for 1 common share.

- The preferred shares are redeemable with a 2% premium above par value and retractable with a discount of 2% below the par value.

Convertible Preferred Shares—Class B

- Preferred shares with a 4% cumulative dividend yield, convertible into common shares at a rate of 1 preferred share for 1 common share.
- The preferred shares are redeemable with a 2% premium above par value.

Common Stock

- Each share of common stock is entitled to one vote. The holders of common stock are also entitled to receive dividends whenever funds are legally available and when and if declared by the board of directors, subject to the prior rights of holders of all classes of stock outstanding.
- The common shares were trading at $16.65 per share at year end.

Employee Stock Options

- The company has issued 10,000 stock options in total to the CEO and CFO. The options are only available to the CEO and CFO, and have an exercise price of $10 per share. The stock options had a fair value of $75,000 at the time of issuance based on an option pricing model. The stock options are expected to provide benefits in terms of future management performance over a three-year service period. The following journal entry was posted to record the stock options:

Compensation Expense	75,000	
Employee Stock Option (debt)		75,000

Tefria Technologies Limited

Tefria Technologies Limited (TTL) is a small, start-up technology company in Ottawa that manufactures portable keyboards for mobile devices and tablets. TTL has been working to perfect a technology that is used in a laser-projection virtual keyboard.

TTL has been investing heavily in research and development, and is constantly having working capital issues. In order to ease the pressure, TTL has taken out a $500,000 working capital loan. The loan is required to be paid back within two years, and carries an interest rate of 1% per month on any outstanding balance. The loan includes a covenant that requires the current ratio to be maintained at least 1.5:1.

You are the controller of TTL, and you are preparing for the December 31, 2020, year-end audit. You know that the shareholders and bank will be paying close attention to the financial statements this year due to the covenant. Accordingly, the CFO would you like to prepare a memo that analyzes the following key accounting issues:

1. TTL is currently being sued for patent infringement by a rival company. TTL's lawyers believe that the patent infringement case is unfounded; however, litigation always includes an element of uncertainty. Accordingly, the lawyers have developed the following payment estimates: 35% chance of no payment, 45% chance of a $100,000 payment, and 20% chance of a $250,000 payment. The case will be settled by March 31, 2021.

2. TTL entered into a forward contract with Marson First Trust to purchase US$100,000 at a rate of C$1.20 per U.S. dollar. The contract is to be settled on June 30, 2021. As of year end, the exchange rate is C$1.10 per U.S. dollar.

3. TTL sold 50,000 laser-projection, virtual keyboards to Mega Mart. Mega Mart paid TTL in cash up front. The keyboards were sold for $30 each, and include a one-year warranty. The warranty is to be serviced by TTL, and not Mega Mart. Considering that the product is relying on relatively new technology, TTL estimates that approximately 5% of all keyboards will require some work. Management has estimated that the average cost per warranty claim will be $15. No claims have been made during the current fiscal year.

4. TTL holds a $500,000 loan with the Royal Legion Bank that is due on January 31, 2021. Management intends to refinance the loan into a five-year blended payment loan. As of year end, the company had received the financing contract, but it had not yet signed the document. The board of directors is expected to formally approve the refinancing at the upcoming meeting on January 10, 2021. The loan is classified as noncurrent.

The CFO reminds you that no journal entries have been posted for the contingency, forward contract, or warranty. The CFO would like you to discuss the proper accounting treatment for the above-noted issues, and to provide journal entries where appropriate. Draft IFRS-compliant financial statements, prior to any adjustments proposed for the above issues, reveal current assets of $2.5 million and current liabilities of $1.1 million.

Required

Prepare the report for the CFO.

Teleflix, Inc.

Teleflix, Inc. is one of the world's leading Internet television networks, with millions of subscribers across the globe. Teleflix's library of digital content offers subscribers millions of hours of TV shows and movies per month, including original series. Members can watch as much as they want, anytime, anywhere, on nearly any Internet-connected screen. Members can play, pause, and resume watching, all without commercials or commitments. The Montreal-based company is organized into three operating segments:

- Domestic Streaming: This segment focuses on revenues generated from Canadian subscribers. Subscribers pay $9.99 per month for unlimited content streaming on any two devices.

- International Streaming: This segment focuses on revenues generated from the United States, United Kingdom, and Australian subscribers. Subscribers purchase a monthly plan that ranges from $7.99 to $14.99 to receive unlimited content.

- Domestic DVD: This segment derives its revenue predominantly from DVD-by-mail subscriptions. The DVD mail service is offered because it is difficult, if not impossible, to obtain a license for new, blockbuster releases in a streaming format. The price per plan varies from $4.99 to $19.99 per month. The plans vary based on the number of DVDs that can be received per month and the overall quality of the video (DVD, Blu-ray, or Blu-ray 3D). Due to the logistics costs, this plan is available only in Canada.

Teleflix is preparing for its 2020 year-end audit. The company is under some financial pressure to meet or exceed analysts' forecast estimates. (Analysts expect that diluted EPS will be $1.75 per share.) Investors are focusing on reported earnings because streaming content is becoming more accessible and competition is heating up. In addition to earnings, analysts will have a close eye on the company's debt to equity ratio, which is currently above industry standards. Considering all that has taken place in the industry, the company's share price has experienced volatility rates of 35% over the past year and is currently trading at $180 per share.

You have recently been hired as an assistant to the controller. The accounting group has put together a draft statement of financial position and operations based on all routine and recurring transactions (Exhibit I). Your first assignment is to help the controller determine the appropriate reporting for the current year's new and nonroutine transactions.

You are provided with a snapshot of the company's relevant accounting policies (Exhibit II) and a file outlining key accounting issues regarding the nonroutine and new transactions (Exhibit III). The controller has requested that you prepare a report that discusses the nonroutine accounting issues and provides a preliminary recommendation. Specifically, the controller would like to understand the impacts of these transactions on the company EPS and debt to equity ratio calculations. The controller reminds you that the income tax expense and deferred tax amounts will be determined by the tax specialist group.

Required

Prepare the report for the controller.

| Exhibit 1 | Draft Financial Statements |

Teleflix, Inc.
Statements of Financial Position
(Unaudited)
(In Thousands)

	DRAFT	AUDITED
	December 31, 2020	**December 31, 2019**
Assets		
Current assets		
Cash and cash equivalents	$ 372,172	$ 178,586
Short-term investments	366,312	281,628
Current content library, net	1,049,782	841,687
Other current assets	93,471	76,623
Total current assets	$1,881,737	$1,378,524
Noncurrent content library, net	1,286,417	926,489
Property, plant, and equipment, net	82,193	81,010
Other noncurrent assets	79,436	55,005
Total assets	$3,329,783	$2,441,028
Liabilities and Shareholders' Equity		
Current liabilities		
Current content liabilities	$1,092,576	$? 840,878
Accounts payable	66,709	53,195
Accrued expenses	33,232	32,691
Deferred revenue	132,739	104,258
Total current liabilities	1,325,256	1,031,022
Noncurrent content liabilities	827,801	662,333
Long-term debt	307,598	123,039
Long-term debt due to related party	0	123,039
Other noncurrent liabilities	48,728	43,476
Total liabilities	$2,509,383	$1,982,909
Shareholders' equity		
Preferred shares	$ 37	$ 34
Common shares	478,278	185,553
Accumulated other comprehensive income (loss)	2,199	1,796
Retained earnings	339,886	270,736
Total shareholders' equity	820,400	458,119
Total liabilities and shareholders' equity	$3,329,783	$2,441,028

Exhibit 1	Draft Financial Statements (Continued)

Teleflix, Inc.
Statements of Operations
(Unaudited)
(In Thousands, Except Per Share Data)

	DRAFT	AUDITED
	December 31, 2020	December 31, 2019
Revenues	$2,691,210	$2,220,413
Cost of revenues	1,917,689	1,631,534
Marketing	289,106	270,199
Technology and development	233,017	202,404
General and administrative	110,920	85,522
Operating income (loss)	$ 140,478	$ 30,754
Other income (expense):		
Interest expense	(14,387)	(12,295)
Interest and other income (expense)	(5,388)	292
Loss on extinguishment of debt	(15,459)	0
Income (loss) before income taxes	105,244	18,751
Provision (benefit) for income taxes	36,094	8,199
Net income (loss)	$ 69,150	$ 10,552
Earnings per share:		
Basic	$1.93	$0.31
Diluted	$1.87	$0.30
Weighted-average common shares outstanding:		
Basic	35,803	34,156
Diluted	36,940	34,803

| Exhibit II | **Accounting Policies** |

Streaming Content

The company licenses rights to stream TV shows, movies, and original content to members for unlimited viewing. These licenses are for a fixed fee and specify license "windows" (time periods in which the content may be shown) that generally range from six months to five years. Payment terms may extend over the license window, or may require more payments, as is typically the case for original content.

The company capitalizes the fee per title and records a corresponding liability when the license period begins, the cost of the title is known, and the title is accepted and available for streaming. For example:

| Current Content Library | xxx |
| Content Liability or Cash | xxx |

The portion available for streaming within one year is recognized as "Current content library" and the remaining portion as "Noncurrent content library." If the cost per title cannot be reasonably estimated, the license fee is not capitalized and costs are expensed as payments are made. However, this does not occur often.

DVD Content Library

The company acquires DVD content for the purpose of renting such content to its members and earning membership rental revenues, and, as such, the company considers its direct purchase DVD library to be a productive asset. Accordingly, the company presents some of its DVD library in "Noncurrent content library, net." The company amortizes its direct purchase DVDs on a straight-line basis over their estimated useful lives, which range from one year to three years. DVDs in the library that have a useful life of one year or less are presented in "Current content library, net" as they will be sold for their salvage value to a discount DVD retailer.

Earnings per Share

Basic earnings per share is calculated using the weighted-average number of outstanding common shares during the period. Diluted earnings per share is calculated using the weighted-average number of outstanding common shares and, when dilutive, potential common shares outstanding during the period.

Potential common shares consist of incremental shares issuable upon the assumed exercise of stock options issued to the executives of companies that have been previously acquired. The calculation of earnings per share is as follows:

	2020	2019
Basic earnings per share:		
Net income	$69,150	$10,552
Shares used in calculation:		
Weighted-average common shares outstanding	35,803	34,156
Basic earnings per share	$1.93	$0.31
Diluted earnings per share:		
Numerator for diluted earnings per share	69,150	10,552
Shares used in calculation:		
Weighted-average common shares outstanding	35,803	34,156
Employee stock options	1,137	647
Weighted-average number of shares	36,940	34,803
Diluted earnings per share	$1.87	$0.30

Exhibit III	Accounting Issues

TeleBox

The Domestic DVD segment has seen significant declines in recent years. The number of DVD subscribers has declined by 56% and 24% over the last two years, respectively. The declining trend is likely due to the availability of many blockbusters through pay-per-view offered by cable providers and the availability of DVDs through different mediums.

Since the Domestic DVD segment has provided a strong contribution to the overall profitability of Teleflix, management decided to explore different options for revamping the service offering. Accordingly, on July 1, 2020, the company launched TeleBox, a digitally automated distribution system that allows subscribers to rent DVDs and Blu-rays at various locations across Canada. The TeleBox is similar to a candy-vending machine, but it allows subscribers to receive and return discs. Discs can be returned at any TeleBox location. During the year, the company launched the concept in several large Canadian cities.

Useful Life of Discs Inventory

Due to the increased wear and tear on the discs from the use of the vending machine system, the useful life of the assets is expected to be reduced. As of year end 2020, approximately $150 million worth of DVD inventory has been transferred to the TeleBoxes. Approximately $60 million of the discs are classified as current. Approximately $90 million of the discs transferred are noncurrent assets that had an average remaining useful life of four years at the beginning of the year and amortization of $22.5 million has been recorded in the financial statements. The useful life of the assets has been revised to three years.

Lease Agreement

Teleflix entered into a lease agreement with Grasshopper Ltd. in order to offset the large, upfront capital costs of the disc vending machines. Grasshopper Ltd. worked with Teleflix to design and develop customized vending machines that are fully integrated into Teleflix's IT systems.

Without the lease agreement, the machines would have required an upfront price tag of $10.5 million. However, the lease agreement allows Teleflix to make annual payments of $1,857,717.61 over a six-year period. The first payment is to be made on July 1, 2021. The vending machines have a 10-year useful life. At the end of the lease term, Teleflix can purchase the equipment for a cost equal to their fair market value. The interest rate implicit in the lease is 6% (which also reflects marginal borrowing rates).

No journal entries have been recorded in regards to the leased assets because no payment has been made.

Long-Term Debt

At the beginning of the year, the company refinanced its long-term debt and related-party debt (of $123,039,000 each) for a new debt issuance with a face value of $300,000,000, coupon rate of 5% (paid annually), and 10-year maturity. The bond yields a market rate of 4.6771% (2% risk-free rate plus a 2.6771% risk premium) and has been recorded at $307,598,000.

The bond offers holders the right to convert $150 in bond face value into a common share. Currently, the company's common shares were trading at $165. If not for the conversion feature, the bonds would have likely traded at par at the time of issuance. The first bond payment will be made on January 1, 2021. Interest has been accrued and recorded in the interest expense line item.

Commitments and Contingencies

In June 2020, ClickFlixes filed a complaint against Teleflix Inc. for patent infringement in the United States District Court. The complaint alleges, among other things, that the company's payment technology used by the TeleBox machines infringes on a patent owned by ClickFlixes. Specifically, ClickFlixes purports that the TeleBox infringes on "Integrated Customer-to-Business Video Rental Automation Payment System" (U.S. Patent No. 123456789) and is seeking monetary damages of $10 million, and the cost of legal fees (approximately $500,000).

The court's decision on the lawsuit is pending the outcome of the U.S. Patent and Trademark Office's re-examination of the patent. The company's lawyers are disputing the allegations of wrongdoing and intend to defend the company vigorously in this matter. Therefore, nothing has been recognized or disclosed in the financial statements.

The company is constantly involved in litigation related to patent infringement. Experience suggests that 55% of the cases are successfully defended, while 35% of the cases result in 50% of damages and costs being paid, and 10% of the cases result in 100% of the damages and costs being paid. The current team of lawyers considers this lawsuit to be in the similar nature of past claims.

Streaming Content Library

The value of the streaming content library is broken down as follows (000's):

Current content library, net	$1,049,782
Noncurrent content library, net	1,286,417
Total content library	$2,336,199
DVD content	$ 350,430
Streaming content	1,985,769
Total content library	$2,336,199

Under the most likely scenario, future cash flows have been estimated at year end for the streaming content as follows ($000's):

1	2	3	Total
1,687,904	397,154	297,865	2,382,923

Exhibit I | Accounting Issues (Continued)

However, if competition escalates and new Internet streaming mediums develop, future cash flows may be much lower ($000's):

1	2	3	Total
1,350,323	317,723	238,292	1,906,338

Management estimates that the most likely scenario will occur with an 80% probability and the pessimistic scenario will occur with a 20% probability.

Share-Based Compensation

At the beginning of the 2020 fiscal year, management of the company received a total of 50,000 call options as part of their compensation package. The options carry a strike price of $175 per share, and can be exercised any time over the next three years. The stock options were issued out of the money (i.e., the shares were trading at $160 per share at the time of issuance) so that there would be no intrinsic value, and therefore no compensation expense. None of the options were exercised at year end. The stock options are expected to have a service period of three years.

Westside Grocery Store

Westside Grocery Store (WGS) is an independent, full-service grocery store in Regina, Saskatchewan. WGS is a family-owned store that was founded in 1968 by Jack and Judy Hill. Originally, Jack and Judy each owned 50% of the common shares of WGS. However, WGS underwent a corporate reorganization in 2009 when Jack and Judy retired. The reorganization resulted in Jack and Judy's common shares being converted into preferred shares, with a new class of common shares being issued to their children, Peter and Penny. Jack and Judy are no longer involved in the day-to-day operations of WGS; however, they have kept their positions on the board of directors. More details on the corporate reorganization can be found in Exhibit I.

Peter and Penny have had some disagreements regarding the management of WGS since they started running the operations in 2016. Much competitive pressure has been felt in recent years due to general economic conditions combined with the constant competitive pressures from the big box retailers. WGS has experienced a steady decline in its gross margin as a result. (See Exhibit II for historical financial statements.) Accordingly, Peter has agreed to purchase Penny's common shares to become the sole owner of WGS.

As a child, Penny never really enjoyed the grocery store business and always wanted to pursue a career in real estate. Upon the sale of her common shares, Penny will make that dream a reality and focus on her real estate career. She will use the proceeds from the common stock sale to help her finance the initial costs of establishing herself as an agent. On the other hand, Peter has always been involved in the grocery store's operations. Peter completed a commerce degree in university, with a major in marketing and a minor in accounting. He is excited to apply his business knowledge in a management role with the hopes of turning around WGS's prospects. He has some ideas regarding new marketing techniques, focusing on niche markets, developing connections with local famers, and partnering with a larger store to distribute lower cost products. Peter firmly believes that these initiatives should help turn WGS around.

Penny and Peter have agreed that the company will be valued based on the net book value of equity as the declining earnings trend may be indicative of no goodwill. (That is, earnings do not support a price premium over and above the net asset value.) Peter has informed Penny that the preliminary financial statements for the 2020 year end suggest a value of $99.58 per common share (common stock, contributed surplus, and retained earnings balances).

Hussain and Fong, LLP is WGS's external accounting firm and you have been involved with WGS's annual financial statement review. As a senior accountant with Hussain and Fong, you are planning this year's engagement, and have met with Penny and Peter. You are aware that the current year's financial statements will be used as part of the common share sale, and spent some extra time with Peter to discuss the accounting issues. Your notes are summarized in Exhibit III.

Since Peter is exclusively involved in the accounting function of WGS, Penny has requested that you prepare a memo that outlines all of the key accounting issues in the current year. She is hoping that you will discuss alternative treatments and provide a recommendation.

Required

Prepare the report requested by Penny.

Exhibit I | Corporate Reorganization

Corporate reorganization

The corporate reorganization was conducted in order to allow Jack and Judy to transfer control and all future growth of the company to Peter and Penny. Essentially, Jack and Judy's common shares ($100 book value) were converted into newly issued preferred shares. The preferred shares were valued at $650,000, which represents the fair value of WGS at the time of the reorganization. A total of $550,000 of the value was in the form of retained earnings, while the remaining $100,000 was goodwill, which was not recorded in the financial statements. Two thousand new common shares were issued equally to Peter and Penny Hill at a value of $1 per share.

Corporate structure

After the reorganization, the corporate structure is summarized as follows:

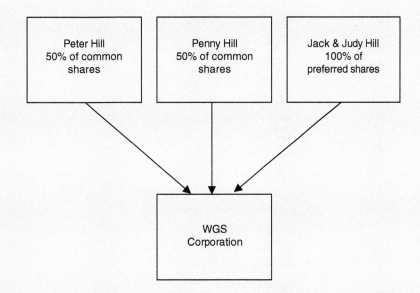

Share characteristics

After the corporate reorganization, the share characteristics are summarized as follows:

- Common shares:
  - Voting: One vote per share
  - Dividend: As declared by the board of directors
  - Redeemable: No
  - Retractable: No

- Preferred shares:
  - Voting: Nonvoting
  - Dividend: 4% dividend yield, cumulative
  - Redeemable: At a value of $650,000
  - Retractable: At a value of $650,000

Exhibit II	Summary of Historical Financial Statements

Westside Grocery Store
Statement of Financial Position (Draft)
For the Year Ended December 31, 2020

Assets

Current assets

Cash and cash equivalents	$ 226,000
Short-term investments	29,000
Accounts receivable	61,800
Credit card receivables	253,800
Inventories	208,400
Prepaid expenses and other assets	7,500
Total current assets	786,500
Fixed assets	910,500
Intangible assets	38,400
Total assets	$1,735,400

Liabilities

Current liabilities

Trade payables and other liabilities	$ 379,700
Provision (note 1)	6,250
Other current liabilities (note 2)	12,500
Total current liabilities	398,450
Contingent liability (note 3)	100,000
Long-term debt (note 4)	445,000
Other noncurrent liabilities (note 5)	42,700
Total liabilities	$ 986,150

Shareholders' Equity

Common share capital	$ 2,000
Preferred share capital	550,100
Retained earnings	185,150
Contributed surplus	12,000
Total shareholders' equity	$ 749,250
Total liabilities and shareholders' equity	$1,735,400

| Exhibit II | Summary of Historical Financial Statements (Continued) |

Westside Grocery Store
Statement of Income (Five-Year Historical Summary)
For the Year Ended December 31

	DRAFT 2020	REVIEWED 2019	REVIEWED 2018	REVIEWED 2017	REVIEWED 2016
Revenues	$2,865,781	$2,954,413	$3,045,787	$3,139,987	$3,237,100
Cost of merchandise inventory sold	2,277,881	2,324,368	2,371,804	2,420,208	2,469,600
Selling, general, and administrative expenses	517,130	544,347	572,997	603,155	634,900
Operating income	70,770	85,698	100,986	116,624	132,600
Net interest expense	44,956	45,410	45,869	46,332	46,800
Refinancing costs (Note 4)	45,000	0	0	0	0
Income before income taxes	(19,186)	40,288	55,117	70,292	85,800
Income taxes (Note 6)	(5,098)	10,706	14,646	18,679	22,800
Net income	$ (14,088)	$ 29,582	$ 40,471	$ 51,613	$ 63,000

Notes (Summary) to Financial Statements

- **Note 1:** The provision represents the estimate for a shopping spree campaign that was initiated in 2020 and will be completed in 2021.

- **Note 2:** Other current liabilities are related to the expected costs related to the next fiscal year's scanning code of practice violations.

- **Note 3:** Contingent liability related to a lawsuit filed by a book publisher claiming that WGS's handling of the sale of a book [see Exhibit III] led to monetary damages. The company's lawyers are vehemently fighting the lawsuit.

- **Note 4:** Represents a principal payment of $445,000 due in four years to GT Capital Group. No principal payments are due until the final payment of $445,000 is made. No interest payments are required (note that the prevailing market rate for similar debt is approximately 2.70%). A total of $45,000 was recorded as refinancing cost in 2020.

- **Note 5:** Other noncurrent liabilities are related to a loyalty rewards program called WGS Points.

- **Note 6:** Income taxes are recorded with the taxes payable method.

Exhibit III	Notes from Meeting with Peter

- Like many other stores, WGS abides by the Scanning Code of Practice, which is overseen by the Competition Bureau of the Canadian government, and is stated as follows: "If the scanned price of a nonprice item is higher than the shelf price or any other displayed price, the customer is entitled to receive the first item free, up to a $10 maximum."

- During the most recent year, WGS had various issues with scanning accuracy, which resulted in approximately $25,000 of free goods being given away. These items were recorded as part of the cost of goods sold. Peter has an IT consultant providing a comprehensive evaluation of the company's IT systems with the goal of rectifying the situation. It is expected to take approximately six months for the IT system to be corrected. Accordingly, Peter has recorded a provision for $12,500 to cover the expected costs of scanning inaccuracies.

- During the Christmas season, Peter created a new promotional campaign called "Flyer Shopping Spree." Customers were eligible to enter into a draw each time they made a purchase during the period of December 10 to 24. The winner of the draw will be allowed to select any 10 items that appear in any of the weekly flyers during the period of January 1, 2021, to March 31, 2021. The draw was held on Boxing Day in the store, and five lucky winners were selected. The minimum and maximum values of items in the flyer are $2.50 to $125, respectively.

- Many of WGS's customers complained to Peter that all other grocery stores offered some sort of loyalty points program. Many big box stores have ramped up the use of loyalty points programs as competition in the retail sector has escalated. Accordingly, Peter launched the WGS Points program. With the help of a local IT firm, WGS Points relies on the use of unique bar codes that are scanned at the point of sale. Customers receive 1 point for every $10 spent in the store. Customers who receive 100 points are automatically mailed a $20 gift card to

use for any merchandise in the store. During the year, WGS Points were awarded on 74.5% of all sales. Industry standards suggest that only 75% of points issued are ever redeemed.

- During the year, WGS began to sell popular novels. WGS received the rights to distribute the highly popular kid's novel, *Harry Poppler*. The novel was scheduled to be released across the globe on April 15, 2020. WGS received its shipment of the books on April 7. The books were to be kept off the floor, and not to be sold to the public, until April 15. On April 9, a WGS employee took a copy of the book and sold it to a popular website. The site posted various pages and discussion around the plot. The publisher of *Harry Poppler* recovered the stolen book and determined that it was part of WGS's shipment. The publisher proceeded to file a lawsuit against WGS for monetary damages. WGS's legal counsel believes that the losses can range from $10,000 to $100,000 and that it is impossible to determine an exact amount at this stage. Regardless of the stolen book, *Harry Poppler* broke various sales records across Canada.

- In the few weeks before the year end, WGS refinanced its long-term debt. Just prior to the refinancing, WGS had a $400,000 balloon payment due on its debt facility with a local bank. Unable to make the payment, WGS refinanced the debt through GT Capital Group (GTCG). GTCG made the $400,000 payment on behalf of WGS in exchange for a promise to repay $445,000 in four years. Consistent with previous creditors, GTCG requires financial statements to be prepared in accordance with ASPE.

Peter recorded the following journal entry to reflect the debt refinancing:

Bank Debt	400,000	
Financing Expense	45,000	
GTCG Debt		445,000

Advanced Financial Accounting

All Kids Play

All Kids Play (AKP) is a not-for-profit entity with the mandate of helping make sports accessible to children of all income levels. AKP was founded by Mario Crosby, a retired professional hockey player, to service communities in Nova Scotia. AKP began operations by gathering donations of gently used hockey equipment and recycling the equipment to children of families with financial need. Given the first year's success, AKP expanded to include football equipment recycling and hockey training camps.

Today, AKP has a dedicated space in a community centre, and is open two days a week. The organization has one part-time staff member who takes care of the daily administration. The remaining services are provided by a strong volunteer contingent who are directly involved in program delivery, which is coordinated by Mario.

In the current year, AKP formalized its board of directors, which is chaired by Sidney Lemieux. Sidney also has a history in professional hockey, but his career was cut short due to injuries. After professional sports, Sidney pursued higher education and is now a lawyer in the community. Under the leadership of Sidney and Mario, AKP has just adopted a strategic plan, and has a clear direction to expand services and create more public awareness of the organization. Mario is excited about the opportunity to promote AKP's vision and mission.

To supplement its current contribution level, AKP plans to research possible government grants and actively fundraise. A committee composed of three board members has been set up to oversee fundraising. The committee has asked that financial and non-financial information on each program be available for potential donors. AKP will soon be accountable to more parties considering the proposed expansion of services, a number of new donors, and greater public exposure.

It is February 2021. Mario has approached your firm to provide AKP with some financial and organizational advice. Mario realizes that some of the current year figures are small, and may not be material, but he would like to develop proper policies for all transactions in order to have a strong financial reporting environment to deal with the significant future growth that is expected. In addition to the strong reporting environment, Mario would like to develop a strong control environment and is contemplating the formation of an audit committee to oversee the reporting process. Mario is unsure of the roles and benefits of an audit committee.

Wayne Limongelli, a senior manager at your firm, has recommended that AKP prepare financial statements in accordance with GAAP. The board has never felt the need to prepare formal financial statements. Monthly trial balance reports were used to monitor operations (Exhibit I). Currently, the financial reporting process does not allow the board or donors to assess whether the funds contributed were used for the intended purpose and there is no clear division between the programs currently being offered: general activities, equipment recycling, training services, and endowments.

You are a senior accountant on the AKP engagement, and will be reporting to Wayne. You have reviewed the recent board minutes and other key information for the operations of the year (Exhibit II). Wayne indicated that, for its December 31, 2020, annual financial statements, the organization will follow not-for-profit organization standards (*CPA Canada Handbook*, Part III). Wayne pointed out that, when accounting policy options are available, it will be necessary to explain the options to the board and make recommendations for AKP. In addition, Wayne would like you to make recommendations to strengthen the control environment and provide some insights regarding the formation of an audit committee.

Required

(a) Prepare the statement of operations and statement of financial position for the year ended December 31, 2020. Include explanations to the board where necessary to explain the choice of accounting policy options available.

(b) Write a memo to Wayne making recommendations to the AKP board on ways to strengthen the control environment and some insights regarding the formation of an audit committee.

Exhibit I	Trial Balance Information for the Year Ended December 31, 2020

Account	Balance	Dr./Cr.	Notes
Cash	10,750	Dr.	
Marketable securities	35,000	Dr.	Investment of the endowment fund
Receivables	2,750	Dr.	User fees for the training program currently outstanding
Hockey equipment	1,750	Dr.	Equipment that is used to run the training program—not to be given away as recycled equipment
Payables for office rent	650	Cr.	
Payables for equipment	700	Cr.	Money owed for equipment purchased from retailer
Deferred revenue	10,000	Cr.	
Pledges collected	7,000	Cr.	$5,000 of the pledges are for the equipment program, the remaining for the training services
Government grant	15,000	Cr.	Government funding for general administration of the programs
Endowment revenue	35,000	Cr.	Endowment from wealthy athlete
Training program fees	7,500	Cr.	Fees collected for the training program
Facilities rentals	3,000	Dr.	Rental of facilities to run training programs
Training program wages	2,000	Dr.	
Office space rental	4,000	Dr.	For general administration of the program
General office expense	1,100	Dr.	For general administration of the program
Equipment warehouse rental	2,000	Dr.	Rental of warehouse space to store equipment that is recycled
Purchased football equipment	3,500	Dr.	
Office administration wages	9,750	Dr.	Administration, cannot be linked to a specific program
Investment income	700	Cr.	Income on the endowment fund investments
Silent auction profit	750	Cr.	
Supplies for equipment fixing	900	Dr.	Fixing equipment that was given away to children in need
Advertising	800	Dr.	For the organization as a whole

Note: This is AKP's second year of operations. The first year of operations resulted in a break-even operation (no surplus or deficit).

| Exhibit II | Description of AKP's Operations |

Administration

AKP's daily administrative tasks are overseen by Michelle Layma-done. Michelle works for AKP on a part-time basis and earned $9,750 in 2020. The remaining services are provided by volunteers, such as Mario and Sidney.

The day-to-day operations are run out of a small office space in a community centre. The community centre charges AKP a fee of $4,000 per year for rent, of which $650 has not been paid as of year end. During the year, AKP incurred $800 in advertising for both programs and to attract general donations. Michelle incurred $1,100 in costs related to office supplies.

Operating Activities

The following is a brief summary of the two main functions of AKP:

- *Equipment Recycling:*   The equipment recycling involves the collection of gently used hockey and football equipment that is provided to children in need. The equipment recycling operations requires the rental of storage space to warehouse the equipment. The storage costs $2,000 per year.

  Most of the equipment is donated to AKP; however, sometimes equipment is purchased. In addition, AKP receives cash donations that are then used to purchase new equipment.

  During the current year, very little football equipment was donated. Accordingly, AKP purchased $3,500 of equipment. The hockey equipment was all donated, and had a market value of $5,000 if purchased by AKP. Many times, the donated equipment needs to be fixed up or adjusted. During the current year, AKP spent $900 to refurbish donated equipment. All of the equipment received and purchased in the current year was given away to needy children.

- *Hockey Training Program:*   The hockey training program involves the delivery of hockey camps during the summer. Participants are charged a fee to participate, but the fee is below what would be charged by a for-profit organization. During 2020, user fees of $7,500 were charged. A total of $2,500 is still outstanding. The receivable collection time can be long because many of the children are from financially challenged families.

  The program requires the rental of ice time at a city-run hockey rink. The rental fees were $3,000 in the current year. In addition, AKP purchased $1,750 worth of equipment that it uses to run the training programs. For example, the equipment includes pylons, pads, shooter tutors, and so on. These items normally last for three or four years. The equipment has been capitalized.

  The program relies on volunteers and paid employees. The paid employees are mostly youth from low-income families who provide administrative support to the trainers. The wages during the year were $2,000. Mario oversees the volunteers who run the training programs. The volunteers are mostly former professional hockey players who want to give back to the community. A total of 250 volunteer hours were provided in 2020. Most of these volunteers could have worked for a for-profit hockey training camp and earned $50 per hour.

Government Grant

During the year, AKP received a government grant of $25,000. The entire $25,000 cash was received during the year, although $15,000 was allocated for 2020 and $10,000 for 2021. AKP recorded the transaction as follows:

Cash	$25,000
Grant revenue	$15,000
Deferred revenue	$10,000

The $15,000 allocated for 2020 was used for operating activities while the $10,000 for the next year is in the bank account.

Endowment Contribution

During the year, AKP received an endowment from Arthur Apps, an active professional hockey player. Arthur donated $35,000 to AKP with the condition that the principal investment cannot be spent. There are no restrictions on the investment income earned by the endowment. During the year, the endowment earned $700, which Mario decided to use for the equipment recycling operations. An interfund transfer from the endowment fund to the equipment fund has been approved by the board.

Forgivable Loan

A wealthy sports enthusiast, who just retired at 65 years of age, has offered to lend AKP $50,000. The terms of the loan are such that the $50,000 must be invested in a fixed-income investment, but the interest can be used for any purpose the organization sees fit. If the donor lives beyond 75 years of age, AKP would have to repay the full $50,000; otherwise, the donation can be kept, and used for any purpose the organization sees fit.

Mario has just accepted the terms and will receive the cash on January 1, 2021. Mario is unsure of how this should be accounted for in next year's financial statements.

Cash Contribution

Eli Brady, a successful professional Canadian football quarterback, is willing to provide a cash contribution of $30,000. The contribution comes with the restriction that it must be used for football equipment. This is a very generous donation and is almost 10 times what AKP would ordinarily spend on football equipment annually. This contribution is expected to be received in 2021. Eli has asked to be kept informed on how this money is spent each year. Mario would like some early guidance on how this can be accounted for in next year's financial statements.

Silent Auction

During the year, Sidney organized a silent auction. Sidney purchased all of the prizes with funds from AKP and then ran the auction. The total prizes cost $2,000 and cash was collected totaling $2,750. The net surplus of $750 was used to fund general operations.

Cranberry Hill

Cranberry Hill (CH) was founded in Quebec in 1983 by Nancy Raine, a former Olympic medalist. Over the years, CH has had significant growth and a loyal following of customers. In the early 2000s, CH went through a major expansion, with Nancy adding warehouse and retail space.

In 2014, CH converted its financial statements to conform with IFRS. Although CH is a private company, Nancy felt that using IFRS would help her to obtain global financing at more competitive rates. She was also interested in expanding her business to Western Canada and felt this would help in doing so.

On January 1, 2019, CH acquired 60% of the common shares of St Anthony's Bikes (SAB), located near St Anthony, Nfld, for $580,000 cash. At the time of acquisition, SAB had retained earnings of $245,000 and common shares of $120,000. SAB was also a private company following IFRS. All of SAB's fair values approximated their carrying values except for the following: Equipment with a net book value of $320,000 (with accumulated depreciation of $80,000) had a fair value of $400,000 and eight years of depreciation remaining; inventory was undervalued by $15,000; and there was an unrecorded patent for a bike mechanism with a value of $40,000. CH expected that the life of the patent was 10 years.

It is now December 31, 2020, and CH is getting ready to prepare its consolidated financial statements for the year. The separate entity statements are shown in Exhibit I. Additional information required to prepare the consolidated statements is shown in Exhibit II.

One of CH's shareholders is Nancy's older brother, Bart. Bart has often asked Nancy why CH prepares consolidated financial statements. Nancy told him she didn't have to, but did because she was following IFRS. Her brother still doesn't understand why any company needed to do so. "Why bother? It seems like a lot of work and unneeded expense. Just give the shareholders all the individual financial statements and let them add things up and figure it out," Bart said. Nancy would like you to prepare a memo that helps her to explain this to her brother.

Required

(a) Prepare the consolidated financial statements for December 31, 2020, and include any information you believe you need to support the numbers used for the financial statements.

(b) Prepare a memo to Nancy so that she can explain to her brother why CH prepares consolidated financial statements. Use examples from real Canadian companies to explain.

| Exhibit 1 | Financial Statements |

Statements of Financial Position
As at December 31, 2020

	CH	SAB
Cash	$ 140,000	$ 35,000
Receivables	80,000	15,000
Note receivable	35,000	0
Inventory	650,000	332,000
Investment in SAB	580,000	0
Property, plant, and equipment	750,000	500,000
Accumulated depreciation	(450,000)	(180,000)
Land	120,000	40,000
	$ 1,905,000	$742,000
Current liabilities	$ 140,000	$200,000
Note payable	0	35,000
Long-term debt	270,000	40,000
Common shares	800,000	120,000
Retained earnings	695,000	347,000
	$1,905,000	$742,000

Statements of Income
For the Year Ended December 31, 2020

	CH	SAB
Revenues	$1,000,000	$650,000
Other revenues	300,000	100,000
Cost of goods sold	845,000	525,000
Gain on sale of land	0	30,000
Administrative expenses	50,000	15,000
Miscellaneous expenses	150,000	35,000
Depreciation expense	90,000	50,000
Income tax expense	66,000	38,000
	$ 99,000	$117,000

Exhibit II   Additional Information

- During 2020, CH sold $80,000 of inventory to SAB, of which half remained unsold at year end. CH has a gross profit rate of 35%. In 2019, CH sold $45,000 of inventory to SAB, of which $20,000 remained at the end of 2019.

- The note receivable is for inventory purchases between SAB and CH.

- During 2020, SAB sold $65,000 of inventory to CH, of which 80% was sold by year end. SAB has a gross profit rate of 30%. SAB didn't sell any inventory to CH during 2019.

- In 2019, CH sold equipment to SAB for $100,000. The equipment is being depreciated over 10 years by SAB. The equipment had a net book value for CH of $80,000 and accumulated depreciation when sold of $40,000.

- In 2020, SAB sold land to CH for $50,000. The land had an original cost of $20,000 and had appreciated in value due to the resurgence of the neighbourhood in Victoria during 2019.

- SAB declared and paid a dividend of $25,000 in 2020. There was no dividend paid in 2019.

- Assume an income tax rate of 40% for both companies.

- Based on information known to SAB and CH, they believe there is an impairment in the patent at the end of 2020 and that it is now only worth $15,000.

- CH consolidates following IFRS and wants to maximize any goodwill on its financial statements.

Delta Society of History

Delta Society of History (DSH) is a non-profit organization that operates a community museum in Red Deer, Alberta. DSH was created in 1918 with the mandate of preserving and interpreting the history of Red Deer and the surrounding area. The museum has a large collection of art, artifacts, and monuments from the area surrounding Red Deer. In addition, DSH generally has two to three major exhibits a year that showcase collections from around Canada, and provides a free lecture series to the community.

DSH receives most of its funding primarily from government grants and contributions from wealthy individuals. In addition, funding is received from membership fees, investment income from endowments, and admission fees. The museum also holds an annual muscle car raffle to generate additional funds.

As a recently qualified professional accountant, you decide that it is time to give back to the community and volunteer your specialized services. You have always maintained an interest in art and history, and feel that being a member of the DSH board of directors would be an interesting experience for a worthwhile cause.

At your first board meeting, the chair of the board welcomes you and expresses her happiness about your decision to join. The chair explains to you that the financial statements of DSH have never been audited in the past, and have always been prepared solely for internal purposes. Special reports on financial information have been prepared and audited annually for restricted contributions.

However, the board is feeling increasing pressure to prepare general purpose financial statements. Accordingly, the chair has asked you to prepare a report that discusses the alternatives available for recognizing the funding received. Exhibit I presents some additional information on the sources of funding. Given the poor economic conditions, the board would like to keep the cost of preparing the financial statements as low as possible.

Aside from the revenue recognition issues, the chair has asked you to assist with the selection of accounting policies for the various other aspects of the museum's operations. Additional details are provided in Exhibit II.

You have agreed to prepare a report for the next board meeting that outlines the specific accounting policies recommended. The chair has made it clear that the financial statements should comply with Part III of the *CPA Canada Handbook*.

Required

Prepare the report for the board of directors.

Exhibit I	Sources of Funding

Revenue for 2020 included the following:

Memberships	$200,000 (note 1)
Admission fees	$75,000 (note 2)
Government grants	$1,250,000
Contributions	$285,000 (note 3)
Endowment fund revenue	$35,000 (note 4)

Note 1—Membership fees are recognized as revenue when money is collected.
Note 2—Admission fees are recognized as money is collected.
Note 3—Contributions are recognized when a pledge is made by the donor. Internal reports segregate the number of restricted and unrestricted contributions. Restricted funds include amounts contributed for a specific purpose and amounts segregated by the board for specific projects or purposes.
Note 4—Endowment fund revenue is recorded as the investment income accrues.

Exhibit II	Additional Information

1. All capital assets are recorded at $1 to have a nominal amount provided on the financial statements. No depreciation is taken on the assets. A recent review of the capital assets indicated the following items. The amounts were estimated by one member of the board of directors:

Automobiles	$70,000
Artwork	Unable to estimate
Building	$375,000
Office equipment	$55,000

2. During 2020, the flooring was replaced. The cost of new flooring was $35,000. This amount was expensed. In addition, a new HVAC unit was installed to protect the artwork from damage due to temperature. The cost was $65,000. To finance the purchase of the new HVAC system, a piece of artwork was sold.

3. Volunteer services are not recorded.

Fun Life Inc.

Contributed by
Nathalie Johnstone and Kristie Dewald
Edwards School of Business, University of Saskatchewan & Alberta School of Business, University of Alberta

Fun Life Inc. (FLI) is a family-owned business, based out of Saskatoon, that sells and repairs recreational vehicles. FLI was founded in 1989 by the sole shareholders, Grant and Kyra Smiley. Both believe their love of outdoor activities and their dedication to the business have been the main reasons for FLI's growth and success. Grant and Kyra are still actively involved in their business, along with their two children, Ayla and Austin. Ayla has joined her mother in the sales office while Austin has worked with his father on the repairs and development side of the business. Recently, Austin developed a new niche market for the business, which involves building customized motorboats. To everyone's surprise, the niche market grew significantly in the past several years, but it has created a few concerns.

It is now January 15, 2021, and you, Alex Sharp, CPA, have joined the company as FLI's controller.

GRANT: Welcome to our business Alex. You have joined us at an exciting time and we could really use your expertise in dealing with some concerns and immediate changes we plan to make.

AUSTIN: Dad and I are pretty excited with the new direction the business has taken. We have increased demand for our customized boats, especially in the United States. Our main concern is with the foreign exchange rate fluctuations. We made two sales to U.S. clients, pricing the contract using our current methods. I feel that we priced each boat accurately but we were surprised when what we received in Canadian dollars was significantly lower when we translated the receipts. In order to sell in the United States, we need to prepare our quotes in U.S. dollars. We had not considered the fluctuation in the exchange rate and so we lost some value when we converted our U.S. dollar payment to Canadian.

KYRA: Austin is correct and this is one of the many reasons we have hired you as controller. We have several new orders from U.S. clients and we expect this market to increase considerably over the next few years. Our goal is to have consistent sales in the United States by 2021. But for now we expect to continue to have sporadic sales over the next few summers while we build our reputation in the United States. I'm concerned with the loss relating to the foreign exchange rate. I hope you can give us some advice on how we can manage the risk.

ALEX: Well, I have some experience with foreign currency transactions and can come up with some options for managing the risk with foreign exchange fluctuations.

GRANT: Excellent. It would be great to know that if the foreign market grows, we can manage the exchange rate risk. We have one more thing that needs your immediate attention. In order to grow our business, we had to borrow funds from the bank. As a requirement of the loan, we now have to prepare consolidated financial statements for our two companies. This is new to us and we are hoping you can help us prepare the consolidated statements the bank is requesting.

KYRA: I have put together some information you may need to prepare the consolidated statements. Exhibit I includes the financial statements for FLI and our subsidiary, MAI. Exhibit II has additional information that Grant put together for you. If you need more information, let me know.

ALEX: No problem dealing with the consolidation process and developing consolidated financial statements. I'll review the information you provide. I'll let you know if I need any additional information in order to prepare the consolidated statements for the bank.

You end the meeting and return to your new office to review the material provided.

Required

Assume the company is following IFRS.

(a) Prepare a memo for Grant and Austin outlining the options available for reducing the risk on the foreign sales. This memo should be no longer than two pages.

(b) Prepare the following consolidated information: a statement of comprehensive income and a statement of financial position. Comparative statements are not required. Provide supporting calculations to prove the balances for the following:

   1. consolidated net income attributable to the parent and noncontrolling interest,

   2. opening consolidated retained earnings,

   3. ending non-controlling interest on the statement of financial position.

(c) Prepare all the necessary journal entries.

Exhibit I — Financial Statements

Statement of Financial Position
For the Year Ended December 31, 2020

	FLI	MAI
Property, plant, and equipment	$2,107,747	$ 907,000
Land	850,000	204,000
Note receivable	150,000	0
Investment in MAI	1,225,200	0
Inventory	596,542	206,000
Accounts receivable	265,000	131,200
Cash	162,551	53,632
Total assets	$5,357,040	$1,501,832
Common shares	$1,650,000	$ 430,000
Retained earnings	1,725,408	166,832
Long-term debt	1,490,000	772,000
Deferred income tax	51,000	5,000
Dividends payable	25,000	28,000
Wages payable	25,700	12,000
Accounts payable	389,932	88,000
Total liabilities	$5,357,040	$1,501,832

Exhibit I	Financial Statements (Continued)

Statement of Income
For the Year Ending December 31, 2020

	FLI	MAI
Sales	$3,298,000	$1,212,000
Interest and other revenue	535,000	125,000
	$3,833,000	$1,337,000
Cost of sales	1,813,900	642,360
Advertising	18,000	11,000
Depreciation	190,700	62,000
Bad debts	12,000	7,500
Foreign exchange loss	15,250	0
Insurance	34,000	24,000
Interest charges	86,000	31,000
Office	75,000	41,900
Professional fees	26,000	12,000
Management fee	0	45,000
Property taxes	7,500	3,200
Repairs and maintenance	18,765	22,100
Salaries and wages	725,000	180,000
Telephone	9,700	8,700
Utilities	28,900	27,225
Total expenses	$3,060,715	$1,117,985
Net income before taxes	$ 772,285	$ 219,015
Income tax (current and deferred)	173,258	48,183
Net income after tax	$ 599,027	$ 170,832

Statement of Shareholders' Equity
For the Year Ending December 31, 2020

	FLI	MAI
Retained earnings, Jan. 1	$1,212,381	$ 81,000
Net income	599,027	170,832
Dividends	(86,000)	(85,000)
Retained earnings, Dec. 31	$1,725,408	$166,832

| *Exhibit II* | Additional Information Gathered by GRANT |

1. FLI paid cash for its purchase of 85,000 common shares of MAI common shares on January 1, 2015. At the time MAI had 100,000 common shares issued and outstanding and the shares were trading for $12.75. At the time of purchase, MAI's common shares were $430,000 and retained earnings were $52,000. The fair value of all the assets and liabilities were equal to book value, except the following:

   - Building had a fair value of $180,000 and a corresponding net book value of $230,000. The fair value difference was not considered to be an indication of a permanent decline in the value of the building. The estimated life was eight years on the date of acquisition.
   - A patent had a fair value of $210,000 with no corresponding net book value. The estimated life of the patent was 15 years on the date of acquisition.
   - Land has a fair value of $500,000 and a corresponding net book value of $210,000. MAI sold one third of this land in 2020 for a gain of $60,000. The gain is recorded in other revenue.

2. In the current year, FLI charged MAI a management fee of $45,000 for services rendered. Of this amount charged to MAI, $15,000 in payment is still outstanding at year end. In 2019, FLI charged MAI a management fee of $22,000.

3. The 2020 ending inventory of FLI contains a profit of $52,000 on merchandise purchased from MAI. FLI purchased a total of $375,000 from MAI in 2020. The 2020 opening inventory of FLI contained a profit of $32,000 on merchandise purchased from MAI. In 2019, FLI purchased a total of $210,000 from MAI. FLI still owes $23,000 to MAI for the purchases in 2020.

4. On July 1, 2020, MAI sold a piece of equipment to FLI for $274,800. The net book value at the time of the sale was $250,000. The equipment had a remaining useful life of eight years at the time of sale.

5. In 2016, FLI sold a piece of land to MAI for a profit of $85,000. MAI sold this land on June 4, 2020.

6. The tax rate for FLI and MAI is 22% for all taxation years. For internal purposes (in its single-entity financial statements), FLI accounts for all of its investments using the cost method.

7. Goodwill is tested for impairment each year. In 2017, goodwill relating to MAI was determined to be impaired by a total of $10,800.

PAN Medical Products Ltd.

Contributed by
Darrell Herauf
Sprott School of Business, Carleton University

PAN Medical Products Ltd., a public company listed on a national stock exchange, designs and manufactures medical products for sale to wholesalers. On January 1, 2020, PAN acquired 80% of the shares of SON Inc., a start-up company listed on a regional venture exchange. PAN issued 100,000 of its own shares in exchange for 800,000 shares of SON. Neither PAN nor SON had any other transactions on this day. The PAN shares and SON shares were trading around $40 and $4.50 per share, respectively, in the last two months of 2019 and first month of 2020.

The condensed statements of financial position for PAN and SON at December 31, 2019, are in Exhibit I. Additional information is in Exhibit II.

Consolidated financial statements will be prepared to combine the financial statements for the two companies. The management of PAN is concerned about the valuation of identifiable assets and goodwill on the consolidated financial statements and how it will affect earnings in future years. It heard that there are two options for measuring non-controlling interest, but does not know the differences between the options or which one would be appropriate for PAN to adopt.

The CFO at PAN has asked you, the controller at PAN, to prepare a memo on how to report the acquisition and to recommend accounting methods and policies that will minimize the debt-to-equity ratio and maximize earnings per share in the first year after the date of acquisition.

Required

Prepare the memo to the CFO.

Exhibit I	Financial Statements

PAN Medical Products Inc.
Condensed Statements of Financial Position
December 31, 2019

	PAN	SON
Current assets	$ 5,000,000	$1,100,000
Property, plant, and equipment—net	11,000,000	800,000
Development costs	0	2,000,000
Intangible assets	3,000,000	0
	$19,000,000	$3,900,000
Liabilities	$10,000,000	$1,600,000
Common shares	2,000,000	3,000,000
Retained earnings (Deficit)	7,000,000	(700,000)
	$19,000,000	$3,900,000

| Exhibit II | Additional Information |

1. On the date of acquisition, all of SON's recorded assets and liabilities had fair values equal to their carrying amounts except for the following:

	Carrying Amount	Fair Value
Land	$ 200,000	$500,000
Building	350,000	400,000
Development costs	2,000,000	Note 2

Additional information:

2. Prior to 2019, all of the research and development costs were expensed. Starting in 2019, the development costs were capitalized because management at SON felt that the main product they had been developing over the past few years was close to being ready for sale. Management feels that a patent could soon be approved and could be worth as much as $3.2 million.

3. SON employs 50 engineers and scientists who are involved with research and development of various biomedical devices. All of the engineers and scientists are highly regarded and have all signed employment contracts. In most cases, their salaries are consistent with market rates. In a few cases, the salaries are considerably less than what is being paid for similar work in other companies. Management at SON estimates that the company will save $220,000 per year for each of the next two years by not having to pay the current market rate for salaries for these employees.

4. The key terms of the employment contracts are as follows:

   a. All intellectual property, prototypes, and products being developed at SON are owned by the company.

   b. The employees have agreed to work for the company for terms of 1–3 years and cannot work for any other organizations during the term of their contract without the prior written consent of the company.

   c. The employees must not discuss or divulge any information about the products or technology being developed at the company with anyone outside of the company during the term of their contract and for one year after leaving the company.

5. Although SON's main activities are researching and developing new products, it does manufacture and sell some products that it had previously developed.

Pure Essentials Inc.

Contributed by
Nathalie Johnstone and Kristie Dewald
Edwards School of Business, University of Saskatchewan & Alberta School of Business, University of Alberta

Pure Essentials Inc. was incorporated in the early 1990s by Dave and June Briske. The company is headquartered in Kamloops, B.C., where it manufactures fruit and vegetable juices that are distributed to retail stores across Canada. Awareness around the health benefits of juicing began to increase about 15 years ago and since then, the company has grown significantly.

The Briskes have three adult children, Brett, Jennifer, and Kyle. All three became actively involved in the business once they completed university degrees. In 2013, Dave and June decided they wanted to slow down and turned the operations of the company over to their children. The children, being much younger and more energetic, wanted to grow the company significantly with an idea to possibly take it public within the next five years. To that end, Pure has invested in other businesses to diversify the company's products and locations. Brett is heading up the acquisitions, Jennifer is overseeing the finances, and Kyle oversees the day-to-day operations in Kamloops.

The siblings are seeking financing, through banks and private lenders, to continue their expansion plans. All potential lenders want to see audited consolidated financial statements for the fiscal year ending September 30, 2020. Jennifer holds a Bachelor of Commerce degree in finance and knows that preparing consolidated statements is well beyond her abilities and those of their staff. As such, they have hired you to oversee the process and assist with the more complex accounting issues.

The following is a summary of the various investments Pure holds.

Fruitful Energy Ltd.

The siblings wanted to expand into the U.S. market; however, receiving approval for new products from the U.S. Food and Drug Administration is a difficult and lengthy process. Early in 2019, Brett found a successful company based in Bakersfield, California, called Fruitful Energy Ltd. The company sells citrus-based fruit juices like lemonade and orange juices. The founders of Fruitful, Kim and Kelly Farrell, liked that Pure was family-owned and operated and agreed to sell 100% of their company. On October 1, 2019, Pure purchased all the outstanding shares of Fruitful for US$6.5 million.

Fruitful had a significant operating line of credit, which carried a very high interest rate. Management of Pure was unable to successfully negotiate lower rates or to find new financing in the United States at an acceptable rate. In order to improve the profitability, on October 1, 2019, Pure borrowed money and lent the funds to Fruitful, which used the money to repay the bank indebtedness that existed at acquisition. Additional information on Fruitful is included in Exhibits I and IV.

Valens Inc.

During 2016, the siblings, along with another investor, incorporated a new company, Valens Inc., for the purpose of developing, producing, and selling healthy snack foods. The company currently sells a variety of energy and protein bars along with a variety of dried fruit and vegetable snacks. In 2016, Pure subscribed for $4 million in share capital, while an organic farmer purchased the remaining $1 million in share capital. The farmer supplies Valens with a variety of fruits and vegetables used in the production of its products. In addition to the investment, both parties agreed to avoid external financing and provided a loan of $4 million split 80/20, the same as the shareholdings. This is the only interest-bearing debt that Valens carries.

Shortly after incorporating, Pure sold some of its equipment to Valens. All intercompany transactions between any related parties are done at fair market value so that each shareholder's interests are protected.

Pure has relationships with suppliers for its juices, but from time to time, it will purchase organic raw materials inventory from Valens. Financial statements and detailed financial information is included in Exhibit II.

EV Packaging

Pure purchased a 30% interest in EV Packaging on September 30, 2017. EV manufactures plastic and glass bottles, which Pure uses for many of its products. EV is working on a process to use recycled materials in its plastic. Pure purchased an equity interest both to retain some influence over its supply of bottles but also because it wants to share in the growth potential of the new product EV is working on.

Information on the purchase and activities of EV in 2020 are contained in Exhibit III.

Required

Prepare a package for the auditors that includes the translated single-entity financial statements and consolidated statements. Financial statements should include a statement of financial position and a statement of comprehensive income. No comparative column for 2019 is required. Assume the effective tax rate for all companies is 25%.

Exhibit 1	Fruitful Energy Ltd. Information

Pure Essentials Inc. purchased 100% of the outstanding shares of Fruitful Energy Ltd. for $6.5 million on October 1, 2019. At that time goodwill was calculated as follows:

	US$	Exchange	C$
Purchase price	$6,500,000	1.1171	$7,261,150
Book value of net assets:			
Share capital	(2,000,000)	1.1171	(2,234,200)
Retained earnings	(3,069,935)	1.1171	(3,429,424)
	1,430,065		1,597,526
Fair value differentials:			
Accounts receivable	126,000	1.1171	140,755
Inventory	(965,000)	1.1171	(1,078,002)
Equipment	(700,000)	1.1171	(781,970)
Land	350,000	1.1171	390,985
Intangible assets	(245,000)	1.1171	(273,690)
Deferred income taxes	358,500	1.1171	400,480
Goodwill	$ 354,565		$ 396,084

Additional information:

- The equipment, at acquisition, had a remaining useful life of seven years. The intangible assets have an indefinite life and relate to the various recipes developed by Fruitful.
- On January 31, 2020, the company sold a parcel of land to an unrelated third party for US$1,114,750 when the exchange rate was 1.2115. The land originally cost US$900,000 and was purchased by Fruitful in 2010 when the exchange rate was 1.002. On June 30, 2020, additional equipment was purchased for US$797,750. Depreciation expense on the new equipment for 2020 was US$149,945. The remainder of depreciation expense recorded relates to the equipment acquired in the initial purchase of Fruitful.
- Management has determined that inventory existing as at September 30, 2019, was purchased when the exchange rate was 1.1218, and inventory existing as at September 30, 2020, was purchased when the exchange rate was 1.3209.
- Prepaid expense relates entirely to prepaid insurance. Fruitful's insurance policy runs from July 1 to June 30 of each year. On June 30, Fruitful prepays the premium for the upcoming year. Premiums are expensed equally over the 12 months they relate to. Spot rates on June 30 were:

June 30, 2019	1.1180
June 30, 2020	1.2474

- General and administrative expenses include depreciation and insurance expenses. All other general and administrative expenses are assumed to have occurred evenly over the year. Dividends were declared and paid on June 30, 2020.
- Fruitful uses the services of a tax accountant to help with the preparation of tax returns and the financial accounting of current and deferred income taxes. She has determined that the appropriate exchange rate to convert deferred income taxes, and any adjustments to deferred income taxes through consolidation, to a Canadian equivalent is 1.3000.
- Pure's auditors have already determined that Fruitful is an integrated subsidiary requiring translation using the Canadian dollar as the functional currency. The exchange rate to convert the U.S. dollar to a Canadian equivalent at September 30, 2020, is 1.3372.

Financial statements of Fruitful are presented as follows:

Exhibit 1	Fruitful Energy Ltd. Information (Continued)

Fruitful Energy Ltd.
Statement of Comprehensive Income
for the years Ending September 30

	2020	2019
	(in US$)	
Sales revenue	$50,931,900	$49,176,800
Cost of sales	(41,824,700)	(40,803,150)
Gross margin	9,107,200	8,373,650
Expense		
Sales and marketing	3,896,785	3,941,000
Distribution expenses	2,271,250	2,450,365
General and administrative	1,995,425	2,136,050
Total expenses	8,163,460	8,527,415
Operating income (loss)	$ 943,740	$ (153,765)
Gain (loss) on sale of property, plant, and equipment	214,750	0
Finance costs	(236,000)	(238,000)
Net income before income taxes	$ 922,490	$ (391,765)
Income taxes (recovery)	(425,000)	156,700
Net income and comprehensive income	$ 497,490	$ (235,065)
Retained earnings—Beginning of year	$ 3,069,935	$ 3,305,000
Dividends	(300,000)	0
Retained earnings—End of year	$ 3,267,425	$ 3,069,935

| Exhibit I | Fruitful Energy Ltd. Information (Continued) |

Fruitful Energy Ltd.
Statement of Financial Position
At September 30

	2020	2019
	(in US$)	
Cash	$ 624,000	$ 149,880
Accounts receivable	3,692,300	3,610,500
Inventory	7,716,000	7,150,750
Prepaid expenses	167,925	192,420
Current assets	$12,200,225	$11,103,550
Property, plant, and equipment, cost	11,284,000	10,486,250
Accumulated depreciation	(6,572,800)	(5,824,965)
Land	3,279,000	4,179,000
Total assets	$20,190,425	$19,943,835
Bank indebtedness	$ 0	$ 1,500,000
Accounts and other payables	7,563,000	6,978,900
Current portion of long-term debt	680,000	680,000
Current liabilities	$ 8,243,000	$ 9,158,900
Due to Pure	$ 1,500,000	$ 0
Long-term debt	4,835,000	5,515,000
Deferred income tax liability	345,000	200,000
Total liabilities	$14,923,000	$14,873,900
Share capital	2,000,000	2,000,000
Retained earnings	3,267,425	3,069,935
Shareholders' equity	$ 5,267,425	$ 5,069,935
Total liabilities and shareholders' equity	$20,190,425	$19,943,835

| Exhibit II | Valens Inc. Information |

On March 1, 2019, Valens was incorporated with an initial share offering of $5 million. On April 1, 2019, Pure sold to Valens equipment for $6.4 million. The equipment had been on Pure's books at an initial cost of $11 million with accumulated depreciation of $3,750,000. The remaining useful life was eight years at the date of sale.

Pure periodically purchases material from Valens. The accountant for Valens determined that total sales to Pure during 2020 were

$2,479,000 and for 2019 were $1,381,000. Valens marks up products by 65%. Pure's accountant determined that at year end, 25% of the purchases from Valens were in ending inventory, whereas only 15% of the purchases were on hand at the end of 2019.

Financial statements of Valens are presented as follows:

Valens Inc.
Statement of Comprehensive Income
For the Years Ending September 30

	2020	2019
	(in C$)	
Sales revenue	$23,284,800	$22,175,980
Cost of sales	(13,970,900)	(13,305,500)
Gross margin	9,313,900	8,870,480
Expense		
Sales and marketing	1,300,000	1,515,000
Distribution expenses	1,845,800	1,699,870
General and administrative	3,560,000	3,148,400
Total expenses	$ 6,705,800	$ 6,363,270
Operating income	$ 2,608,100	$ 2,507,210
Gain (loss) on sale of property, plant, and equipment	(86,000)	147,000
Finance costs	(147,000)	(152,000)
Net income before income taxes	$ 2,375,100	$ 2,502,210
Income taxes	(594,000)	625,500
Net income and comprehensive income	$ 1,781,100	$ 3,127,710
Retained earnings—Beginning of year	11,595,960	8,468,250
Dividends	(356,000)	0
Retained earnings—End of year	$13,021,060	$11,595,960

Exhibit II   Valens Inc. Information (Continued)

Valens Inc.
Statement of Financial Position
At September 30

	2020	2019
	(in C$)	
Cash	$ 1,250,000	$ 1,876,000
Accounts receivable	2,011,820	1,847,900
Inventory	2,562,000	2,217,580
Prepaid expenses	50,000	41,000
Current assets	$ 5,873,820	$ 5,982,480
Property, plant, and equipment, cost	24,700,000	23,850,000
Accumulated depreciation	(14,820,000)	(14,382,920)
Land	7,200,000	7,200,000
Total assets	$22,953,820	$22,649,560
Accounts and other payables	$ 3,019,360	$ 3,323,600
Current portion of long-term debt	830,000	830,000
Current liabilities	$ 3,849,360	$ 4,153,600
Long-term debt	$ 870,000	$ 1,700,000
Deferred income tax liability	213,400	200,000
Total liabilities	$ 4,932,760	$ 6,053,600
Share capital	5,000,000	5,000,000
Retained earnings	13,021,060	11,595,960
Shareholders' equity	$18,021,060	$16,595,960
Total liabilities and shareholders' equity	$22,953,820	$22,649,560

| Exhibit III | EV Packaging Information |

On September 30, 2017, EV Packaging issued 90,000 new common shares to Pure for $1.2 million. Prior to the issue, EV had 210,000 common shares outstanding, giving Pure a 30% interest. Pure also appoints two members to the eight-person board of directors and has been contributing business support to management of EV as they research and develop their new bottles. Pure has been accounting for its investment in EV using the cost method. However, to comply with potential financers' requests for GAAP-compliant financial statements, you correctly believe they should be using the equity method. The purchase documents show that on September 30, 2017, EV's shareholders' equity accounts were:

Share capital	$ 525,000
Retained earnings	1,789,000

All assets and liabilities were equal to the book values except for inventory, which had a fair value $160,000 greater than book value and an intangible asset relating to the new plastic process with a fair value of $1.5 million and a book value of $650,000.

During the 2020 fiscal year, EV recorded a loss on the writedown of intangible assets of $149,500 relating to the earliest development expenditures.

Pure purchases inventory from EV every year. A summary of purchases and amounts in ending inventory for the year is:

2019—purchases	$7,000,000
2019—profit in ending inventory	$56,000
2020—purchases	$7,380,000
2020—profit in ending inventory	$31,900

EV Packaging Inc.
Statement of Retained Earnings
For the Years Ending September 30, 2020, and 2019

	2020	2019
Opening retained earnings	$3,608,170	$2,701,400
Net income	887,665	985,620
Dividends	(71,000)	(78,850)
Ending retained earnings	$4,424,835	$3,608,170

The company did not pay dividends in 2018.

Exhibit IV | **Pure Nonconsolidated Statements**

Statement of Comprehensive Income
For the Years Ending September 30

	2020	2019
Sales revenue	$152,795,000	$147,529,000
Cost of sales	(125,474,000)	(122,311,000)
Gross margin	27,321,000	25,218,000
Expenses: Sales and marketing	$ 11,699,000	$ 12,721,000
Distribution expenses	6,813,000	6,352,000
General and administrative	5,987,000	5,410,000
Total expenses	$ 24,499,000	$ 24,483,000
Operating income	$ 2,822,000	$ 735,000
Gain (loss) on sale of property, plant, and equipment	0	(57,000)
Investment income	854,220	
Finance costs	(708,000)	(714,000)
Net income before income taxes	$ 2,968,220	$ (36,000)
Income taxes	(847,000)	(348,000)
Net income and comprehensive income	$ 2,121,220	$ (384,000)
Retained earnings—Beginning of year	$ 45,080,150	$ 45,464,150
Dividends	(1,200,000)	(0)
Retained earnings—End of year	$ 46,001,370	$ 45,080,150

Exhibit IV — Pure Nonconsolidated Statements (Continued)

Statement of Financial Position
At September 30

	2020	2019
Cash	$ 3,031,220	$ 721,000
Accounts receivable	14,047,000	13,672,000
Inventory	29,149,000	31,794,000
Prepaid expenses	502,000	579,000
Current assets	$46,729,220	$46,766,000
Notes receivable	$ 3,365,800	$ 2,024,000
Investments, at cost	12,461,150	12,461,150
Property, plant, and equipment, cost	52,598,320	53,093,000
Accumulated depreciation	(21,309,520)	(19,432,000)
Land	2,244,000	2,244,000
Intangible assets, net	1,061,000	1,084,000
Total assets	$97,149,970	$98,240,150
Accounts and other payables	$22,954,600	$20,479,000
Current portion of long-term debt	4,989,300	5,100,000
Current liabilities	$27,943,900	$25,579,000
Long-term debt	$15,472,700	$20,462,000
Deferred income tax liability	4,035,000	3,422,000
Total liabilities	$47,451,600	$49,463,000
Share capital	3,697,000	3,697,000
Retained earnings	46,001,370	45,080,150
Shareholders' equity	$49,698,370	$48,777,150
Total liabilities and shareholders' equity	$97,149,970	$98,240,150

Tykes and Tots Child Centre

After completing your professional accounting exams, you noticed that you have some extra time. As a result, you decided to volunteer to help others in community. Recently, you accepted the volunteer position as treasurer of the Tykes and Tots Child Centre (TTCC) and have just returned from your first meeting (on February 1, 2021) with Melanie Manning, the executive director of TTCC.

TTCC just completed its first year of operations, ending December 31, 2020, and Melanie just recently assumed the role of executive director.

At an initial meeting with Melanie, she informed you that one of her major concerns with the financial statements is in regards to the information provided to TTCC's various users. Specifically, she is concerned about the statement of operations. She would like you to review the statement of operations, considering its users, and provide recommendations that may lead to enhanced relevance of information.

Next, Melanie would like to make sure that the financial statements are compliant with the standards outlined in Part III of the *CPA Canada Handbook* for not-for-profit organizations.

Lastly, Melanie would be very happy to see a summary of your recommendations regarding the financial statement preparation, along with your recommendations on any individual compliance issues. She is hoping to see a draft of the statement of operations after your recommendations. Currently, TTCC's board of directors believes that all activities are generating a surplus because the organization as a whole generated a surplus of $90,750, but Melanie is unsure if this is actually true.

At the end of the meeting, Melanie provides you with a file of information to help you get started. The file is organized as follows:

Exhibit	Description of Information
I	Description of TTCC and its operations
II	Draft statement of operations for the year ended December 31, 2020
III	Notes on accounting practices
IV	Extracts from the financial statements for the Get Fit Foundation for the year ended December 31, 2020

Required

Prepare a report that will address the needs of Melanie.

Exhibit I

Description of Operations

TTCC is a not-for-profit organization incorporated under the provincial Corporations Act as a corporation without share capital. TTCC's mandate is to provide daycare services to low-income families and families with a need for daycare services in Victoria, British Columbia.

TTCC has three main programs: daycare services, early literacy, and after-hours activities. The following is a brief summary of each program.

Daycare Services Program

This program is offered to low-income families and runs from 8:30 a.m. to 4:00 p.m. The daycare centre provides the children with a welcoming and nurturing environment. Daily activities include playing games, reading, and drawing. The children also receive two snacks and lunch. The daycare centre has a rented facility in a central location, and has children from all around the city.

The daycare service receives most of its funding from a sizable grant from the province of B.C. ($325,000 in the current year, with $25,000 allotted for general administration). The daycare also charges a small user fee for each child in order to help offset additional costs. Recently, the daycare also received a small grant ($55,000 in the current year) from the City of Victoria.

In addition to rental and meal expenses, the daycare's most significant cost is the wages of the daycare providers.

Early Literacy Program

Early literacy specialists work with children in order to promote literacy and numeracy. The program provides various resources, workshops, activities, and consultation for parents. The program is funded mainly by the federal government, along with revenues from a small user fee.

During the year, the Early Literacy Program received a $150,000 contribution that is to be used to fund operations equally over the current year (2020) and next year.

After-Hours Activities Program

These are activities that are offered from 4:00 p.m. to 8:00 p.m., and include things such as indoor and outdoor sports, and a reading club. These activities provide a location for parents to bring their children outside of class time. Many parents who work shifts into the evening take advantage of these activities.

This after-hours program is funded by user fees. The TTCC board tries hard to keep costs down in order to keep user fees at an acceptable low level, and therefore it relies significantly on volunteers. Operations are also subsidized by an annual fundraising campaign.

Endowments

During the year, TTCC received an endowment of $100,000 from a wealthy individual in the community. The conditions of the endowment are that the principal amount must remain invested in perpetuity; however, the investment income generated by the endowment can be used to help offset the costs related to the after-hours program. During the year, the investments generated a return of $7,000.

Administration

TTCC, like most not-for-profit organizations, is thinly administered because the board prefers to devote as much of TTCC's resources as possible to its charitable objectives rather than to administration. There is no professional accountant on staff and the annual financial statements prepared by the bookkeeper is the primary document used by the board and the executive director for decision-making.

Advertising campaigns are undertaken each year for $5,000, and advertise the TTCC as a whole as opposed to any program. The building used by the organization is rented for $150,000 per year, of which 75% is used by daycare activities, 15% is used by after-hours activities, and 10% by early literacy activities.

Annual Silent Auction

TTCC holds an annual silent auction. All proceeds from the auction are allocated to the after-hours program, and the auction is advertised as such. During 2020, the silent auction was a success and resulted in a $30,000 net surplus (revenues of $90,000 less costs of $60,000 for purchased items).

Donated Goods and Services

TTCC received various donated goods and services. For example, the silent auction benefited from donated auction prizes (which would have had to be purchased otherwise) and the after-hours program received many donated services from individuals who provide instructing and coaching of various sports.

Capital Assets

During 2020, TTCC purchased $7,000 worth of office equipment, which has been expensed. The equipment includes computers and other office devices. This equipment is used for general operations and administration.

Aside from office equipment, which has a seven-year useful life, TTCC purchased $48,000 in daycare furniture and fixtures, which have a useful life of 12 years, and $25,000 in after-hours activity equipment, which has a 10-year useful life.

Get Fit Foundation

In 2020, TTCC incorporated the Get Fit Foundation as a non-profit organization without share capital. The articles of incorporation stipulate that TTCC can appoint four of the five members on the foundation's board of directors.

The foundation provides sports equipment recycling services to children who cannot afford to purchase equipment to play sports. In addition, the foundation provides subsidies to low-income families to help offset the annual fees of playing organized sports. TTCC advanced $35,000 to the foundation in its first year of operations.

Exhibit II ‖ Draft Statement of Operations

Tykes and Tots Child Centre

Statement of Operations

December 31, 2020

Revenue

Grant—Federal government	$150,000
Grant—Province of British Columbia	325,000
Grant—City of Victoria	55,000
User fees collected	60,000
Investment income	7,000
Endowment	100,000
Silent auction	30,000
	$727,000

Expenditures

Advertising	$ 5,000
Equipment purchases	80,000
Food and drinks (for snacks and meals)	25,000
Office supplies	1,250
Rent expense	150,000
Wages and benefits	375,000
	$636,250
Excess (deficiency) of revenue over expenditure for the year	$ 90,750

Exhibit III ‖ Notes on Accounting Practices

Note 1—Revenue Recognition Policy

- Revenues are recorded in the accounts by source (government, donations, etc.) when the cash is received. Grants and pledges are recorded when pledges or grants are announced.

Note 2—Donated Goods and Services

- Donated goods and services are not recorded in the accounts.

Note 3—Expenditure Classification

- Expenditures are recorded to each account solely based on the type of expenditure (salaries, supplies, etc.). No further subclassification is provided in the financial statements.
- The following additional information is therefore disclosed:
  - User fees: $27,500 of the user fees were collected for the daycare program and for the after-hours program (each), and $5,000 was collected for the early literacy program.

- Office supplies are shared by all programs, and cannot be allocated.
- Wages and benefits were incurred as follows: 70% for daycare services, 10% for early literacy activities, 15% for after-hours programs, and 5% for administrative services.

Note 4—Capital Assets

- Capital assets are not recorded in the financial statements (accordingly, there is no depreciation recorded). The cost of furniture and equipment is charged to operations when the expenditure is made.

Note 5—Inventory

- Similar to capital assets, no inventory of supplies is maintained. Expenditures are charged to operations when the purchase is made.

| Exhibit IV | Extracts from the Financial Statements of the Get Fit Foundation |

Get Fit Foundation
Statement of Operations
December 31, 2020

Revenues

Government grants	$145,000
Advance from TTCC	35,000
Donations	3,500
User fees	2,800
	$186,300

Expenses

Advertising	$ 1,500
Furniture and equipment	275
Miscellaneous	600
Purchased services	25,000
Rent, utilities, and taxes	8,000
Salaries and benefits	17,500
Supplies	2,500
Travel	2,500
	$ 57,875
Excess (deficiency) of revenue over expenditure for the year	$128,425

Capstone Cases

All Extreme Wrestling

All Extreme Wrestling (AEW) is a large, multinational entertainment company that delivers wrestling content year-round to a global audience. AEW delivers its content through various media, such as cable television, pay-per-view (PPV), the Internet, and books. AEW's mission statement is:

> To be an international leader in the creation and delivery of wresting-related entertainment content across various platforms.

AEW started out in 1965 as a small, regional wrestling company in Calgary, Alberta. AEW hosted live wrestling events in various cities in Alberta. Generally, the company would rely upon Canadian wrestling talent, occasionally attracting a large headlining superstar from the United States or Japan. In 1975, AEW expanded to offer live shows across Canada. The company's big break came in 1981 when it landed a television deal to broadcast its wrestling program once a week, live from various locations across Canada. The television deal led to a more international audience and a rapid expansion into the United States.

AEW experienced significant growth during the 1980s and early 1990s. However, the company felt some growing pains during the mid-1990s when the general public began to suspect that wrestling was staged. At this point, the company decided to rebrand itself as an entertainment company, as opposed to a competitive wrestling company. AEW was open about the fact that the wrestling matches were staged, and instead focused on detailed storylines, extreme wrestling stunts, and comedic characters. In addition, AEW immediately embraced the Internet as a means of delivering content and connecting with its audiences.

In 2004, AEW went public and is now traded on the Toronto and New York stock exchanges. The company has experienced steady growth since the Internet era, and its share price has reflected the strong performance.

After years of strong performance, fiscal 2020 appears to be ushering in a new period of challenges. Transition from pay-per-view events to Internet subscription speciality programming, the continual challenge posed by Internet piracy, and drug scandals have begun to take their toll on the company. In addition, new companies are beginning to challenge AEW's status as an industry leader.

The most challenging issue has been the company's development and launch of the AEW Network (AEWN). AEW is a monthly subscription-based speciality channel that provides subscribers with 24/7 access to AEW material. AEWN is available through most cable providers, AEW's website, or a mobile app. Subscribers pay $9.99 per month for AEWN, and can cancel any time after a minimum of six months. AEWN offers subscriber access to the monthly PPV events, and therefore, AEWN subscribers reduce the number of PPV purchases.

After spending significant amounts to develop the AEWN technology and acquire additional content to build up historical libraries, the network launched during the most recent fiscal quarter. Analysts were concerned with the low number of subscribers and the backlash from cable providers about losing PPV revenue. Some cable providers have threatened to drop AEW content due to the competition provided by AEWN.

The market has punished AEW's share price for the preliminary poor results from the launch of AEWN. The shares are down 16% from their all-time high of $42 per share since the third-quarter financial statements were released. Further declines, of up to 50% of the market capitalization, are expected if analysts' consensus earnings estimates for the fiscal year are not achieved.

The poor performance of the AEWN has resulted in a corporate shake-up, and many of the executive-level management team has resigned. The CEO, Owen Daniels, has recently hired you as the new CFO. Owen is the company's founder and visionary. He is expecting that analysts' expectations will be met once fourth quarter earnings are released.

Owen hands you the AEW's previous four years of annual financial statements, along with the financial results for the first three quarters of this fiscal year, 2020 (Exhibit I). Owen has received a report from the accounting group that shows fourth-quarter profit (after taxes) of $40.5 million. However, the figures do not include the impacts of various accounting issues. Owen provides you with a file of outstanding accounting issues as prepared by the previous CFO before his resignation (Exhibit II) that have yet to be reflected in fourth-quarter earnings.

Owen would you like you to prepare a report that provides a recommendation for the appropriate treatment of each accounting issue. In addition, Owen would like you to provide an estimate for annual earnings per share. Analysts are expecting the annual EPS to be $0.05 per share.

Required

Prepare the report for Owen. Note that the company's marginal tax rate is 26.4% and the discount rate for discounting cash flows is 4%.

Exhibit 1 **Financial Statements**

All Extreme Wrestling
Statement of Financial Position ('000s)

For the year ended December 31	2016 Y	2017 Y	2018 Y	2019 Y	2020 (Q1–Q3)
Assets					
Current assets					
Cash and cash equivalents	$ 45,268	$ 34,031	$ 42,820	$ 21,337	$ 16,886
Short-term investments, net	62,967	66,952	55,967	49,581	59,870
Accounts receivable (net of allowance for doubtful accounts)	44,850	43,997	42,218	46,542	70,962
Inventory	1,353	1,075	1,148	1,863	3,917
Prepaid expenses and other current assets	13,521	9,375	9,899	10,468	15,308
Total current assets	$167,959	$155,430	$152,052	$129,791	$166,943
Property, plant, and equipment, net	52,511	62,603	66,234	86,538	118,163
Feature film production assets, net	36,470	15,295	15,359	10,385	23,513
Television production assets, net	0	163	4,105	6,984	7,994
Investment securities	9,749	6,584	3,384	5,380	10,443
Other assets, net	2,836	5,395	6,125	6,286	25,256
Total assets	$269,525	$245,470	$247,259	$245,364	$352,310
Liabilities and Shareholders' Equity					
Current liabilities					
Current portion of long-term debt	$ 758	$ 818	$ 0	$ 2,756	$ 4,179
Accounts payable and accrued expenses	27,826	30,006	31,738	31,043	60,848
Deferred income	18,362	14,074	18,549	19,522	30,885
Total current liabilities	$ 46,946	$ 44,898	$ 50,287	$ 53,321	$ 95,912
Long-term debt	10,820	3,886	5,895	19,624	25,346
Noncurrent deferred income	6,406	5,338	0	0	6,638
Commitments and contingencies	0	0	0	0	0
Shareholders' equity					
Class A common shares	218,398	219,584	221,757	225,137	342,971
Class B convertible common shares	300	300	300	300	300
Accumulated other comprehensive income	2,038	2,115	2,613	2,277	2,526
Accumulated deficit	(15,383)	(30,651)	(33,593)	(55,295)	(121,381)
Total shareholders' equity	$205,353	$191,348	$191,077	$172,419	$224,416
Total liabilities and shareholders' equity	$269,525	$245,470	$247,259	$245,364	$352,310

| Exhibit I | Financial Statements (Continued) |

All Extreme Wrestling
Statement of Income ('000s, Except Per Share Data)

For the year ended December 31	2016 Y	2017 Y	2018 Y	2019 Y	2020 (Q1–Q3)
Net revenues	$309,673	$313,736	$313,795	$329,327	$274,125
Cost of revenues (including amortization and impairments of feature film and television production assets)	177,833	204,339	184,417	209,426	227,552
Selling, general, and administrative expenses	70,921	75,684	88,393	100,219	94,528
Depreciation and amortization	7,590	9,712	12,982	15,864	12,563
Operating (loss) income	53,329	24,001	28,003	3,818	(60,518)
Investment income, net	1,327	1,332	1,420	925	447
Interest expense	(169)	(404)	(1,105)	(1,132)	(963)
Other income (expense), net	(1,365)	(1,017)	(646)	(628)	(38)
(Loss) income before income taxes	53,122	23,912	27,672	2,983	(61,071)
(Benefit from) provision for income taxes	18,469	7,812	7,295	1,192	(12,389)
Net (loss) income	$ 34,653	$ 16,100	$ 20,377	$ 1,791	$(48,683)
(Loss) Earnings per share					
Basic and diluted	$0.71	$0.33	$0.42	$0.04	$(1.00)
Weighted average common shares outstanding					
Basic	48,345	48,113	48,361	48,584	48,719
Diluted	48,822	48,532	48,612	48,870	48,719
Dividends declared per common share (Classes A and B)	0	0.64633	0.4797	0.48072	0.35721

Consolidated Statements of Comprehensive Income

Net (loss) income	$34,653	$16,100	$20,377	$1,791	$(48,683)
Other comprehensive income (loss)					
Foreign currency translation adjustment	124	(27)	101	(91)	101
Change in unrealized holding gain (loss) on available-for-sale securities (net of tax (benefit)/expense)	394	161	476	(244)	(2)
Reclassification adjustment for gains realized in net income—available-for-sale securities (net of tax expense)	(21)	(57)	(79)	(1)	150
Total other comprehensive income (loss)	497	77	498	(336)	249
Comprehensive (loss) income	$35,150	$16,177	$20,875	$1,455	$(48,434)

Exhibit II   Additional Information

AEW Network Subscriptions

In the third quarter of 2020, AEW launched the AEWN and 496,668 paid subscribers signed up to receive the service. The breakdown of new subscribers over the three months in the third quarter is as follows:

Month 1	Month 2	Month 3	Total
372,501	99,334	24,833	496,668

Subscribers pay $9.99 at the beginning of each month and must purchase a minimum of six months of service. Subscribers who cancel before the minimum six-month period are charged a cancellation fee equal to the number of remaining months to reach the minimum time period times the monthly fee.

In addition to the monthly fee, subscribers can purchase additional content on a PPV basis. Each month features a unique program that can be purchased for $2.99. For example, the first three months of content featured a documentary on the history of AEW, a backstage look at AEW, and a documentary on AEW's largest superstars. A total of 72,251 PPV items were purchased during the third quarter.

Television Contract

During the third quarter, AEW reached a new agreement with the Japan Sports Channel (JSC) whereby JSC will be the exclusive provider of AEW's flagship weekly episodic wrestling program in Japan for the next three years. The agreement was signed with JSC at the beginning of month two and was effective immediately. JSC has already begun broadcasting AEW content on its network. The terms of the agreement require AEW to provide JSC with weekly wrestling content in exchange for a $3-million upfront fee, and an annual royalty of $0.75 per viewer. The third quarter has seen approximately 1.3 million viewers; however, the actual number of viewers will be determined by Japan's television rating agency. It could take up to six months to determine the exact number of viewers.

Feature Film and Television Productions

The following is the breakdown of the feature film and television production intangible assets ('000s):

	Feature Film Productions	Television Productions
In release	$ 9,640	$3,357
Completed but not released	3,292	1,918
In production	8,650	2,719
In development	1,881	0
	$23,463	$7,994

The feature film productions are movies and documentaries developed by AEW for distribution through AEWN, DVD sales, PPV, or online downloads. The "in release" and "completed but not released"

categories are expected to generate annual revenues of a total of $3.5 million annually over the next five years (for both the feature film and television categories combined, respectively).

The "in production" category for feature film productions includes AEW's portion of the development costs of a new Hollywood movie featuring a former AEW heavyweight champion and a big movie star. The movie is expected to debut in the fourth quarter of 2020, and AEW is entitled to receive 3.5% of gross revenues from the movies but must incur $1.5 million in advertising fees in each of the next two years. The movie is expected to earn gross revenues of $360 million over a two-year period, with 75% earned in the 2021 fiscal year.

The "in development" category includes two documentaries that are currently being developed for release in the 2021 fiscal year. One documentary showcases the rise to stardom of Chris Francios, a former AEW heavyweight champion. The second documentary features Owen Daniels's journey in taking AEW from a small, regional wrestling company to a large, multinational entertainment company. Each documentary represents half of the total development costs.

The television productions consist of episodic series. The amounts capitalized include development costs, production costs, overhead costs, and employee salaries. The "in production" costs are related to a new program being created to run every Thursday night that features young and up-and-coming wrestlers. The program is called "Are You Strong Enough?" Owen is hopeful that this new program will be a hit. The "in release" and "completed but not released" categories of television products are expected to generate annual revenues of $1,750,000 in each of the next four years.

Legal Proceeding

AEW has been sued by Crazy-Man Steve Ostroski, a former wrestler with AEW. Crazy-Man is a four-time heavyweight champion, and a fan favorite. Crazy-Man left AEW after a heated contract dispute. Now, he is suing AEW for royalties related to his character's and name's use in digital and movie content. Crazy-Man had a unique contract with AEW that allowed him to retain ownership and creative control over his name and character. AEW lawyers are trying to settle the case for $500,000. If AEW loses, it may be required to pay a 5% royalty on all content sold that includes Crazy-Man's name or character. The following is a listing of the content that includes Crazy-Man's name:

Title	Selling Price	Expected Units Sold	Number of Years Units Will Be Sold Over
Documentary: *Wrestling with Scars*	$14.99	125,000	Three years
Video game: *AEW 2020*	$34.99	175,000	One year
Coffee table book: *AEW Legends*	$29.99	280,000	Four years
Feature film: *The Warrior*	$19.99	135,000	Two years

Exhibit II | Additional Information (Continued)

There is a 50% chance that Crazy-Man will settle for $500,000.

Steroid Use Allegations

Recently, the wrestling industry has received some negative attention. Many wrestlers have passed away at very young ages and in tragic manners. The past quarter has been especially challenging as former AEW superstar Chris Francios went on a crime spree. Chris's legal defense is arguing that his time with AEW led to excessive head injuries and the use of steroids and other narcotics that have significantly impacted his mental state. AEW has not been named in any lawsuit thus far, but national media has picked up the story, resulting in much negative publicity. There is also a rumor that there could be some level of government investigation regarding the use of narcotics in the industry and excessive numbers of wrestler deaths. Owen is clearly concerned about this issue.

Investment Securities

At the end of the third quarter, AEW made an investment in a regional wrestling company (Total Wrestling Action, TWA). AEW paid $5 million for a 9% stake in TWA. The two wrestling companies are planning to work together to share wrestling talent, co-promote events, and share other resources. AEW sees TWA as a developmental company that can provide much-needed new talent to AEW's main roster of superstars.

AEW has the ability to elect 3 of the 10 board members. Currently, Owen and two other AEW executives are sitting on TWA's board. As of its third quarter of 2020, TWA's fair value was estimated to be $5.2 million. TWA earned income of $8.5 million during the third quarter, and paid dividends of $1 million.

The investment is currently reported at its cost basis as part of the investment securities.

Long-Term Debt

On March 1, AEW issued long-term debt in the form of a bond with a face value of $7 million. The bonds were issued at par and have a coupon rate and market rate of 5%. The bonds pay interest semi-annually and mature after 10 years.

The company's management believes that interest rates will increase in the next few years as the economy begins to accelerate and inflation becomes more of a concern. Accordingly, AEW management is planning to redeem the bonds within a two- to three-year period and therefore it elected to measure the bonds at fair value.

The first interest payment has been made. The market yield for similar bonds at year end was 4.11%.

BuyThings.com

BuyThings.com (BT) opened its virtual doors in 2013. In the beginning, the company focused on being an online retailer of various products, such as books and video games. The company experienced significant growth during its first five years of operations. Recently, the company's sales have plateaued and management began to seek new sources of revenues.

During fiscal 2020, BT's board of directors and the management team developed a new strategic plan to stimulate growth and create shareholder wealth. The strategic plan was finalized in May 2020 and received unanimous board support at a meeting in July 2020. During the most recent fiscal year of 2020, BT's management implemented the strategic plan by moving into two new markets and restructuring activities across three distinct, yet similar, operating segments. BT now seeks to be a customer-focused company across the following three segments:

- Online retailing: The first segment serves customers through a diverse product and service range from various large brands. For example, BT sells bestselling books, movies, video games, music, and electronic devices. This operating segment focuses on variety of selection, low prices, and home shopping convenience.

- Content enabling: BT also offers services that enable individuals from across the globe to sell their products on BT's website and to fulfill orders through BT's purchasing information system. This segment focuses on providing high levels of visibility and market reach to musicians, authors, filmmakers, app developers, and other content developers to publish and sell their intellectual property.

- Electronic device manufacturing: BT manufactures and sells electronic devices. The only device developed and currently for sale is an e-book reader called eReads. Customers can buy eReads and downloadable books through BT's website.

In addition, BT began to provide advertising services, such as banner ads, to businesses looking to advertise on BT's website.

In order to provide management with an incentive to fully implement the strategic plan and maximize shareholder wealth, the board of directors voted to provide management with a bonus of 5% of 2021 net income if both 2021 revenue and net income experienced growth of 15% over 2020.

You are a manager in the internal audit department and are preparing to report to the audit committee on the accounting policies adopted by management during the most recent year. The audit committee is eager to review your report because the strategic plan has resulted in many new, nonroutine transactions. Therefore, the audit committee would like to feel comfortable that the financial statements present fairly the results of operations before the external auditors begin their review. In addition, the audit committee would like to provide information to the compensation committee to help determine the bonus benchmarks that will be used for the management team's 2021 bonus.

You begin drafting your report by reviewing draft financial statements (Exhibit I) and summary notes of all of the new transactions related to the new operations (Exhibit II).

Required

Prepare the report for the audit committee.

| Exhibit I | Draft Financial Statements |

Buythings.Com
Consolidated Statements of Operations
(Unaudited)
(In Thousands, Except Per Share Data)

	Draft	Audited
	December 31, 2020	**December 31, 2019**
Online retail product sales	$28,825	$24,083
Electronic device sales	0	0
E-book downloads	198	0
Content enabling sales	1,200	0
Banner advertising	260	0
Total sales	$30,483	$24,083
Operating expenses		
Cost of sales	$21,019	$17,765
Fulfillment	3,330	2,490
Marketing	1,215	934
Development costs	2,055	0
Website design	1,948	1,771
General and administrative	438	348
Content enabling services fees	780	62
Total operating expenses	$30,785	$23,370
Income from operations	(302)	713
Interest expense	(55)	16
Interest and other income	15	(36)
Other income (expense)	(53)	(31)
Income (loss) before income taxes	(395)	662
Provision (benefit) for income taxes	(62)	(166)
Equity-method investment activity, net of tax	87	(60)
Net income (loss)	$ (370)	$ 436
Earnings per share:		
Basic	$ (2.09)	$ 2.46
Diluted	$ (2.06)	$ 2.42
Weighted-average common shares outstanding:		
Basic	177	177
Diluted	180	180

*Other comprehensive income statement excluded for simplicity.

| Exhibit I | Draft Financial Statements (Continued) |

Buythings.Com
Consolidated Statements of Financial Position
(Unaudited)
(In Thousands)

	Draft	Audited
	December 31, 2020	December 31, 2019
Assets		
Current assets:		
Cash and cash equivalents	$ 3,359	$ 3,136
Marketable securities	1,470	1,305
Inventories	2,875	2,340
Accounts receivable, net	1,849	1,481
Total current assets	$ 9,553	$ 8,262
Property, plant, and equipment, net	4,248	2,739
Goodwill	1,779	1,629
Total assets	$15,580	$12,630
Liabilities and Shareholders' Equity		
Current liabilities:		
Accounts payable	$ 5,871	$ 5,167
Accrued expenses	2,595	1,898
Unearned revenue	450	307
Total current liabilities	$ 8,916	$ 7,372
Long-term debt	1,738	1,696
Other long-term liabilities	1,646	883
Commitments and contingencies	0	0
Total liabilities	$12,300	$ 9,951
Shareholders' equity:		
Common shares	$ 2,358	$ 1,389
Accumulated other comprehensive income (loss)	72	70
Retained earnings	850	1,220
Total shareholders' equity	3,280	2,679
Total liabilities and shareholders' equity	$15,580	$12,630

Exhibit II | Notes on New Transactions

Content Enabling Services

Starting on September 1, 2020, BT began publishing content created by authors, musicians, app developers, and filmmakers. The content creators must log in to BT's website to create a profile, upload their intellectual property, and set a selling price. BT performs an internal review of the content before it becomes publicly available to ensure that it complies with all policies and codes of conduct. During the year, $1.2 million of content was sold through BT's website. BT retained 35% of the sales price, with the remaining 65% going to the content creator.

eReads Development

During the year, BT developed an e-reader called eReads. eReads allows users to download and read content from BT's website (or other websites), such as e-books and magazines. The device features a touch screen, sound capability, and various lighting options.

The initial design and prototype for the eReads device was purchased on May 15, 2020, for $1 million from Techno Solutions, a small technology company in Waterloo, Ontario. The purchase agreement has two significant clauses: (1) If the prototype was not fully developed into an operational reader, Techno Solutions would be required to refund 50% of the purchase price to BT; and (2) if the prototype is fully developed and commercialized, BT must pay Techno Solutions a royalty of 1% of all future sales in perpetuity.

BT undertook the following additional steps in 2020 in order to fully develop and commercialize the e-reader:

Date	Process	Cost
May–June	Developing and implementing the touch screen feature	$1,275,000
June–July	Developing and implementing lighting and sound features	300,000
July–August	Quality assurance testing and pilot testing in select markets	105,000
August	Designing the packaging, logo, brand name, etc.	75,000
September	Marketing and advertisements to create brand awareness	300,000
	Total development costs (including initial design purchase)	$2,055,000

eReads Sales

BT began selling the e-reader in November 2020. As an initial promotion, BT offered customers the e-reader with 10 downloads of selected e-books for the initial purchase price of $60. Customers can download the e-books anytime over the next two years. In addition, customers have a 90-day, no-questions-asked, money-back satisfaction guarantee. However, any downloaded books will reduce the refund price by $1.80.

The promotion was a great success because it offered customers much value. (The e-reader normally sells for $70 while e-books sell for $3 each.) By year end 2020, in just two months, a total of 32,000 e-readers were purchased under the promotion and 110,000 e-books were downloaded. BT has no history with the money-back guarantee. Industry standards suggest that 15% of new electronic devices are returned under such guarantees. None of the e-readers have been returned as of year end.

Lawsuit

During 2020, Ethos Limited filed a complaint against BT for patent infringement in the United States District Court. The complaint alleges that, among other things, BT's payment system infringes on patents owned by Ethos Limited (Patent No. 422421) and seeks injunctive relief, monetary damages ($750,000), costs ($20,000), and legal fees ($55,000). BT disputes the allegations of any wrongdoing and intends to defend itself vigorously in this matter.

Vendor Agreements

During 2020, BT created agreements with many online retail vendors. The agreements allow BT to recover funds for co-operative marketing efforts, promotions, and volume rebates for certain products. The following two agreements were signed:

- Co-operative marketing: On March 1, BT signed an agreement with a large publisher to recover marketing costs. The agreement required BT to incur $500,000 in advertising costs related to the publisher's content in order to trigger a 20% rebate. BT reached the threshold and a total of $100,000 was received and recorded as part of the online retail product sales account.

- Volume rebate: On October 1, BT signed a volume rebate with a large movie distributor whereby BT will receive a volume rebate of 10% of all purchases if $1 million in inventory is purchased during a 12-month period. Once the threshold is reached, the 12-month period restarts and a new rebate can be received. The agreement is effective for a five-year period and an unlimited number of rebates can be earned during the life of the agreement. As of year end, a total of $960,000 in inventory was purchased from the vendor. No rebate has been received.

Banner Advertising Swaps

BT began offering banner advertising as an additional source of revenue. BT also swapped banner advertising in the following two transactions:

- BT provided Tek-Rite Computers with banner advertising in 2020, normally valued at $130,000, in exchange for 1,000 tablet computers. The tablets will be sold through BT's retail website for $150 each. BT could purchase these tablets from Tek-Rite Computers for $130 each.

- BT provided a large book publisher with banner advertising in exchange for banner advertising on the publisher's website. The fair value of the advertising provided by BT is equal to the fair value of the advertising received ($130,000). BT would not have paid for banner advertising of this nature if cash was to be used as payment.

BT's management is excited about banner advertising, and specifically, banner advertising swaps. Management is planning to expand these transactions in the future.

Calgary Rush Ltd.

Today is March 15, 2021. Your partner called you, CPA, into her office to discuss a new, special engagement. Your firm has been engaged to assist a group of investors, led by Jason McGill, with a business acquisition. Jason is interested in buying the Calgary Rush Ltd. (CR), a wholly owned subsidiary of Flames Sports Entertainment (FSE). CR owns a minor-league professional hockey team. The hockey team has been rather successful on the ice, winning three championships in its first five years in the league.

The partner tells you that she and Jason have scheduled a meeting with the rest of the investors next week to finalize an offer to be presented to FSE for the purchase of CR's shares. At an initial meeting a week ago, Bryan dropped off excerpts from the purchase price calculation agreement (Exhibit I) and financial statements (Exhibit II). Subsequent to the meeting, the partner, with the consent of FSE and the investor group, met with the management and staff of CR. Notes from both meetings are collected in Exhibit III.

Based on the financial statements obtained, and the purchase price equation, Jason said to your partner: "FSE's management expressed that it is expecting to receive between approximately $1.4 to $1.8 million for CR. I'm not sure whether the investor group will continue to run CR the same way that FSE did, but FSE's management used the 2020 financial statements as a starting point in determining their expected price."

The partner tells you: "Our primary task is to review the financial statements of CR to determine compliance with GAAP. Based on the information we have obtained thus far, please prepare a report outlining any GAAP issues and a recommended treatment, along with any reasonable alternative treatments where applicable. Because of the relatively small size of CR, its financial statements have never been audited. Secondly, can you please calculate purchase price based on the GAAP adjusted net income that Jason can use in the meeting next week."

Required

Prepare the report for the partner.

Purchase Price Agreement Excerpts

Purchase Price Calculation

The final purchase price is to be determined based on using an earnings multiple approach, whereby the total net income for the most recent fiscal year is multiplied by the earnings multiple as follows:

$$\text{Net Income}^1 \times \text{Earnings Multiple} = \text{Purchase Price}$$

Earnings Multiple

An earnings multiple of between 3 and 4 is common for companies owning minor-league professional hockey teams.

Net Income

Net income must be determined based on generally accepted accounting principles.

[1]Calculated in accordance with Part II of the *CPA Canada Handbook*

Exhibit II | Financial Statements

CR Ltd.
Statement of Financial Position
As At December 31
(Unaudited)

	2020	2019
Current assets		
Cash	$ 29,400	$ 27,000
Temporary investments	120,000	120,000
Accounts receivable	271,400	163,400
Employee receivable	70,000	45,000
Prepaid insurance	25,000	0
	515,800	355,400
Property, plant, and equipment (net)	237,600	93,000
Franchise rights	1,000,000	950,000
	1,753,400	1,398,400
Current liabilities		
Accounts payable	20,000	31,000
Due to FSE Corp.	55,280	150,000
	75,280	181,000
Share capital (common shares)	7,000	7,000
Share capital (preferred shares)	3,000	3,000
Retained earnings	1,668,120	1,207,400
	1,678,120	1,217,400
	$1,753,400	$1,398,400

CR Ltd.
Excerpt from the Income Statement
for the Year Ended December 31
(Unaudited)

	2020	2019
Income before taxes	$768,720	$860,386
Income taxes	307,400	344,200
	40%	40%
Net income	$461,320	$516,186
Dividends on preferred shares	$ 600	

Exhibit III **Notes from Meeting with Jason McGill and Employees at CR Ltd.**

1. In 2011, FSE purchased a minor-league professional hockey franchise in Calgary and paid $800,000 in initial league fees. The hockey operations were immediately incorporated in a new subsidiary company, CR Ltd. Recently, FSE made a decision to return to its core business of major league sports and to sell CR. CR's year end is the same as FSE's year end, December 31.

2. The hockey season runs from September to April, with the team playing 80 games—40 at home and 40 away. Attendance in the first part of the season is low but, by January, attendance for home games is usually close to capacity of 6,000 seats. About half of the home games are played by the end of December of each year.

3. All tickets are general admission tickets, with single game seats selling for $6.00. Season ticket holders, which number around 2,000, pay $200 for the 40 home games in August and September. Any season tickets not used cannot be transferred for another game, no refunds are offered, and the tickets are nontransferable and nonrefundable. Theo Bennett, the team's general manager, has instructed the bookkeeper to record all season ticket sales as revenue when the customer pays for the tickets. Playoff tickets are sold apart from the season ticket package, although season ticket holders are given the right of first refusal to purchase playoff tickets for their seats.

4. Theo describes his relationship with advertisers as excellent, although he admits that the approaches he uses are sometimes unique. Some of the advertising revenue comes in through the exchange of products or services instead of cash. Advertising revenue is generated through the sale of space on the rink boards, displays on the ice surface, and announcements during the game, etc.

   For example, one advertiser, Alberta Tech, supplied 15 laptops, with a carrying value of $10,000, on the condition that they be given away at specifically scheduled home games during the season, in exchange for an advertising sign on the boards behind the goalie net. The fair value of the advertising given was $15,000. Theo credited $15,000 of revenue and debited $15,000 prepaid advertising on this sale when the transfer took place. As at December 31, there were 10 laptops still on hand. The laptops are expensed, and the prepaid advertising reduced, as they are given away.

5. CR's largest advertiser is FSE. It has the premier advertising space in centre ice. FSE pays $60,000 per year for this advertising space, which is about $40,000 more than what the space would cost in other minor-league arenas. CR records advertising revenue each year in the amount of $60,000.

6. Theo believes that the value of the franchise has increased over the years that CR has owned the team. Consequently, Theo has asked the bookkeeper to increase the value of the franchise on the statement of financial position each year to reflect his estimate of the increase in market value. The journal entry's credit has been posted to gain on intangible asset.

7. On January 1, 2019, CR issued 3,000 redeemable and retractable preferred shares at a value of $1 per share. The shares are redeemable by CR at any time after January 2023. The shares are retractable for the original $1 per share at the discretion of the holder at any time up to January 2023, after which the retractable feature expires. The preferred shares require the payment of a mandatory $2 per share during the retraction period, after which the dividends become noncumulative and are paid at the discretion of the board only.

8. The arena where the team plays is owned by the city and leased by CR. The lease expires on June 30, 2023. CR is responsible for all operating expenses, including maintaining the ice surface and all equipment necessary to maintain the arena and parking lot. While the lease payments are relatively low ($100,000 per year), the facility desperately needed about $250,000 in renovations, particularly the concession stands and the home and visitors dressing rooms. CR had been pushing the city to do the renovations for several years, but the city was reluctant to spend the money and had not done anything.

   Theo got tired of waiting. On July 1, 2020, he took it upon himself to spend about $150,000 on improvements, which have been set up as a receivable. Since the work should have been done by the city, he is now battling with the city to recoup this "receivable" from them. He is frustrated because there is still another $100,000 of upgrades to go. If the arena is not completely upgraded, Theo is fearful the league will step in and force the franchise to move to another city. It is unlikely that the city will reimburse Theo for any incurred or future upgrade costs.

9. CR has temporary investments that are being carried at cost. Theo has confessed that he has not adopted the accounting standards for financial instruments. The temporary investments are being carried at cost on the financial statements. The market value of the investments are as follows:

2020		2019	
Cost	Market value	Cost	Market value
$100,000	$150,000	$100,000	$110,000

Candy Apple Technologies

Candy Apple Technologies (CAT) is relatively new company that designs video games and applications for mobile devices. Users are able to download a game or application onto a mobile device for a fee that normally ranges from 99 cents to $4.99. In addition, users can play the company's games over the Internet.

The company was established by Thomas Waboose and Petra Bior, one year after they completed a degree in computer sciences. Thomas and Petra are excellent programmers, and have been playing video games since they were children. After designing a mobile device game for an undergraduate course assignment, the two friends decided to start up CAT. The company's games have been well received by the market, and have been downloaded by over 5 million users across the globe. In addition, the company's applications are also considered to be high quality.

The company experienced significant growth in its first five years of operations, and decided to go public. Two analysts are currently following CAT's shares, which are trading at $13, and are preparing their first recommendation. CAT is scheduled to release its financial results in two weeks during a conference call. Based on the results released by industry competitors, analysts are expecting the company to report revenue of $7 million and earnings of $1.5 million in the current year.

You are the senior manager with Singh and Islam, LLP, the auditors of CAT. Recently, you met with Thomas and Petra to discuss the following transactions that took place during the year:

- CAT entered into an agreement with Eastern Sports Corp. (ESC). The terms of the agreement required CAT to provide in-game advertising to ESC in exchange for ESC providing CAT with in-game advertising on its website. CAT normally does not sell advertising space in its games, and likely would not have been able to sell the advertising for cash. Since this is a new transaction for CAT, the fair value is difficult to estimate, but management believes the advertising is worth $200,000. ESC normally sells in-game advertising, and estimates the fair value of the advertising provided is $250,000. It is unlikely that CAT management would have paid cash for the advertising received. The transaction has been recorded as a credit to revenue and a debit to advertising expense for $200,000.

- The company recently began selling the games of smaller companies on its website. The games are sold for $1 (credit card payments only), with 95 cents going to the game designing company and 5 cents being retained by CAT. The selling price of the game is established by the game designer. The game designer retains any continuing commitment to the customer after the game is purchased (e.g., game updates, modifications). During the year, 1 million games were downloaded, resulting in CAT recording $1 million in revenue and $950,000 in cost of goods sold.

- CAT began selling two-year, nonrefundable memberships. The memberships are sold for $75 and allow users to download any 100 games during the two-year period. During the year, 15,000 memberships were sold. Accordingly, members can download up to a maximum of 1.5 million games under the membership. On average, a member downloads 85 games. During the current year, a total of 475,000 games were downloaded under the agreement. Management decided to record revenue of $1,125,000 during the current year as CAT has no further work required to service the memberships. Currently, CAT has over 200 games in its library available for download.

- During the year, the company purchased the rights to develop a game based on a popular comic book hero. CAT paid $175,000 for this exclusive right, and incurred an additional $475,000 in programming costs to create the game, and $205,000 in promotional costs. CAT capitalized $855,000 as an intangible asset. The following are the expected downloads for the game, which will be sold for $1.99:

		Downloads		
	Probability	Year 1	Year 2	Year 3
Optimistic	25%	300,000	200,000	55,000
Average	60%	165,000	90,000	20,000
Pessimistic	15%	75,000	50,000	5,000

- CAT purchased 30-year bonds of another public company for $500,000. The bonds were purchased in the prior year and classified as FV-NI as the fair value was increasing as rates decreased. During the current year, the bonds declined in value by $40,000 as central banks began to raise rates in order to combat inflation. At the beginning of the year, management reclassified the bonds to amortized cost as the company plans on holding the bonds until maturity, and the bond is a pure debt instrument.

- At the beginning of the year, CAT issued 100,000 redeemable preferred shares to the public for $5 each. The preferred shares have a dividend yield of 7%. The preferred shares must be redeemed if the common share price exceeds $20 per share. Dividends of $35,000 were declared and paid during the year.

- During the year, CAT was named in a patent infringement lawsuit in regards to the use of various trademarked logos. The company's lawyers believe that there is a 50% chance that the case will be settled with no damages to be paid by CAT. However, there is a chance that the company may have to pay between $100,000 and $200,000 in damages. As of year end, both the $100,000 and $200,000 amounts are equally likely (50% each).

Draft financial statements reveal revenue and earnings of $7,478,000 and $2,257,000, respectively. Management displayed their excitement for their ability to meet analysts' revenue and earnings expectation. The partner has asked you to prepare a memo for the audit file that discusses the appropriate accounting treatment of the above-noted transactions. The memo will be used as part of the audit planning process.

Required

Prepare the memo.

Interstellar Explorations Ltd.

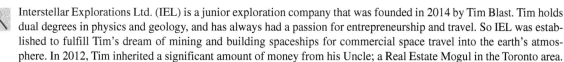

Interstellar Explorations Ltd. (IEL) is a junior exploration company that was founded in 2014 by Tim Blast. Tim holds dual degrees in physics and geology, and has always had a passion for entrepreneurship and travel. So IEL was established to fulfill Tim's dream of mining and building spaceships for commercial space travel into the earth's atmosphere. In 2012, Tim inherited a significant amount of money from his Uncle; a Real Estate Mogul in the Toronto area.

After completing his Master's Degree from Laurentian, Tim decided to venture out on his own; and Interstellar Explorations Limited was created. Based on a research project, he worked on while completing his Master's Degree, Tim is convinced that minerals found in the far Canadian North have the same chemical make-up as asteroidal and lunar materials. Research has shown that lunar materials will make propellants that are far better and safer than the current propellants used in Spacecraft rocket boosters.

IEL was incorporated in January 2016. Tim injected $7 million of his own money into IEL in return for all of the 2,000,000 common shares.

With the money, IEL purchased all of the assets of Star Traks (ST) for $2,500,000. The assets included a building, equipment, and patents. ST was founded to build small commercial spacecraft capable of bringing four to eight passengers into space and then safely back to earth. ST was never able to be viable because they lacked the proper rockets to safely get out of the earth's atmosphere and back again. However, their patents for the creation of the actual ship have been proven to be quite viable and useful for IEL.

In 2017, IEL began negotiating the purchase of 2,000 acres of land up in the Northern tip of Nunavut for $1,000,000. Key portions of the agreement IEL signed with the Territory of Nunavut is detailed in Exhibit I.

IEL currently has two key patents on its books. The first patent is recorded at $325,000 (purchased from Star Traks) and is for the spacecraft design. The second patent is a manufacturing patent that covers the processes of the refined minerals into the necessary propellant. This patent is recorded at $95,000 based on internal costs to register the patent.

Very little happened with IEL until January 1, 2020, when mine development and equipment purchasing began happening quickly. In June, 2020, Tim decided that a fulltime controller was needed to head his young company. As a result, you, a recent CPA, were hired.

Your most important task is to recommend accounting policies, with support, for some of the key activities that IEL has currently undertaken, along with recommendations for some of the planned future activities. You should also ensure you examine any subsequent measurement issues of items currently on the financial statements. Tim would like you to prepare a report to him that addresses the issues, alternatives, and your recommendations.

Details of assumptions, other key information, and key activities for the year follow:

Assumptions

- Audited financial statements for 2016 to December 2019 were completed and an unmodified opinion was given in every year. No mining activity occurred during this time frame and no space ships were manufactured; you may assume that all activities prior to January 2020 have been dealt with to the satisfaction of the auditors.

- The auditors are the same ones that IEL has had since inception.

- IEL is currently a private company but at the recommendation of their auditors, they have always chosen policies based upon eventually going public.

Other Information

- Based on your research, you expect that the patent on the spacecraft has projected cash flows for the next 8 years of $50,000 per year and that the patent on the propellant has projected cash flows of $10,000 for the next 10 years. Fair value, less costs to sell for the Star Traks patent is estimated to be $320,000 and the second patent at $85,000.

Required

Prepare the report to Tim.

Key Activities During 2020

Twilight Technologies

In March 2020, Tim incorporated a Holding Company and purchased 60% of the outstanding shares of Twilight Technologies (TT). Tim personally holds 100% ownership in the Holding Company. TT manufactures high-end computer components. Tim believes that TT will eventually be able to manufacture and sell these computer components to IEL, to be used in the spaceships. Currently TT sells much of its equipment to organizations such as NASA and Intelligence Agencies.

Financing

IEL anticipates needing more funding as its mining activities are expected to increase dramatically in 2021. As a result, IEL has entered into the following arrangements during 2020:

Preferred Shares

IEL sold 100,000 preferred shares at $20 to 10 key investors (each one investing equally). The preferred shares pay a $2 cumulative dividend and have a unique redeemable feature. IEL believes it will have its first space flight in 2026, as long as the mineral extraction goes according to plan. Beginning in 2026, preferred shareholders may redeem 5,000 preferred shares for one ticket on the spacecraft. The redemption period ends in 2031. Any preferred shares not redeemed by 2031 will be purchased back by IEL at a rate of $15 per share. The tickets will be good for any flight from 2026 until 2046 at which time, they will expire with no return. The preferred shares were purchased within 24 hours of being announced, mostly by wealthy business individuals and celebrities.

Common Shares

IEL expects to go public in 2021 as news of its use of minerals to provide the necessary propellant have created huge press releases. Tim expects to sell off 45% of IEL and underwriters are expecting an initial offering price of $55 per share.

Debt Financing

In order to manage the quickly escalating costs of mining, IEL obtained a revolving line of credit, secured by its patents for $4,000,000. The line of credit carries a 6% interest rate due to the riskiness of IEL's operations. Annual audited financial statements within 90 days of year end are a requirement of the loan along with a current ratio covenant of a minimum of 1:1. Current rates of return can be found in Exhibit II.

Revenue

Mineral Extraction

IEL expects to extract and process the minerals in the mine for use in their rocket boosters; however, this will account for only 60% of the minerals extracted. IEL has determined that the minerals, unrefined, are also commercially viable for several other businesses and they expect to sell the balance of the 40% immediately upon extraction. The current market rate for similar minerals is 0.94 cents per tonne. Initial estimates project the following extraction by IEL over the next eight years:

Year	Estimated Tonnes (unrefined)
2019	3,000,000
2020	12,000,000
2021	13,000,000
2022	10,000,000
2023	10,000,000
2024	10,000,000
2025	7,000,000
2026	3,000,000
Total	68,000,000

Space Travel

A significant goal of Tim's is to use IEL to produce the propellant needed for his rockets and spacecraft. There is a huge and lucrative market for individuals wanting to experience a ride in space. The current market price for a future ride in space is $200,000 per ticket. In addition to any tickets that might be redeemed by the investors, IEL has already sold 10 tickets to other individuals wishing to be the first in line for a seat.

The tickets had to be paid for upfront with expected travel to begin in 2026. Should a customer wish not to travel and a seat was available, they would forfeit their ticket; tickets are not transferable. Should IEL not be able to provide a seat; either due to delays or the inability to fly, the entire ticket would become refundable (at the holder's option) in 2036.

Exhibit I	Nunavut Agreement—Key Highlights

- Land was purchased for $2,000,000.
- As a part of the sale, IEL agreed to restore the site after mining was done. At the end of the eight year life, IEL must ensure the land is restored. The estimated cost of doing so is $1,800,000 at that time.
- In agreeing to sell the land to IEL, Nunavut required a contingent fee clause to be added to the sale contract. The clause requires IEL to pay Nunavut 2% of the market value of the estimated total minerals extracted on a yearly basis beginning January 1, 2023. The fee does not become payable until January 2024 based upon amounts extracted for the year ended December 31, 2023. There will be no fee payable for any minerals extracted in 2021 or 2022. This fee was an agreement required as part of the sale of the land. IEL also agreed to the demands made by Nunavut to pay the yearly fee regardless of whether or not they extracted the estimated minerals from the land.

Exhibit II	Current Rates of Return	
Treasury Bill		1%
Long-term Government of Canada Bond		2%
Corporate Bond AAA		5%

Northern Arts Ltd.

Northern Arts Ltd. (NAL) is a developer and distributor of video games. The company became public three years ago, and now trades on the Toronto Stock Exchange under the ticker NAL. Its main source of revenue is packaged video games, although the company has begun to earn more significant revenues from mobile device games and online gaming.

The video game industry is characterized by its many participants frequently launching new games, which may be new game concepts or sequels of popular game franchises. NAL has five popular sports game franchises, and two role-playing franchises. In addition, NAL is always developing and offering new products in the hopes that it too will become a franchise title. The fierce competition in the industry is based on product quality and features, timing of product releases, brand-name recognition, availability and quality of in-game content, access to distribution channels, effectiveness of marketing, and price.

Many analysts have been following NAL's stock since its initial public offering. The following are the analysts' expectation of NAL's EPS, along with the reported earnings:

	2020	2019	2018
Expectation	0.07	0.05	(0.15)
Actual	?	(0.03)	(0.11)
Surprise	?	(0.08)	0.04

NAL missed earnings expectations in 2019, but exceeded expectations in 2018. NAL's share price reacts significantly to the earnings surprise. The following chart outlines NAL's share price over the past three years, and highlights the earnings announcement dates:

Management of NAL does not want to disappoint the analysts again this year, following fiscal 2019's large, negative earnings surprise. The most recent run-up in share price is the result of analysts' expectations that NAL can continue to grow earnings and report positive earnings. These expectations are based on a combination of management issuing positive earnings guidance, positive earnings surprises reported by many industry competitors, and the growth potential offered by the mobile gaming industry.

Olivares and Samson, LLP has been NAL's auditor since inception and you have been the audit senior on the file for the past three years. Recently, Pedro Rodriguez, the partner in charge of the audit, met with management of NAL to discuss the upcoming year-end audit. Management displayed their pleasure with the current year's financial performance as EPS exceeded the analysts' estimate.

Pedro has called you into his office to discuss the results of his meeting. He has provided you with the draft financial statements (Exhibit I), along with his notes from the meeting (Exhibit II). Pedro has asked that you prepare a report addressing the accounting issues that can be used at the next meeting between Pedro and NAL management.

Required

Prepare the report.

| Exhibit I | Draft Financial Statements |

NAL Entertainment Ltd.
Statement of Financial Position

As at December 31 (unaudited)	2020
Assets	
Current	
Cash	$ 129,870
Marketable securities	342,110
Accounts receivable	225,660
Inventory	176,780
Other assets	34,210
	908,630
Goodwill	125,780
Property, plant, and equipment, net	1,455,000
Intangible assets, net	10,231,507
	$12,720,917
Liabilities and shareholders' equity	
Current	
Accounts payable	134,550
Accrued and other liabilities	345,200
Deferred net revenue (packaged goods and digital content)	2,456,880
	2,936,630
Bonds outstanding (7%), issued at par	4,956,780
Common shares	5,035,850
Retained earnings (accumulated deficit)	(208,343)
	4,827,507
	$12,720,917

| Exhibit 1 | Draft Financial Statements (Continued) |

NAL Entertainment Ltd.
Income Statement

For the year ended December 31	2020 (Unaudited)	2019 (Audited)	2018 (Audited)
Sales	$ 3,475,690	$ 2,780,552	$ 1,946,386
Cost of sales	1,459,790	1,195,637	836,946
Gross profit	2,015,900	1,584,915	1,109,440
Expenses			
Marketing and sales	524,134	570,569	513,512
General and administrative	161,272	158,047	154,886
Research and development	463,657	459,020	440,660
Amortization of intangibles	533,297	522,631	517,405
Acquisition-related contingent consideration (note 1)	(28,000)	8,000	0
Goodwill impairment	0	5,000	0
Total operating expenses	1,654,360	1,723,268	1,626,463
Operating income (loss)	361,540	(138,353)	(517,022)
Gain (losses) on marketable securities	12,455	(4,400)	1,200
Income (loss) before taxes	373,995	(142,753)	(515,822)
Provision for (benefit from) income taxes	104,719	(39,971)	(144,430)
Net income (loss)	269,276	(102,782)	(371,392)
EPS	0.08	(0.03)	(0.11)
Weighted-average number of shares outstanding	3,500,000	3,430,000	3,361,400
Opening balance—retained earnings	(477,619)	(374,837)	(3,445)
Net income	269,276	(102,782)	(371,392)
Dividends	0	0	0
Closing balance—retained earnings	$ (208,343)	$ (477,619)	$ (374,837)

Note 1—Contingent consideration for a football game franchise purchased in 2019.

| Exhibit II | Noted from Meeting with NAL's Management |

- During the year, the board of directors approved a new compensation package for management. The new package moves away from cash-based compensation toward stock-based compensation. Details on the new stock-based compensation program will be provided to Pedro at the next meeting.

- The intangible asset breakdown is as follows:

	Gross Amount	Accumulated Amortization	Net
Acquired technology	$ 1,924,560	$ 213,840	$ 1,710,720
Licences	765,000	85,000	680,000
Software	8,960,900	1,120,113	7,840,788
	$11,650,460	$1,418,953	$10,231,508

- The software intangible asset is broken down as follows:

Hockey game franchise	$1,004,567
Golf game franchise	780,976
Wrestling game franchise	756,780
Baseball game franchise	765,890
Soccer game franchise	556,662
Mobile strategy game	490,500
Mythical Legend game franchise	1,750,890
Antique Legacy game franchise	1,734,523
	$7,840,788

- The NBV of the property, plant, and equipment is utilized in operations as follows:

Acquired technology	$ 260,597
Sports game franchise	588,744
Mobile games	74,719
Role-playing game franchise	530,940
	$1,455,000

- The sporting games, as a combined unit, are expected to sell the following copies:

Year	1	2	3	4	5	6	7
Copies sold	120,000	110,000	100,000	100,000	100,000	90,000	90,000

The sporting games have sold for an average of $50 per copy, and generally result in costs of $750,000 annually for updates.

- Management believes that the licences are used by each unit based on the extent of their intangible assets.

- The role-playing games, as a combined unit, are expected to sell the following copies:

Year	1	2	3	4	5	6	7
Copies sold	45,000	20,000	15,000	125,000	85,000	35,000	15,000

The role-playing games have sold for an average of $35 per copy, and with no annual costs required for upgrades. The large increase in sales in Year 4 is based on the expectation that both role-playing games will have developed and published a sequel game in the continuing storyline. The cost of developing the sequel is $1,750,000.

- During the year, NAL capitalized costs related to the development of a new strategy game concept for mobile devices. The following expenses were capitalized:

| Exhibit II | Noted from Meeting with NAL's Management (Continued) |

New Mobile Device Game—Capitalized Costs

• Market research related to popular military game features:	$ 75,000
• Design of characters and writing story line:	115,000
• Programming and coding of game play:	235,000
• Pilot testing and error analysis:	17,500
• Marketing and promotional material:	48,000
	$490,500

Given the fierce competition in the mobile device gaming industry, combined with a short gaming life span, management is uncertain about the future revenues to be earned by the new game; however, management does believe that the game will be successful if priced at $1.99 per download. Management has developed the following forecast of downloads:

		Downloads		
	Probability	Year 1	Year 2	Year 3
Optimistic	10%	300,000	200,000	55,000
Average	65%	165,000	90,000	20,000
Pessimistic	25%	75,000	50,000	5,000
Probability Weighted Average		156,000	91,000	19,750

- The acquired technology resulted from the acquisition of a successful professional football game franchise from SQUARE CUBE Software (SCS). NAL purchased the software for $1,924,560 cash on the assumption that 30,000 copies would be sold annually. The agreement includes a contingent consideration clause whereby NAL must pay SCS a royalty of 5% of sales on any copy sold in excess of 30,000. Conversely, SCS must pay NAL a 5% fee if 30,000 copies are not sold. The 5% fee is calculated based on the difference between 30,000 and the number of copies sold, assuming that each copy would sell at $40.

- Given a recent lockout in professional football, the popularity of the sport has declined. Only 23,000 copies of the football game were sold during the past year. The following forecast is available for future sales:

Year	1	2	3	4	5	6	7
Copies sold	25,000	27,500	30,000	30,000	30,000	30,000	30,000

Each copy is expected to sell for an average of $40 per game. In addition, it is expected to cost $300,000 each year in maintenance in order to upgrade the game play, rosters, functionality, cover design, etc.

- NAL shipped 10,000 copies of the above noted football game to a new retailer. The games were shipped in early December in hopes that the retailer could promote and sell the units over the holiday season. In order to entice the retailer to take on such a large number of units, NAL provided a general right of return on any unsold copies up to January 15, 2021. As a result of the right of return, NAL did not recognize any revenue on the sale. Based on experience with other retailers, it is very likely that at least half of the order will be sold to customers.

- Included in the inventory balance are 7,500 units of NAL's basketball franchise game with a cost of $17.50 per game. The cover of the basketball game is a superstar who is known for his great on-court play, along with his "bad boy" attitude. Just prior to the year end, the superstar was arrested as a result of a domestic disturbance. It is unclear if the superstar will miss any time on the court as a result of this incident; however, many parent groups have began protesting the fact that the superstar is included on the cover of the game. The impact of this event on the resale value of the game is unknown.

- The marketable security breakdown is as follows:

	2020 FV
Equities	$245,788
Fixed-income	78,665
Short-term treasuries	17,657
	$342,110

The marketable securities are classified as fair value through profit or loss. During the year, NAL realized gains of $12,455 on securities that were sold. The fair value of the securities still held by NAL at the beginning of the period was $306,978.

Radiant Fireplace and BBQ Inc.[1]

Radiant Fireplace and BBQ Inc. (RFB) was founded in 1968 by Brad Piper. Over the next two decades, RFB became a leader in wood fireplaces and natural gas fireplaces. In 2001, RFB began to focus exclusively on natural gas fireplaces and gas barbeques. By 2008, RFB had grown to the point that increased production was necessary. Products were now in demand across North America. In order to obtain the financing needed for expansion, Brad decided to take the company public in 2009. The initial public offering resulted in Brad maintaining 60% ownership in RFB, with 40% of the company being widely held. Brad completed the first expansion in 2010.

RFB has been a client of your accounting firm since 2016. Sales have steadily increased since you began as the audit senior. You are now manager on the annual audit. RFB is traded on the TSX and there have never been any major issues with the annual audit. In early 2020, Brad decided it was time to step away from some of the day-to-day operational activities of RFB. He wanted to focus on production and take some time off and travel with his wife. In order to ensure that operations ran smoothly, Brad hired a controller, Margie Douglas, to oversee the financial operations of RFB. He also wanted Margie to increase sales of RFB's in order to take advantage of the increased production capacity and to utilize sunk costs. Margie was a recent CPA, gaining most of her articling hours at a nonprofit organization in a small town about an hour away. In addition to Margie's base salary, Brad offered her a bonus of 8% of income before tax that exceeded $5 million. Brad chose $5 million as the baseline amount because that has been the average over the last four years and he really wanted to motivate Margie to do well in his absence. Margie signed the contact and began working in March 2020.

Brad went ahead with another expansion plan during 2020 in order to meet the increasing production demand. In order to finance the expansion, Brad entered into several agreements and asked Margie to ensure that the amounts were recorded correctly. These transactions are detailed in Exhibit I.

It is now early February 2021 and you are working on the audit for RFB's 2020 fiscal year end. In discussions with Margie, you have found out that the second expansion completed in the middle of June has been very favorable. "Our sales have really increased as a result of the expanded facilities," Margie comments. "In fact I have managed to sign some interesting contracts this year, even with Brad away so much." The unaudited income before tax for the year ended December 31, 2020, is currently at $6.2 million. As a result of this favorable outcome, Margie has booked a bonus liability in the amount of $96,000.

You have been asked by the partner in charge of the audit to examine the transactions in Exhibit I and provide her with your recommendations on the accounting treatment along with any other concerns you may have. Assume an income tax rate of 40% and that it has been RFB's policy to take a year's worth of depreciation in the year of acquisition and none in the year of disposal.

Required

Prepare the report for the partner in charge of the audit.

---

[1]The casebook authors would like to thank Valorie Leonard, Laurentian University, for her feedback on this case.

Exhibit I | Radiant Fireplace and BBQ Inc. Transactions

Nickelback Fire

In October 2020, RFB purchased 18% of Nickelback Fire (NF) for $630,000. NF is a private company producing piping for natural gas fireplaces. RFB felt that NF's production facilities would be a good match for the company. RFB has one member on the 12-member board of directors. NF declared a $100,000 dividend in November 2020 and recorded net income and comprehensive income of $600,000 for its December 31, 2020, year end. Margie believes that NF is a very important investment for RFB and hopes to persuade NF to put more RFB members on the board in the future. Margie recorded the investment in NF by picking up RFB's share of NF's income for the year. Your quick research shows that there is very little information regarding similar types of companies.

Plant Expansion

The plant expansion involved the building of a new 9,200 square-metre (100,000 square-foot) facility. The total cost of the building was $4.5 million. The building qualifies as a class 1 asset for capital cost allowance (CCA) purposes with the enhanced deduction (therefore allowing it a 10% CCA rate). The building was put in use July 1, 2020. Margie determined that the new building had a useful life of 30 years. Margie recorded depreciation in the amount of $75,000. You note that no deferred taxes have been recorded. Research showed that a typical facility of this nature generally has a 20-year useful life.

Financing

In order to finance the entire plant expansion, RFB issued $3 million of bonds on July 1, 2020. The bonds are five-year bonds with semi-annual interest payments of 3%. The current market rate was 4% at the time of issuance. Brad mentioned to Margie that they would watch interest rates and if things changed, he would be investigating the possibility of redeeming them. RFB does have the ability to redeem the bonds at any time without any penalty. At year end, Margie recorded the interest expense and payment made on December 31, 2020, for $45,000. The current yield rate for very similar bonds remains at 4% as of year end.

The balance of the financing was raised through the issuance of 10,000 cumulative preferred shares with a dividend rate of $5 per share. The preferred shares are retractable at the option of the holder at any time after 2020. Dividends were declared and paid by December 2020. The dividends were recorded through retained earnings.

Production Contracts

In an attempt to increase revenues, Margie entered into two production contracts in geographical areas previously untapped by NFB. NFB completed a contract for Birmingham Heat totaling $380,000. The contract called for the production of several hundred specialty fireplaces. Production of the fireplaces was completed on December 15, 2020, and shipped via Merck Liners FOB shipping point on December 28. On January 5, 2021, Margie found out that the fireplaces had still not arrived at Birmingham Heat due to a customs issue. Birmingham Heat hopes to have the issue resolved in two weeks.

The second contract called for the production of $420,000 of fireplaces and barbecues to Maldovia Heat Inc., located in a small country overseas. The products were delivered to the overseas company on December 18, 2020. On December 22, political unrest toppled the government in the country. The new government that was installed has refused to allow any monies to leave the country.

Margie has recorded the revenue and related receivable for both contracts for the year ended December 31, 2020.

Production Accident

In October 2020, RFB found out that one of the air tubes used in its barbecues was incorrectly made. As a result, several customers throughout Western Canada and the Northeastern United States became ill or were injured. There is currently a lawsuit pending that may result in claims being paid out. When your partner asked Margie about insurance, she stated that she had downgraded the insurance this year, saving the company $100,000. In doing so, exposure of damages as a result of these tubes is not covered. Margie has not recorded any amount yet in the financial statements because the lawsuit has yet to go to trial. Documentation from the lawyers suggests that there is a 5% probability that there will be no amount payable for the claim, a 25% chance that $200,000 would have to be paid, a 50% chance that $500,000 would be due, and a 20% chance that $700,000 in claims will have to be paid.

Westhouse Publishing Enterprises

Westhouse Publishing Enterprises (WPE) is a private company that publishes a wide variety of books, including textbooks, hardcover books, and paperbacks. You, a CPA, have been providing a variety of consulting services (including accounting, finance, and controls) to WPE over the past 10 years.

It is now February 7, 2021, and you have been approached by Angela Pumpet, the CEO and sole shareholder of WPE. WPE is considering a strategic acquisition of E-Readerz Ltd. (ERL). ERL is a mid-sized private Canadian company that produces e-readers for e-books. WPE will be purchasing all of ERL's shares. The preliminary purchase price has been determined based on revenue and income multiples. Revenue and income must be determined in accordance with GAAP.

Currently, ERL's financial statements are prepared in accordance with ASPE, while WPE uses IFRS. Both companies have a December 31 year end. Upon acquisition, WPE will convert ERL's financial statements to IFRS so that consolidated financial statements can be more easily prepared.

Angela would like you to review ERL's most recent financial information and identify any differences between ASPE and IFRS. Angela is concerned that ERL will need to complete a full retrospective adjustment to ERL's financial statements the first time that IFRS is adopted.

In order to complete this task, Angela provides you with excerpts from the notes to ERL's most recent unaudited financial statements (Exhibit I) and summary notes from a meeting between Angela and ERL's management team (Exhibit II).

Angela would like your report to discuss each identified difference in the following format:

Difference: Will this affect recognition, measurement, presentation, and/or disclosure?

ASPE standard: Briefly discuss the ASPE standard.

IFRS standard: Briefly discuss the related IFRS standard, and provide alternatives with IFRS for going forward (if any).

Implication: How can this affect the purchase price?

In addition to discussing the differences between ASPE and IFRS, Angela would like your insights on the appropriate accounting for a few unique transactions (Exhibit III).

Required

Prepare the report for Angela.

Exhibit I	Excerpts from ERL's Notes to Financial Statements

Note 1: Property, plant, and equipment

Property, plant, and equipment (PPE) are recorded at cost less accumulated depreciation. Depreciation is estimated on a straight-line basis over the estimated useful life of each class. The following schedule summarizes the company's PPE:

	Cost	Accumulated Depreciation	2020 Net Book Value	2019 Net Book Value	Remaining Useful Life (Years)
Land	$ 43,273	$ 0	$ 43,273	$ 43,273	n/a
Building	2,985,222	1,641,872	1,343,350	1,612,020	20
Equipment	1,422,200	782,210	639,990	767,988	15
Computer	245,211	134,866	110,345	132,414	7
Furniture and fixtures	78,521	43,187	35,334	42,401	7
Vehicles	35,895	19,742	16,153	19,384	6
	$4,810,322	$2,621,877	$2,188,445	$2,617,480	

Note 2: Impairment testing

Long-lived assets are reviewed for impairment upon the occurrence of events or changes in circumstances indicating that the carrying value of the asset may not be recoverable, as measured by comparing their net book value with the estimated undiscounted future cash flows generated by their use. Impaired assets are recorded at fair value, determined principally using discounted future cash flows expected from their use and eventual disposition. During the year, impairment testing was conducted and no impairment was recorded. All PPE is seen as a single cash-generating unit and a 5% discount rate is used to present value cash flows.

Note 3: Development costs

ERL expenses the development costs. For example, costs associated with the development of the Pages e-reader were expensed in the most recent year.

Note 4: Operating lease

Leases that are classified as operating leases are expensed over the passage of time.

Note 5: Financial assets

The company has various strategic and nonstrategic assets that are being measured at fair value. Any changes in fair value are recorded in net income. The following is a summary of the financial assets:

Investment	Cost	Fair Value
Portfolio investments	$752,000	$852,000
Shares in Books Ltd.	$254,000	$375,000

The investments in Books Ltd. represent 8% of the total shares outstanding. ERL does significant business with Books Ltd. and is looking to acquire a strategic investment position over the next three years.

Exhibit II	**Summary Notes from Meeting with ERL's Management**

Pages E-reader Development

During the year, ERL developed Pages. The Pages device is an advanced e-reader as it has a new touch screen technology that is superior to those of competitors. ERL incurred the following costs in 2020 for the development of the Pages device.

Time Period (2020)	Activities	Costs Incurred
January	Researching and designing concepts	$300,000
Feb.–Mar.	Developing pilot and programming technology, updating the touch screen technology	$225,000
Apr.	Completing design, proving concept	$ 85,000
May	Board approves the new e-reader to be completed and sold	nil
June–July	Market trials completed and market response strong	$175,000
Aug.–Oct.	Packaging completed, patents filed, logos created, technology tested for bugs	$225,000
Nov.	Product is packaged and shipped to stores for holiday season	$ 85,000

The company is expected to generate additional cash flows of $275,000 in each of the next five years.

Fair Value of Capital Assets

ERZ obtained an appraisal of its capital assets in order to facilitate the purchase price agreement with WPE.

	Fair Value
Land	$ 75,728
Building	2,350,863
Equipment	1,119,983
Computer	193,104
Furniture and fixtures	61,835
Vehicles	28,268
	$3,829,781

The appraiser also identified the following components of the building:

	Fair Value	Net Book Value	Useful Life (Years)
Roof	$ 305,612	$174,636	7
Windows	493,681	282,104	12
Structure	775,785	443,306	25
Heating/ cooling system	164,560	94,035	10
Total	$1,739,638	$994,081	

All remaining items are considered to be part of the general building (not an identifiable component) with an estimated useful life of 10 years.

| Exhibit II | Summary Notes from Meeting with ERL's Management (Continued) |

Impairment Testing

The following cash flow information was used to test the recoverability of the PPE ($2,188,445):

Year	1	2	3	4	5	6	7	Total
Net cash flow	$350,000	350,000	350,000	350,000	350,000	350,000	350,000	$2,450,000

Operating Lease

During the year, ERL entered into a lease agreement for the manufacturing equipment required to produce the Pages device. The equipment is specialized to integrate with ERL's existing manufacturing equipment and information systems. The lease is for five years (11-year useful life), with annual lease payments of $252,000 (present value of minimum lease payments = $1,091,028). ERL could have purchased the asset for $1.5 million outright. There is no purchase option and the lease will revert to the lessor at the end of the lease term. This lease is being treated as an operating lease.

| Exhibit III | Unique Accounting Issues |

Sale to Wordz Book Store

ERL made a large shipment of e-readers to Wordz Book Store in December 2020. The sales agreement required Wordz to pay half of the amount upfront, with the remaining balance to be paid only when the e-readers are sold. Any e-readers that are not sold after four months can be returned to ERL for a full refund. ERL entered into this agreement because management believes with a high level of certainty that Wordz's large outlet network and turnover of e-readers will ensure that the entire shipment will be sold. ERL has recorded the entire contract amount of $1,750,000 as revenue in the current year.

Advertising Agreement between WPE and ERL

Prior to the acquisition discussions, WPE and ERL entered in an agreement whereby WPE would provide advertising to ERL on its website in exchange for ERL providing free e-reader advertising to WPL. The advertising WPE provided was free banner ads on the e-book download website, while the advertising provided by ERL to WPE was in-text banners in e-readers and in free e-books. The market value of the advertising provided by WPE is $225,000 while the market value of the advertising provided by ERL is $250,000. ERL recorded the transaction as advertising revenue of $225,000 and advertising expense of $225,000. Neither WPE nor ERL have paid cash for such advertising in the past.

Whiteware Industries

Whiteware Industries (WI) is a closely held company owned by the Mahood family. The company has a long history dating back to the early 1900s. The company manufactures small household appliances, such as toasters, blenders, coffee makers, and indoor grills. WI's products are well known for their quality and affordability.

Recently, the company has been experiencing poor financial results due increased competition, lack of new product development, and the increasing power of the retailers in the supply chain. As a result, Dennis Mahood, the former CEO, was recently relieved of his duties.

On September 1, 2020, the board of directors elected to hire Allan Peters as the new CEO. Allan is a well known turnaround specialist and is the first person outside of the Mahood family to become CEO of WI.

It is now January 7, 2021, and WI is preparing for its December 31, 2020 year-end financial statement audit. WI is a long standing client of the public accounting firm of Lebeau and Liang, LLP. You are the senior accountant with Lebeau and Liang, LLP who is responsible for WI's audit. The partner in charge of the audit recently met with Allan, and has provided you with a copy of the draft financial statements (Exhibit I) and notes from her meeting with Allan (Exhibit II). The partner has asked you to prepare a memo to the audit file that addresses your concerns regarding any financial accounting issues.

Required

Prepare the report for the audit file.

Exhibit I   **Draft Financial Statements**

Whiteware Industries
Statement of Financial Position

As at December 31 (unaudited)	2020
Assets	
Current	
Cash	$ 50,675
Marketable securities	115,200
Accounts receivable	174,930
Inventory	837,040
Other assets	250,000
	1,427,845
Property, plant, and equipment, net	1,300,000
	$2,727,845
Liabilities and shareholders' equity	
Current	
Accounts payable	$ 104,305
Accrued and other liabilities	267,595
Deferred revenue	345,900
	717,800
Long-term debt	659,000
Common shares	1,098,258
Retained earnings	252,787
	1,351,045
	$2,727,845

| Exhibit I | Draft Financial Statements (Continued) |

Whiteware Industries
Income Statement

For the Year Ended December 31 (unaudited)	2020
Sales	$2,775,990
Cost of sales	1,499,035
Gross profit	1,276,955
Expenses	
Depreciation and amortization	155,490
General and administrative	534,500
Marketing and sales	459,704
Office expense	395,980
Wages and benefits, administration	515,000
Total operating expenses	$1,905,184
Operating income (loss)	$ (628,229)
Gain (loss) on marketable securities	12,455
Impairment loss on capital assets	(327,900)
Income (loss) before taxes	(943,674)
Provision for (benefit from) income taxes	(264,229)
Net income (loss)	(679,445)
Opening balance—retained earnings	932,232
Net income	(679,445)
Dividends	0
Closing balance—retained earnings	$ 252,787

| Exhibit II | Notes from the Partners' Meeting with Allan |

- Allan signed a 16-month contract on September 1, 2020. Allan was paid an upfront signing bonus of $80,000, a monthly salary of $2,000, and a bonus of 15% of 2021 net income. The signing bonus was paid in September, and expensed in fiscal 2020 as part of the wages and benefits, administration. The bonus is not repayable if Allan leaves prior to the 16 months.

- On August 1, 2020, WI entered into a sales agreement with Big Box Outlets, a large Canadian retailer. Under the terms of the agreement, WI shipped 70,000 coffee makers to Big Box Outlets, which placed the products in special display booths throughout its stores in Canada. Big Box Outlets is able to return any unsold appliances to WI up to February 1, 2021 (just after the holiday season). The coffee makers are sold to retailers for $22 each and have a cost of $10 each.

  Past history under similar arrangements suggests that at least 60% of the appliances are sold during the holiday season (i.e., just before New Year's Eve). Allan has decided not to record any revenue until the right of return period lapses.

Year:	1	2	3	4	5	6	7
Cash Flow:	350,000	350,000	450,000	450,000	300,000	300,000	250,000

  The fair value of the capital assets, less costs to sell, is estimated to be $1.3 million. The net book value of the property, plant, and equipment was $1,627,900 prior to Allan recording an impairment loss of $327,900.

- WI operates a small number of outlet stores that distribute their products. Allan has accrued a $100,000 liability for the closing of two unprofitable stores. Allan is currently unsure which stores will be closed, but is very sure that two stores will be closed in 2021, resulting in severance pay and other closing costs. The expense has been included in the general and administrative expenses.

- In fiscal 2019, 10,000 can openers held in inventory were written down from their historical cost of $5.50 each to their net realizable value of $4.00. The writedown was a result of a decrease in demand for the product due to child safety concerns. In fiscal 2020, a total of 5,000 of these can openers were sold. The can openers were sold for $7.50 each as it appears that the child safety concerns have subsided.

- On December 1, the company paid $250,000 in order to undertake a large marketing campaign. The marketing campaign is intended to help re-brand the company's products and to increase customer awareness of the company's product offering. The marketing campaign began in December and will run for four months over the Internet, television, radio, and on billboards. The entire $250,000 is included in the marketing and sales expense.

- There were no additions or dispositions in the marketable securities from 2019. The marketable securities are being held until 2021, at which point they will be used to help fund an expansion of the company's product offering. The following additional details are available regarding the marketable securities, with no entries posted in the current year:

- On July 1, 2020, WI exchanged 10,000 coffee makers to TeleCo, a large telecom company, in exchange for $280,000 worth of telecom services. The coffee makers have a cost of $14 and a retail value that ranges between $25 and $30 per unit. TeleCo plans to use the coffee makers in the staffrooms of its offices across North America. Allan posted the following journal entry:

Other Assets	250,000	
Inventory		250,000

- Given the recent poor financial performance, Allan decided to conduct an asset impairment test. The controller estimated that the following net cash flows are expected to be generated from the property, plant, and equipment (a reasonable discount rate is 8%):

	2020 FV	2019 FV
Equities	$155,788	$145,788
Fixed-income	81,665	78,665
Short-term treasuries	41,244	40,747
	$278,697	$265,200

- During the year, WI designed and developed a new technology for a toaster that toasts bread more evenly than the toasters on the market. The following costs were incurred during the year related to the toaster:

New Toaster Technology—Costs Expensed

• Developing heat insulation technology:	$ 35,450
• Developing inner toaster technology:	95,900
• Design of toaster outer casing:	37,500
• Patenting of toaster technology:	21,500
• Testing the prototypes prior to commercialization:	48,000
	$238,350

The toaster technology is expected to generate additional net cash flows of $35,000 for the next five years. Allan has expensed all of the costs as part of general and administrative expenses.

- On November 1, WI was sued by a competitor for a patent infringement suit. Legal counsel suggests that WI will be liable to make a payment. There is a 30% chance of a $50,000 payment, a 50% chance of a $100,000 payment, and a 20% chance of a $150,000 payment. Allan recorded a $150,000 contingent liability.

Integrative Cases

Canadian Airborn Technologies (CAT)

You, CPA, recently hired by Blackrock Investment Ltd.'s (BIL) internal audit department, are sitting in your office and planning for your upcoming meeting with the head of internal audit. It is January 20, 2021. You just returned from a week visiting Canadian Airborn Technologies (CAT), BIL's newest subsidiary.

CAT has been part of the BIL group of companies since late in 2019 and up to now had never been visited by internal auditors. As is standard practice at BIL, the internal audit department visits the subsidiary companies once a year to check on the functioning of the accounting systems and internal controls and to make sure that policies and procedures are being adhered to.

This was your first assignment and you thought it was a tough one because you have to prepare a report not only addressing the internal audit findings but also discussing the financial reporting issues you found related to IFRS.

As you sit down to write your report, you once again review the material gathered in your investigation. Exhibit I is a brief history of CAT; Exhibit II contains notes from your meeting with Mike Peterson, CAT's president; Exhibit III is a summary of the development costs incurred during 2020; Exhibit IV provides CAT's financial statements for the year ended December 31, 2020; and Exhibit V contains other information you gathered.

| Exhibit I | Brief History of Canadian Airborn Technologies (CAT)) |

Mike Peterson is an amateur inventor. He developed a new technology for air cleaning that is especially useful for spaces that do not have central forced air heating and cooling. The technology is more effective at removing airborne pollutants than any existing technology. Air was formed in 2016. Mike's goal for the company was to develop and market a new method for residential and commercial air cleaning. In 2018, Mike built and tested commercial prototypes for the new technology, which performed very well under difficult conditions. Because of the increase in asthma in children and the perceived decrease in air quality in many parts of Canada, Mike knew his technology would be very successful.

While Mike was convinced that the product would be successful, he did not have the resources to take the project any further. He was unsuccessful in obtaining financing from banks or venture capitalists and could not find anyone interested in purchasing an equity stake in CAT. Mike was about to give up when, in November 2018, he had a chance meeting with the chief executive officer of BIL, Frank Inster, at a local meeting of the asthma association. Mr. Inster is the father of two children who have severe asthma and Mike was demonstrating his product. Mr. Inster took an immediate interest. Mike loaned Mr. Inster his prototypes; Mr. Inster was very pleased that they helped improve his children's symptoms. Based on his personal experiences with the prototypes, Mr. Inster saw that the product had significant market potential and agreed to get involved in developing and marketing it.

In late 2019, Mike sold all the outstanding shares in CAT to BIL for $250,000. BIL agreed to finance the remaining research and development necessary to complete the product and bring it to market. The sale agreement required that Mike remain as president of CAT until December 31, 2010, to complete development of the product and launch it. Mr. Inster believed that Mike' knowledge was vital for the product's success. Mike' agreement with BIL stipulates that he receive a salary of $50,000 per year. In addition, he is to receive a bonus of $1 million if (a) the product is successfully brought to market, (b) at least 10,000 units of the product are sold at a minimum average price of $65 per unit by December 31, 2020, and (c) CAT generates a profit for the year ended December 31, 2020.

| Exhibit II | Notes from Meeting with Mike Peterson |

Mike explained that, from the time BIL acquired CAT until the end of 2019, his effort was directed toward refining the product. During that time, $300,000 was spent on improvements to the product and the full amount was expensed. CAT reported a loss for tax purposes of $424,000.

In early 2020, everything came together. All the glitches with the product were solved, and testing results were consistent and met the specifications. Sure that the product would be successful, Mike then turned all of his attention to selling the product.

In January and February 2020, marketing studies and production feasibility studies were carried out. In late April, Mike made a presentation to Frank Inster and received commitment of the funds required to get production underway. The manufacturing process is quite straightforward and relatively inexpensive, requiring only about $800,000 for manufacturing and assembly equipment. Despite a number of initial problems, the first full production run occurred in July. The first 900 units produced did not meet specifications and could not be shipped. The first shipment of units to customers was in August. Mike explained that the 900 units with specification problems are currently in inventory and he expects that, when time permits, they will be repaired and sold.

Mike said that he agreed to stay on with CAT for an additional three months (until March 31, 2021) by which time a new president for CAT should be hired. He said that Frank Inster did all he could to convince him to stay on longer but Mike explained that he is an inventor at heart, not a manager, and that, with the right president, CAT would continue its success.

Mike was very satisfied with initial demand for the product. He had arranged contracts with a number of national and local distributors, and early feedback from the distributors was favorable. However, Mike thought that the initial orders made by the distributors were unrealistically low and that they would quickly run out of inventory, which would cost CAT significant sales because customers might buy a competitor's product.

Mike thinks that market penetration is a key and he is not prepared to miss any sales. As a result, he often shipped significantly more units to distributors than ordered. While Mike assured any distributors that objected that they would see that the extra units were merited, he allowed them to delay payment until six months after delivery. At that time, they have to pay in full or return any unsold units shipped in excess of the initial amount ordered. Mike' first priority is getting product out the door. Once orders are sent to the shipping department, Mike wants the goods shipped within a day or two. Mike keeps production operating at full capacity to ensure that there is enough inventory in place to meet the anticipated demand.

Mike acknowledged that paperwork was a bit sloppy. Because of the strong demand for CAT's product, Mike had little time to pay attention to administrative tasks, devoting his time instead to selling and to making sure production was kept on schedule and orders were shipped on time. He pointed out that BIL had kept CAT on a fairly tight budget and, as a result, he was understaffed in the office.

Mike expects the paperwork to flow better once everyone gets used to the computer system and its glitches are fixed. The computer system was mandated by BIL and was installed by a small company recommended by BIL. The system was installed in May 2020. Mike complained that the computer company simply showed up one day, installed the system without any discussion of what was wanted or needed, and then left. It was never heard from again, except to render the bill.

Exhibit III	Summary of Development Costs During 2020

Costs incurred from January to March 2020:	
Marketing surveys	$ 65,000
Consultant's report on air quality issues	80,000
Search costs for production facility	70,000
Feasibility study for production facility	92,000
Costs incurred from April to July 2020:	
Cost of setting up production facility	37,000
Training of production staff	48,000
Costs incurred from August to December 2020:	
Production cost overruns during first three months of production	97,000
Selling, marketing, and promotion costs	118,000
Total development costs incurred	$607,000

Exhibit IV	Canadian Airborn Technologies

Extracts from the Internal Financial Statements
Balance Sheet
As at December 31, 2020

Assets	
Current assets	
Cash	$ 75,000
Accounts receivable	475,000
Inventory	303,620
Other current assets	35,000
	888,620
Property, plant, and equipment	767,650
Development costs	607,000
	$2,263,270

Liabilities	
Current liabilities	
Accounts payable and accrued liabilities	$ 302,000
Loan from parent company	2,500,000
	2,802,000

Shareholder's deficiency	
Share capital	278,670
Deficit	(817,400)
	(538,730)
	$2,263,270

| Exhibit IV | Canadian Airborn Technologies (Continued) |

Extracts from the Internal Financial Statements

Income Statement

For the year ended December 31, 2020

Revenue	$770,352
Cost of goods sold	295,352
Gross margin	475,000
Amortization of equipment	32,000
Selling, general, and administrative costs	201,000
Income before income taxes	242,000
Income taxes	75,400
Net income	$166,600

- CAT recognizes revenue when merchandise is shipped to customers. This method is consistent with BIL's standard accounting policy for other manufactured products.
- Amortization of the equipment began in August 2020 and is calculated on a straight-line basis over 10 years.

| Exhibit V | Other Findings |

CAT shipped the first units to customers in August 2020. Total units shipped during 2020 were 11,672. No other products are produced by CAT.

During 2020, CAT shipped 500 units as demonstration models to potential customers and to a variety of lung and asthma associations. The units were treated as sales with a selling price of $0.

Discussion with the accounts receivable clerk found considerable dissatisfaction with CAT's computer accounting system. When the clerk tried to reconcile the receivables list to the general ledger, she found that the listing sometimes had the same invoice number assigned to more than one shipment. The clerk said that she knows "for a fact" that different numbers were assigned but the computer seems to have its own ideas.

She also complained about difficulties with the monthly bank reconciliation, explaining that the accounting system keeps reporting as outstanding, cheques that have cleared the bank. "No matter how hard I try, I can't figure out how to get those cheques off the computer-generated list. Now when I do the bank reconciliation, I ignore the outstanding cheque list generated by the system because I have no confidence in it. Instead, I rely on a manual record that I keep."

The accounts payable clerk complained that many of the outstanding payables balances are not true payables but that they cannot be removed from the system. He explained that Air uses a purchase order system. He thinks that the problem might be that the receiver enters the receipt of the back-ordered items as a new-order receipt instead of going back to the original order. When the accounts payable clerk tried to fix the problem using the "over/under shipment"

menu item, access was denied. So, he has had to leave the old balances on the aged accounts payable report. The accounts payable clerk is frustrated because he is sure that there is an easier way to handle the shipments but can't figure it out.

Other members of CAT's staff complained that they weren't consulted in the development of the computer system and that they didn't receive any training. It seemed that they were supposed to figure it out for themselves. Some people complained that the system doesn't produce the information they need to do their jobs properly, generating useless reports instead. Some of these people have figured out how to circumvent the system to obtain the information they need.

From discussions with the shipper, there appear to be significant problems in the shipping department. The shipper seems overworked and extremely dissatisfied with the way shipping is managed. The shipper has been involved in shipping for 15 years and has never seen a mess like CAT's. It's virtually impossible for him to keep up with the orders that have to be shipped. "I'd say I'm two to three weeks behind getting orders out." The shipper said that he could use more help in the department, but he could probably get the job done if Mr. Shayne didn't get involved in what gets sent out. "It seems he's down here every day telling me to add a few more units to this order and to that order. The shipping documents are almost useless. I'd say that most orders go out of here with a different number of units than what is recorded on the shipping documents I receive from sales. In fact, they're so useless I don't even bother filing them anymore. I just toss them into that box in the corner."

| *Exhibit V* | **Other Findings (Continued)** |

Review of the accounting system showed that the billing process is initiated as soon as an order is confirmed and sent to the shipping department. Trade receivables and sales are recorded at that time.

Inventory records are perpetual. The inventory is reduced when goods are shipped. The shipper maintains a log of units shipped and the log is used to update the inventory records each day.

CAT operates in a rented facility. The production department occupies about 45% of the building, storage 25%, and offices and administration the rest. The full amount of rent is treated as a product cost and included in inventory. BIL's accounting policies state that only the rental cost associated with production should be inventoried. CAT also includes the cost of office staff, managers, and production supervisors in the cost of inventory.

CKER[1] Radio

In the fall of 2020, eight wealthy business people from the same ethnic background founded a committee (CKER committee) to obtain a radio licence from the Canadian RadioTelevision and Telecommunications Commission (CRTC). Their goal is to start a nonprofit, ethnic community radio station for their area. They plan to call the station CKER-FM Ethnic Radio (CKER). It will broadcast ethnic music, news, and sports from their country of origin, cultural information, ethnic cooking, and other such programs, seven days a week.

The station's capital requirements are to be financed by memberships, donations, and various types of loans. It is expected that on-going operations will be supported by advertising paid for by business people from that ethnic community and by the larger business community targeting that ethnic audience, as well as by donations and memberships.

It is now March 2021, and the CRTC has announced that hearings will start in one month on a number of broadcasting licence applications, including the CKER committee's application. The CKER committee members are fairly confident about the viability of their proposal; however, they have decided to seek the advice of a professional accounting firm to assist with the endeavor. The CKER committee has engaged Maria & Casano, Chartered Professional Accountants, for the assignment, as three of the five partners of the firm are from the same ethnic community. The partner in charge of the assignment has stated that the firm will donate half its fee for the work.

You, CPA, work for Maria & Casano and have been put in charge of the assignment. You have met with the CKER committee and various volunteers associated with the project. Information gathered on the station start-up is contained in Exhibit I. Exhibit II provides other information on the CKER committee's proposal. The partner has asked you to prepare a draft report to the committee members discussing the viability of the proposed radio station over the initial three-year period. Since the committee is fairly confident that they will receive the licence, the partner has also asked you to recommend accounting policies for the transactions that CKER is contemplating. Note that CKER is planning to adopt Accounting Standards for Not-for-Profits ("ASNPO") as outlined in the *CPA Canada Handbook – Part III*. Your report must also cover other significant is issues that the station will face after it commences operations.

Required

Prepare the draft report.

<table>
<tr><td>Exhibit I</td><td>Information on Station Start-Up</td></tr>
</table>

1. Costs to date have totaled $50,000 and are mostly transportation and meeting costs, as well as postage. These costs have been paid for personally by the CKER committee members.

2. To approve the license application, the CRTC must see written commitments to finance the station's start-up costs and operating losses in the first two years. Remaining costs to obtain the license, excluding donated legal work, are expected to be about $8,000 and will be paid by CK.ER committee members.

3. If the CRTC approves the license application, the CKER committee will immediately set up a nonprofit organization and apply to Canada Revenue Agency for charitable status, which it will likely receive.

4. Fairly exhaustive efforts to obtain commercial financing have failed. As a result, four wealthy individuals have volunteered to provide CKER with the financing for the startup costs. They will each personally borrow $25,000 from financial institutions and give the funds to the station. These individuals expect the loans to be cost free to them, as the station will make the interest and principal payments.

5. A "Reverse Life-Time Contribution" program will also be instituted. Under this program, a donor will pay the station a capital sum of at least $50,000. The station can do whatever it wants with the funds, but it will repay the donor an equal annual amount calculated as the capital sum divided by 90 years less the individual's age at the time of contribution. Upon the death of the donor, the station will retain the balance of the funds. Currently, a 64-year-old station supporter has committed $78,000, and seven other individuals are considering this method of assisting the station.

6. Initially, the station is to broadcast with a 2,500 watt signal. It is hoped that within three to four years it will be possible to obtain commercial financing for a second transmitter that will boost the power of the signal and the broadcast range.

---

[1] Adapted with permission from the Canadian Institute of Chartered Accountants 1996 Uniform Final Examination. Permission granted by the Canadian Chartered Professional Accountants. Any edits or modifications from the original materials are the sole responsibility of the authors, and have not been endorsed, reviewed or approved by the Canadian Chartered Professional Accountants.

Exhibit II # Other Information About Plans for Station

1. The CKER committee has analyzed census and other data to determine the potential market for the station. Engineering studies have mapped out the area that will be covered by the broadcast signal. There are about 1.1 million people in the target listening area. The latest Canadian census shows that 14% of the population comes from the target ethnic group. A number of surveys have shown that, of a given population, nearly 80% listen regularly to the radio. By applying a conservative factor of 50% to these findings, the CKER committee has arrived at a listenership figure of 5.6% or about 62,000 people. The CKER committee has found that about one in five of the businesses in the area are run by members of the ethnic community, many of whom would like a medium for reaching their own people through direct advertising.

2. The amount of time expected to be devoted to commercials per hour is four minutes in year one, five minutes in year two, and six minutes in year three. Advertising cost per minute, discounted to 25% below the current market rate, will be:

Prime time (6 hours a day)	$40
Regular time (10 hours a day)	$30
Off-peak (8 hours a day)	$25

Advertising time will be sold by sales people whose remuneration will be a 15% commission.

3. Miscellaneous revenue from renting out the recording studio when not in use by CKER could approach $3,000 per month in year three but will start out at about $2,200 per month.

4. At least 120 people have committed to pay a $125 annual membership fee. Membership carries no special privileges other than to be identified as a supporter of the station. Membership is expected to grow by 20% per year.

5. Start-up capital expenditures are as follows: transmission equipment $61,000; broadcast studio equipment $62,000; and production studio equipment $40,000. Administration and other costs, including rent, are expected to total about $1,237,000 per year and will not increase when advertising sales increase.

6. The Committee believes that there are HST implications related to running the station, since it is a nonprofit venture.

7. About one-third of the person-hours needed to run the station are expected to come from volunteers.

Hot Spot Ltd.

Hot Spot Ltd. (HSL) is an Internet-based company. The Company's main activity is running a Hindi-based Internet search engine, with a specific focus on content from the Republic of India. The Company is based out of Canada and was founded in 2010 by Bryan and Kim, two recently graduated computer science students.

The following is a summary of some of the major aspects of HSL's operations:

- Although there are other Hindi-based search engines, Bryan and Kim have developed a new and innovative technology that optimizes search results in a manner that is superior to other engines. The search engine requires users to login in and then uses a neural network and fuzzy logic to optimize search results for individual user accounts based on past searches. Users can rate the search results in order to further optimize future searchers.

- The Company generates revenues by selling advertising space that appears on a side bar of the search results screen. The advertising rates vary based on the time (day posts are more expensive than night posts), size, and other features of the posting.

- The Company is relatively new to the market, but its market share has been increasing steadily since its inception.

Recently, Bryan and Kim have been approached with a purchase offer by SearchCo., a larger, more established Internet search engine. SearchCo. has offered to purchase 100% of the outstanding shares of HSL for $900,000.

Bryan and Kim are unsure of how to proceed and have hired Lento and Lento LLP to provide some advice. You are a senior analyst with the Financial Advisory Service group of Lento and Lento, LLP. The partner in charge of the file has asked you to prepare a preliminary estimate of HSL's equity value in order to assess the reasonability of the purchase offer. In order to complete the engagement, the partner has provided you with the following information:

- Historical financial statements (Exhibit I);
- Information on comparable public companies (Exhibit II);
- Notes from a discussion with Bryan and Kim (Exhibit III).

Required

Prepare a preliminary estimate of value and assess the reasonableness of the offer. The partner has asked you to focus on the capitalized cash flow and hold off on any discounted cash flow methodology at this stage. The partner also requested that both the entity and equity approaches be utilized and reconciled to assess the reasonableness of the conclusion.

Exhibit I | Historical Balance Sheet and Income Statement

Hot Spot Limited
Balance Sheet
As at December 31, 2020, and 2019

ASSETS	2020	2019
Current assets		
Cash and cash equivalents	245,675	345,700
Receivables	48,595	55,785
Due from related party	25,000	25,000
Prepaid insurance	24,550	22,450
	343,820	448,935
Property and equipment	550,000	675,000
Intangible assets	850,000	850,000
	1,743,820	1,973,935
LIABILITIES AND SHAREHOLDERS' EQUITY		
Current liabilities		
Accounts payable and accrued liabilities	59,960	408,880
Due to related party	20,000	22,000
	79,960	430,880
Long-term debt	900,000	1,200,000
Shareholders' equity		
Share capital	64,480	200
Retained earnings	699,380	342,855
	763,860	343,055
	1,743,820	1,973,935

| Exhibit I | Historical Balance Sheet and Income Statement (Continued) |

Hot Spot Limited
Income statement
As at December 31, 2020, and 2019

	2020	2019
Revenues		
Online advertising services	844,330	755,670
Other services	35,675	34,555
	880,005	790,225
Operating costs		
Traffic acquisition costs	120,560	117,560
Bandwidth costs	66,785	65,780
Depreciation	59,500	62,750
Interest expense	52,500	67,500
Operational costs	38,900	45,670
Share-based compensation	45,000	45,000
Selling, general, and administration	8,215	7,680
Research and development	57,860	55,600
	449,320	467,540
Operating profit	430,685	322,685
Other income (expenses)		
Interest income	10,560	12,500
Gain (loss) on disposal of capital assets	4,750	(3,500)
Foreign exchange gain (loss)	23,130	18,770
	38,440	27,770
Income before income taxes	469,125	350,455
Income taxes	(112,600)	(84,100)
Net income	356,525	266,355
Retained earnings, beginning of the year	342,855	76,500
Retained earnings, end of the year	699,380	342,855

Exhibit II | **Comparable Public Company and Market Information**

- The following are multiple details for public companies that are in a similar industry:

Company Name	Trading Data			Market Capitalization			Performance Metrics					Enterprise Value Multiples				Equity Value Multiples	
	Trading Price	O/S Shares (millions)	Market Cap (millions)	Net Debt (millions)	EV	EBITDA	EBIT	Sales	EPS	Book value	EV / EBITDA	EV / EBIT	EV / Sales	EV / Book value	Price / Earnings	Price / Book value
	A	B	C = [A × B]	D	E = [C + D]	F	G	H	I	J	K = E/F	L = E/G	M = E/H	N = E/J	O = A/I	P = C/J
Baidu	141	267.32	37,622	12	37,634	667	601	1,171	2.53	1244	56.42	62.62	32.14	30.25	55.63	30.24
Yahoo!	16	1,262.59	20,113	142	20,255	1,752	1,070	6,324	0.82	12596	11.56	18.93	3.20	1.61	19.43	1.60
Google	616	323.18	199,081	379	199,460	12,192	10,796	29,321	30.86	46241	16.36	18.48	6.80	4.31	19.96	4.31
Microsoft	27	8,378.23	224,034	21,391	245,425	30,837	28,071	69,943	2.75	57083	7.96	8.74	3.51	4.30	9.72	3.92
Average											23.08	27.19	11.41	10.12	26.19	10.02

- The following market characteristics exist, given current market conditions:

Risk-free rate	2.00%
Equity risk premium	5.40%
Industry premium	6.00%

- The Company's β is 2.2.
- The Company is much smaller than many of the public companies listed above. Historical evidence suggests that company size has an inverse relationship with the cost of equity capital. Given the small size of the Company, a size premium of 4% is reasonable.

Exhibit III	Discussion with Bryan and Kim

- The fair market value of the property and equipment has been estimated to be approximately $675,000.

- Included in the property and equipment is a vacant parcel of land with an appraised value of $55,000. The land is next to the Company's head office and was required to be purchased with the office building. Sales fees are estimated to be 5%.

- The UCC of the capital assets is $455,000. The average CCA rate of the capital assets is 28%.

- An appropriate current ratio for the company is 1.5:1.

- The foreign exchange gain (loss) arises from advertising sales made in other countries.

- A total of $3,500 ($2,750) of interest income in 2020 (2019) was earned on the cash balance.

- Both Bryan and Kim have taken compensation only in the form of stock-based compensation. The stock options received were valued at $45,000 combined for Bryan and Kim in 2019 and 2020. However, Bryan and Kim have provided services to the Company that have a fair value of $55,000 each in 2020 and 2019.

- Included in the 2020 operational costs is $5,000 in legal fees that were paid to settle a patent infringement lawsuit.

- HSL's marginal tax rate is 24%, which is expected to continue in the foreseeable future.

- Bryan and Kim estimate that it will cost approximately $57,000 in expenditures, on average, each year in order to maintain the asset base. The average CCA rate for these capital assets is 28%.

- Included in the 2020 traffic acquisition costs is $15,000 for payments to a fraudulent company that provided no benefits to HSL.

- Baring any significant developments or major marketing efforts, sales are expected to increase at a rate of 3% into the future.

- The Company's cost of debt is 5%.

Indie LP

Indie LP (ILP) is an independent music producer and distributor of Canadian hip-hop music. The Company was formed in 1995 by two successful Canadian rap artists. Since its inception, ILP has helped launch the career of many Canadian artists. ILP has recording studies in Toronto, Montreal, and Vancouver.

Recently, the two founding owners have had a dispute in regard to the future direction of the Company. One owner would like to continue to focus only on Canadian hip-hop artists, while the other would like to pursue international artists from various genres of music. The dispute has reached the stage where both owners can no longer coexist. Accordingly, one shareholder will be bought out by the other shareholder.

Your firm, a small business valuation boutique, has been hired to prepare a valuation of the Company, which will be used as part of the negotiations between the owners. You have been provided with some additional information (Exhibit I), along with a copy of the most recent financial statements (Exhibit II).

Required

Prepare a preliminary estimate of value. At this stage, you can ignore any tax shield calculations.

Exhibit I	Additional Company Information

- The fair value of the property and equipment is $875,000.
- A working capital of 1:1 is normal for this Company. Any additional working capital is excess.
- Cash balances are earning interest at 2% per annum over the past two years.
- The following additional information is available for sustaining capital reinvestment:

	Replacement Cost	Useful Life
Land	120,000	n/a
Building	250,000	25
Equipment	560,000	12

- An appropriate weighted-average cost of capital would range between 23% and 25%.
- The wages and benefits on the financial statements are all paid to the two owners. The fair value of their services, if replaced, would be $85,000 combined.
- Included in the 2019 sales are one-time sales worth $20,000, which are not expected to recur in the future.
- The owners are currently using corporate vehicles for personal use. Expenses in the income statement related to personal vehicle usage is approximately $30,000 annually.

Exhibit II | Historical Balance Sheet and Income Statement

Indie LP
Balance Sheet
As at December 31

ASSETS	2020	2019
Current assets		
Cash and cash equivalents	559,080	345,700
Receivables	678,900	655,785
Prepaids and other assets	145,150	122,450
	1,383,130	1,123,935
Property and equipment	750,750	675,000
Intangible assets	250,900	250,900
	2,384,780	2,049,835
LIABILITIES AND SHAREHOLDERS' EQUITY		
Current liabilities		
Accounts payable and accrued liabilities	1,130,385	1,172,345
Deferred revenue	156,000	22,000
	1,286,385	1,194,345
Long-term debt	450,000	500,000
Shareholders' equity		
Share capital	10,000	10,000
Retained earnings	638,395	345,490
	648,395	355,490
	2,384,780	2,049,835

| Exhibit II | Historical Balance Sheet and Income Statement (Continued) |

Indie LP
Income Statement
As at December 31

	2020	2019
Revenues		
Sales of CDs	650,760	640,675
Online downloads	250,760	225,760
	901,520	866,435
Operating costs		
Cost of goods sold	115,000	113,218
Depreciation	87,000	85,652
Interest expense	33,250	32,735
Operational costs	112,090	110,353
Wages and benefits	150,000	150,000
Selling, general, and administration	8,215	8,088
	505,555	500,045
Operating profit	395,965	366,390
Other income (expenses)		
Interest income	10,560	12,500
Income before income taxes	385,405	353,890
Income taxes (24%)	(92,500)	(84,900)
Net income	292,905	268,990
Retained earnings, beginning of the year	345,490	76,500
Retained earnings, end of the year	638,395	345,490

Louis Developments Limited

Louis Developments Limited (LDL) acquired land 10 years ago to develop a revenue producing property in a growing area of a city. The project was scheduled for completion in August 2019 after a 21-month construction period. LDL entered into a lease in May 2017 with a private school for students up to the sixth grade. The lease took effect in August 2019. LDL planned to lease the remaining space to three main categories of tenants:

- companies desiring retail space in a shopping centre,
- companies wanting to lease space in an office tower, and
- a movie theater chain.

The space did not actually become available for occupancy until early January 2020. The five-month delay was caused by a major architectural error that had not been discovered until contractors submitted their bids for construction of the project. A new design became necessary, which led to the five-month delay. As a result, LDL sued the architects on grounds of breach of contract for all losses caused by the delay. The architects informed their insurance company of the lawsuit.

It is now September 2020. The insurance company has admitted that it is liable for the errors of the architectural firm. The insurance company has engaged your firm, CPA & Co., to prepare a report evaluating the claim that was submitted by LDL in January 2020 and providing an estimate of what CPA & Co. believes the claim should be.

The partner in charge of the engagement has asked you, CPA, to prepare the report, including the revised estimate of claim. In addition, the partner has asked you to prepare a memo to her indicating the procedures that would be required to support the revised claim and specifying the nature of assurance that could be provided to the insurance company.

You were able to assemble the additional data (Exhibit I) and the claim that was submitted by LDL (Exhibit II).

Required

Prepare your report to the insurance company and the memo to the partner.

Exhibit I   Additional Data

1. The economic lite of the project is estimated as 40–50 years.

2. The contract with the theater chain requires a rental payment of 6% of movie ticket revenue and 3% of soft drink, popcorn, and other concession revenue. The theater chain lease is for 10 years from the date of opening of the group of six theaters (the theaters opened in January 2020).

3. Before the delay, LDL budgeted construction costs for the project at $90 million. Actual construction costs amounted to $92 million for the project. According to the predelay plan, the fair value of the completed project was expected to be $102 million. Upon completion, the property was appraised at S108 million, based on an assumed 95% occupancy rate for the shopping centre and office tower.

4. The income statement of LDL for the year ended July 31, 2020, shows (in thousands of dollars):

Revenue		
Shopping centre	$7,740	
Office tower	3,580	
School	0	
Theatres	65	11,385
Expenses		
Operating costs	$4,210	
Interest	4,025	
Leasing costs	2,690	
Property taxes	2,170	
Tenant inducements	2,130	
Amortization	780	
Financing placement cost	550	16,555
Loss before income taxes		$5,170

5. To lease retail and office space, LDL paid part of the cost of tenants' leasehold improvements and offered free rent periods. The cost of these inducements is expensed and included in "tenant inducements" on LDL's income statement. Other costs of leasing a project and similar start-up expenditures such as wages of leasing stuff, commissions, advertising, and most overheads are included in "leasing costs."

6. Before the delay, planned financing for the project was mainly debt, including a $20 million first mortgage 25-year bond at 12% per annum. As a result of a change in market conditions, a 25-year $20 million first mortgage bond at 10.5% was sold on October 17, 2018, two months earlier than was noted in the pre-delay plan.

7. The insurance company has agreed to indemnify LDL to "the financial position in which it would have been had there been no delay."

8. Virtually all leases for retail stores in the shopping centre charge a minimal rent plus a percentage based on net sales of the store.

Exhibit II	Claim for Project Delay

The total claim is for out-of-pocket expenditures of $4.688 million plus lost revenues of $13.410 million.

Part A—Expenditures incurred as a result of the delay (in thousands of dollars):

Cost of drafting new construction plans required because the design was changed	$62
Additional fee charged by architects for the changes (not yet paid)	75
Advertising required	
Announcement of delay	2
Opening of shopping centre	88
To lease office space	108
Payment to school for one-year delay in opening the school (September 2019 to September 2020)	10
Various expenditures from August 1 to January I for five-month delay period:	
Property taxes	465
Insurance	1,040
Maintenance of facilities	325
Leasing staff, wages, and benefits	196
Management salaries	200
Other	457
Financing cost	
Placement cost	550
Interest on first mortgage bond $20 million × 12% × 5 months	1,000
Estimated cost of preparing insurance claim	
LDL staff time	50
External accounting firm	60
	$4,688

Part B—Estimated revenues lost as a result of the delay (in thousands of dollars):

	Revenue forecast* for the year ended July 31, 2020	
	If project was open for use on:	
	August 1, 2019	January 1, 2020
Revenue		
Shopping centre	$15,800	$8,260
Office tower	12,200	6,700
School	180	0
Theatres	340	150
	$28,520	$15,110
Lost revenue (difference between the two numbers)		$13,410

*Both revenue forecasts were made after the completion of the building in January 2020 and were submitted to the architects.

Mid-Town Manufacturing Inc.

On January 13, 2021, you arrive to your desk at 8:30AM on a Monday morning after a long weekend. As soon as you sit down you receive a phone call from the managing partner. The partner calls you into her office for an urgent client matter:

> *Over the course of the weekend, I met with the Farhan Lalji, 50% owner and sole-operator of Mid-Town Manufacturing Inc. (MTM). Farhan has been having significant difficulties with his brother, Rajan Lalji, about the future operations of MTM. Rajan owns the other 50% of the common shares but is not active in the day-to-day operations of the business.*

> *After a significant dispute, Rajan exercised his shotgun clause and offered Farhan $250,000 for his 50% common share interest. Under the agreement of the shotgun clause, Farhan can either sell his shares for the offered price or purchase Rajan's common shares for the same offered price.*

> *Rajan feels this is a reasonable and fair offer as it represents approximate 1.5 times Farhan's portion of the book value of equity. Therefore, goodwill has been included even though MTM's experienced a lack of profitability.*

> *Farhan was taken by surprise by the shotgun offer, but, must respond within three-business days. Baring a response, Farhan will be forced to sell his common shares to Rajan for the offered price.*

> *Farhan has contacted me in a panic to discuss whether or not he should sell his common shares or purchase Rajan's common shares for the offered price. I need you to put aside all of your other commitments and make this your first priority. I would like you prepare a report that I can present to Farhan that outlines which course of action he should pursue as supported by a valuation calculation.*

> *What makes this engagement more complicated is the fact that the financial statements have not been audited, and have historically been prepared by Rajan for internal purposes only. The shareholder's agreement requires the financial statements to be prepared in accordance with ASPE. It may be worthwhile for you to start by looking through the financial statements to determine if there are any ASPE compliance issues, and then proceed to prepare the valuation calculation.*

As you leave the partner's office, you take with you some notes that the partner had taken based on a discussion with Farhan (Exhibit I), the preliminary 2020 financial statements (Exhibit II) and some notes reviewed by Rajan while preparing the financial statements (Exhibit III). You sit down and review all of the information.

Required

Prepare the report.

Exhibit I	Notes from Discussion with Fahran

- MTM operates a drill bit manufacturing and servicing business. In the current year, the Company designed and patented a unique drill bit, which will be sold exclusively to junior mining and exploration. The new drill bit is expected to double the gross profit derived from parts sales.

- Historically, the MTM sold most of their drill bits to companies in the Sudbury nickel belt area. However, recent interest in Northwestern Ontario's Ring of Fire has lead to a more diversified customer base.

- MTM was founded by Aadarsh Lalji, the father of Farhan and Rajan. Aadarsh retired three years ago and passed the business on to his two sons. However, Rajan decide against working at MTM and pursued a career in accounting and finance. Farhan runs the business and is paid $50,000 each year. Rajan collects $20,000 per annum even though he is not actively involved in the business.

- Sales in 2020 and 2019 are understated by $100,000 and $125,000, respectively, due to an employee theft. A trusted employee was diverting the cash from the sale of parts and services into his own bank account. The large amounts appeared on the bank reconciliation as outstanding deposits but were not followed up on by Farhan until the fraud reached approximately $225,000. The employee was released and has been charged. The employee is required to pay back the $225,000 over a five-year period. No journal entries have been recorded for the diverted sales and resulting receivable. The sales will be recorded as the cash is received from the employee. The funds received from the employee are not required to fund the day to day operations of MTM.

- At the end of 2020, Farhan signed a new contract with Primo Mining Exploration (PME), a large junior mining company. The contract is for five years, and renewable for another five years, and allows for MTM to be the exclusive drill bit service provider for PME's exploration activities. Farhan expects that this new contract will increase the gross profit from the service line of business by 20% for the foreseeable future.

- Telephone expenses are for the cell phones of Farhan, Aadarsh, and Rajan. All three have plans of equal status and used the phone an equal amount.

- MTM is eligible for the small business tax rate (14.5%) going forward.

- The shareholders' agreement specifies a multiple in the range of 4–4.5 should be applied to normalized debt-free cash flows.[1] Both Rajan and Farhan agreed to this multiple when the shareholders agreement was signed.

- Both Rajan and Farhan agreed that sustaining capital reinvestment (SCR) would be approximately $20,000 per year. Rajan had done a quick calculation of the present value of the SCR tax shield which is $1,440.

- Capital assets have a fair value of $400,000 of which $50,000 is redundant (i.e., vehicles and real estate property that are used for nonbusiness activities by Rajan). The redundant vehicles result in additional costs of $3,000 per annum. The undepreciated capital cost (UCC) of the operating assets (less land) is approximately $250,000.

- A current ratio in the range of 1:1 to 2:1 is normal for this type of industry.

---

[1] Debt-free cash flows is defined as normalized EBITDA less taxes and sustaining capital reinvestment.

Exhibit II	Summary Financial Statements

Mid-Town Manufacturing Inc.
Statement of Financial Position (Unaudited)
As at December 31

	2020	2019
ASSETS		
Current assets		
Cash and cash equivalents	0	2,607
Receivables	85,995	90,101
Inventories	282,677	318,896
	368,672	411,604
Property and equipment	318,201	318,853
	686,873	730,457
LIABILITIES AND SHAREHOLDERS' EQUITY		
Current liabilities		
Accounts payable and accrued liabilities	158,721	163,633
Bank indebtedness	20,905	0
Demand loan	90,000	110,000
Current portion of LTD	17,941	14,295
	287,567	287,928
Long-term debt	86,809	92,935
	374,376	380,863
Shareholders' equity		
Share capital	100	100
Retained earnings	312,397	349,494
	686,873	730,457

Mid-Town Manufacturing Inc.
Statement of Operations
As at December 31

	2020	2019
Sales (Schedule 1)	1,311,057	1,237,854
Cost of sales (Schedule 1)	1,062,486	1,090,718
Gross profit	248,571	147,136
Interest and other income	44,165	42,285
Operating and administrative expenses (Schedule 2)	329,431	310,107
Loss before other items	(36,695)	(120,686)
Loss on disposal equipment	(402)	(7,212)
Net loss	(37,097)	(127,898)
Retained earnings, beginning of the year	349,494	477,392
Net loss	(37,097)	(127,898)
Retained earnings, end of the year	312,397	349,494

Exhibit II | Summary Financial Statements (Continued)

Mid-Town Manufacturing Inc.
Schedule 1—Sales and Cost of Sales
Year Ended December 31

	Parts	Service	2020 Total	2019 Total
Sales	944,892	366,165	1,311,057	1,237,854
Cost of sales				
Opening inventory	318,896	0	318,896	343,915
Purchases	837,202	0	837,202	851,405
	1,156,098	0	1,156,098	1,195,320
Ending inventory	282,677	0	282,677	318,896
	873,421	0	873,421	876,424
Other direct expenses				
Labour	0	161,612	161,612	194,583
Freight	27,453	0	27,453	19,711
Cost of sales	900,874	161,612	1,062,486	1,090,718
Gross profit	44,018	204,553	248,571	147,136

Mid-Town Manufacturing Inc.
Schedule 2 - Operating and Administrative Expenses
As at December 31

Expenses	2020	2019
Administrative and parts wages	163,242	162,442
Advertising	773	676
Amortization	20,666	20,044
Bad debts (recovery)	33,179	−31,541
Diesel, gas, and oil	6,079	4,753
Insurance	12,520	12,100
Interest and bank charges	9,651	8,003
Interest on long-term debt and demand loan	12,522	14,253
Office and general	9,414	10,724
Professional fees	9,500	9,400
Property taxes	8,071	7,976
Repairs and maintenance	0	38,438
Shop supplies	10,132	22,036
Telephone	4,883	5,461
Training	100	72
Travel—Rajan Personal	12,988	12,301
Utilities	15,711	12,969
	329,431	310,107

| Exhibit II | Summary Financial Statements (Continued) |

Mid-Town Manufacturing Inc.
Note—Property, plant, and equipment
as on December 31

	Cost	Accumulated Amortization	2020 Net BV	2019 Net BV
Land	43,273	0	43,273	43,273
Building	305,303	80,638	224,665	234,026
Equipment	146,701	118,727	27,974	34,967
Computer	3,653	3,288	365	522
Furniture and fixtures	25,758	21,868	3,890	4,862
Vehicles	21,217	3,183	18,034	1,203
	545,905	227,704	318,201	318,853

| Exhibit III | Notes from Financial Statement Preparation |

Related party transactions

(a) During the year, MTM exchanged manufacturing equipment with Temco Manufacturing, a related company. The equipment given up had a net book value of $50,000 and a fair value of $65,000, while the equipment received had a net book value of $40,000 and a fair value of $55,000. Both Temco and MTM are owned by the same shareholders. The fair values were estimated by Rajan.

(b) MTM is involved in various sales transactions with related companies. The sales are all at normal terms and conditions. During 2020 (2019), a total of $35,000 ($32,500) in sales were made to related parties. All cash was collected on the sales.

(c) All related party transactions are measured at exchange amount.

Contingency

The Company has been named in a trial by Magma Resources. Magma Resources has stated that the Company provided faulty drill bits, which caused damage in excess of $100,000. Legal counsel has suggested that the full $100,000 in damages is unlikely to be paid by the Company; however, a 25–50% conegligence outcome is likely.

Income taxes

(a) The Company uses the taxes payable method for reporting income tax expenses.

(b) The Company has losses available for income tax purposes totaling $170,637. This amount can be used to reduce taxable income of future years. If not used, $55,600 of these losses will expire in 2021, $99,816 will expire in 2022, and the remaining $15,211 will expire in 2023.

Northern College Student Union

Northern College Student Union ("NCSU") is considering opening up another coffee shop on campus, called the Northern College Coffee Shop ("NCCS"). As a recent graduate of the business program, and a newly qualified CPA, you have decided to volunteer your time to help the NCSU executive determine whether the expansion is viable. NCSU is a non-for-profit student union that seeks to provide critical services for Northern College students and a voice for students in various settings. Their main goal with this project is provide students with more options for purchasing coffee and snacks and to create employment opportunities for students. NCCS has voluntarily adopted IFRS for preparing their financial statements.

The NCSU executive has provided you with some information regarding the new coffee shop (Exhibit I). In this regard, the executive wants to know:

1. What price of baked goods would result in a break-even first year of operations; and

2. If the coffee shop is viable over a three-year period and if the price of baked goods is fixed to $2.50 over the three-year period.

Some members of the NCSU executive have put together a potential promotional plan for the proposed new coffee shop (Exhibit II). The executive is unsure of the appropriate revenue recognition policies related to the promotional plan. The executive would appreciate some illustrative journal entries for single coffee sale and the redemption of the free coffee based on your recommended conclusion.

The NCSU executive have also contacted various government officials in order to explore the possibility of obtaining a grant in order to help fund the new coffee shop. Details of a possible grant are outlined in Exhibit III.

Prepare a report that can be used by the NCSU Executive.

Exhibit I | Information on Potential Coffee Shop

Based on information from their other coffee shops on campus, the NCSU has compiled the following expectations:

- 20,000 coffees are expected to be sold per year.
- The average price per coffee is expected to be $2.00. There is not much flexibility with the price of coffee due to the competitive landscape.
- 15,000 baked goods are expected to be sold per year.
- The price of the baked goods has yet to be determined.

- The variable cost per coffee cup is expected to be $0.40.
- The variable cost per baked good is expected to be $0.75.
- All other costs related to space rental, wages, insurance, utilities, etc. are expected to be $62,000.

The total sales of coffee and baked goods are expected to increase by 10% in each of Year 2 and Year 3. All costs are expected to remain the same over the three-year period.

Exhibit II | Promotional Plans

In order to ensure that the figures in Exhibit I materialize, the executive has come up with the following promotional plan:

- **Loyalty cards**—NCCS would provide customers with a "punch card" that will count the number of coffees purchased.
  - After 10 coffee purchases, a customer will be entitled to a free coffee.

- On average, 50% of coffee customers will use the loyalty program and redeem their punch cards.

Exhibit III | Government Grant

The Ontario Government is willing to provide NCSU with a nonrepayable grant of $1,000 per year, over the next three years, if the following conditions are met annually:

- A minimum of three new positions are created for individuals that are 21 years of age, or younger;
- The three employees are paid a minimum of $16 per hour and work a minimum of 50 hours each, annually.

- Annual reporting that the above two conditions have been satisfied is required in order for the annual grant to be forgiven.

NCSU's President stated that the Executive will use the annual audited financial statements for the NCSU to satisfy the reporting compliance requirement.

Overlook Video Stores Inc. (OVS)

Overlook Video Stores Inc. (OVS) is a privately held chain of DVD rental stores headquartered in Toronto. The company was incorporated in 1992 and has gone from a single store in Toronto to over 30 stores throughout Ontario.

Harford & Harford and LLP (H&H), a mid-sized professional services firm, have been the auditors for OVS since its inception. You, CPA, are the audit senior on the OVS audit for the year ending December 31, 2020. On December 1, 2020, Alice Harford, the engagement partner, calls you into her office to explain that the audit will need to begin in early January 2021 because OVS's bank is eager to see the audited financial statements.

"I would like you to prepare the audit planning memo for the OVS audit. OVS has experienced some changes, and I want to make sure we consider those in our audit plan. The controller of OVS has faxed us the interim financial statements for the 11 months ended November 30, 2020 (Exhibit I). These should help you in your audit plan. Please be sure to consider OVS's financial reporting issues when drafting your audit planning memo and suggest ways to audit them.

"I met with Victor Ziegler, the controlling shareholder and CEO of OVS, a few months ago and he told me about OVS's new initiatives for the current year. Here are my notes from that meeting (Exhibit II). There are some new accounting issues that have arisen as a result of these initiatives. I would like you to look at them and provide your recommendations on the accounting treatments to adopt. I would also like from you to prepare a separate report that we can provide to Victor to help him make a decision regarding a new initiative that is being considered for next year (Exhibit III).

"I also met with OVS's Chief Information Officer, Nick Nightingale. He provided a description of OVS's expansion during 2020 into the Internet-based video game rental market through a program called Games By Mail. Here are my notes from my meeting with Nick (Exhibit IV). Please review them and provide your recommendations for improving the system. I will pass on your comments to our Information Technology (IT) partner so that she can include them in a report she is preparing for Victor. Victor has asked our IT partner to meet with him to discuss the information technology issues related to the Internet-based rental system."

"Lastly, I met with the Chair of OVS's board of directors, Malcolm Brodie. He discussed how the board is trying to transform itself in light of OVS's recent expansion efforts and the disruptive forces in the industry. There are no minutes from the board's meeting in the current year; however, I was able to put together some rough notes based on my meeting with Malcolm (Exhibit V). Please review the board composition and prepare a separate report for me to provide to Malcolm that outlines any issues and your recommendations for improvement."

Required

1. Prepare an audit planning memo for Alice Harford that discusses the audit and reporting issues.
2. Prepare a report for Victor Ziegler that assesses the Rent Box initiative.
3. Prepare a report for the IT partner that discusses the issues with OVS's IT system.
4. Prepare a report for Alice Harford that discusses the issues with OVS's board of directors.

Exhibit I	Overlook Video Stores INC.

Excerpts from the Balance Sheet
(in Thousands of Dollars)

	Nov. 30 2020	Dec. 31 2019
Assets	(Unaudited)	(Audited)
Current assets		
Cash	21	35
Accounts receivable (no late fees)	3,210	-
Inventory – DVDs for rent	7,935	6,545
Inventory – New DVDs for sale	2,315	2,119
Inventory – Previously viewed DVDs for sale	3,526	-
Inventory – video games for rent	2,849	1,517
	19,856	10,216
Property, plant, and equipment	40,355	31,105
Database development costs	425	-
Website	8,512	-
	69,148	41,321
Liabilities		
Current liabilities		
Accounts payable	652	3,569
Current portion of long-term debt	2,937	-
	3,589	3,569
Long-term debt	26,430	-
Due to shareholders	4,532	6,483
	34,551	10,052
Shareholders' equity		
Common shares	100	100
Retained earnings	34,497	31,169
	34,597	31,269
	69,148	41,321

| Exhibit 1 | Overlook Video Stores INC. (Continued) |

Excerpts from the Income and Retained Earnings Statement
(in Thousands of Dollars)

	11 months ended Nov. 30 2020	Dec. 31 2019
	(Unaudited)	(Audited)
Revenues		
Rentals	15,477	14,613
Sales	6,321	5,946
Games by mail	7,432	-
No late fees	3,539	-
Government grant	50	-
Other	537	419
	34,356	20,978
Expenses		
Advertising	3,124	2,460
Amortization	659	450
Bank charges	11	11
Business and property taxes	140	149
Cost of goods sold	8,797	4,757
Insurance	125	105
Interest on long-term debt	1,325	-
Professional and consulting fees	691	710
Rent and office	1,286	1,246
Repairs and maintenance	569	498
Utilities	1,542	1,612
Wages and benefits	10,540	8,465
	28,809	20,463
Income before taxes	5,547	515
Income taxes	2,219	206
Net income	3,328	309
Retained earnings, beginning of the period	31,169	30,860
Retained earnings, end of the period	34,497	31,169

Exhibit II	Notes from Meeting with Victor Ziegler on Current Year Initiatives

After years of slow and steady growth, OVS began expanding in two directions. First, OVS opened 10 new video stores in 2020. In the past, OVS had only opened one store per year. Second, OVS moved into the Internet-based video game rental business by launching a new website, www.GamesByMail.ca. The expansion was financed by a 10-year term loan from OVS's bank. Victor noted that the bank now seems concerned with the profitability of the company. Given all the extra hours worked this year, Victor will be receiving a bonus of 2% of net income.

No Late Fees

OVS introduced a new program called "No Late Fees" during 2020. Since people are often reluctant to rent movies because they cannot return them on time, OVS eliminated late fees for its customers. However, to prevent abuse of this program, after 30 days if the movie is not returned, the outstanding movie is considered sold to the customer who rented it. The next time the customer comes to the store, there will be a charge of $25, the price of purchasing a new DVD, on the customer's account and they have the right to keep the DVD.

The program has been "tremendously successful," according to Victor. It has both increased rental revenue and increased sales of DVDs, since many customers keep their DVDs beyond the 30 days. However, Victor conceded that it has upset some customers who believed that OVS had truly eliminated all forms of late fees. Most customers who were charged for an over-30-day DVD have refused to pay for it and simply returned the DVD to an OVS store. Others have yet to pay for the DVD and have yet to return it.

Exchange with Blockster Home Video

During the year, OVS exchanged $1,000 cash and various New DVD inventory with a cost of $85,000 and a fair value of $96,000 with Blockster Home Video in exchange for 3,000 Model XT500 DVD players. OVS is going to sell the DVD players to its customers. The XT500s can be purchased from various suppliers, with a price range of $25 to $38 per unit. OVS sold DVDs similar to those traded to its customers for $15 per unit last month. OVS has not recorded this transaction, as Victor said "it's really like nothing happened," he tells you. "We gave them inventory and they gave us inventory. That's why I didn't record anything."

Games by Mail—Rental Program

When customers first subscribe to the Games By Mail service at the store, they supply their credit card number and agree that it will be charged $30 at the end of each month until they cancel their subscription. To rent a video game, customers log on to the website using a user ID and password provided to them.

Once logged on, customers can choose up to 40 video games to have in their "wish list." Customers can flag as urgent certain video game.

The customer is mailed his or her initial four video games from the OVS warehouse in Toronto. These are selected automatically by the system based on availability of video games in the rental inventory, while giving priority to those video games marked as urgent by the customer. Once the customer is finished playing a particular video game, he or she returns it by mail in a postage-paid envelope. OVS then sends the customer the next video game on the list. During the introduction period of May 2020, OVS offered new customers the option of paying $500 up front for three years of video games rentals by mail and 5,000 customers took advantage of this option due to its substantial savings.

Games By Mail—Database Development

OVS has spent more than $425,000 to date researching and developing a patented database used to track orders and returns of video games from the Games by Mail program. The database is fully integrated with the website. Victor Ziegler has determined that other companies, in various lines of business, could make use of this technology. Essentially, OVS has developed an off-the-shelf packaged inventory tracking database that other businesses can purchase. It seems that OVS has spent $175,000 on research and an additional $250,000 on development. OVS capitalized the full $425,000 as an asset on the balance sheet. A breakdown of the costs is as follows:

Development costs:	
Salaries of researchers	$50,000
Salaries of office administration staff	$20,000
Allocation of direct overhead utility cost	$20,000
Allocation of building amortization (Note 1)	$50,000
Amortization of equipment used in development process	$60,000
Materials used in the lap during development	$50,000
	$250,000

Note 1—the amortization of the building was based on a 20% allocation, since the development lab accounts for approximately 20% of the building.

The present value of the revenues and expenses from database are $1.35 and $1.13 million, respectively.

RentPoints

In January of 2020, OVS introduced a customer reward program called RentPoints. For every dollar a customer spends with OVS,

| Exhibit II | Notes from Meeting with Victor Ziegler on Current Year Initiatives (Continued) |

they get one RentPoint added to their OVS account. The point-of-sale system in OVS's stores automatically tracks the points each time a customer rents or purchases DVDs or video games.

Customers can then redeem RentPoints for selected rewards. For example, 1,000 RentPoints can be redeemed for a new DVD, or 250,000 RentPoints can be redeemed for a trip for two to Hollywood. Although Victor believes the program has been very popular, to date, only 92,000 RentPoints have been redeemed. Victor has faith that more people will eventually redeem their points since the points do not expire. However, he is now wondering if he should continue the program, since so few people have taken advantage of it.

Previously viewed DVDs

In the past, a wholesaler purchased all of OVS's previously viewed DVDs. Now, due to its expansion, OVS first sells all the previously viewed DVDs it can to the wholesaler. OVS then offers the remaining previously viewed DVDs for sale to its customers at discounted prices. Each of these remaining DVDs is scanned and its cost is transferred from "Inventory–DVDs for Rent" to "Inventory–Previously Viewed DVDs for Sale." When a new movie is released on DVD, OVS must order at least 20 copies of it for each store, at an average cost of $20 per DVD. Within two months, demand for the movie has diminished so that only five copies per store are necessary. As a result, OVS must sell off 15 copies per store for about $10 each.

| Exhibit III | Notes from Meeting with Victor Ziegler on Possible Future Initiative |

OVS is evaluating the purchase of 20 Rent Boxes, which would be located in highly populated areas within the City of Toronto. Rent Boxes allow for the rental of DVDs and video games via rental kiosks. Rent Boxes allow a customer to select a DVD or video game, pay for the rental, and receive the physical copy of the DVD or game all from a self-serve rental kiosk. It is similar to a vending machine but for renting DVDs and video games. Customers must return the DVD or video game to the same Rent Box after a specified number of days. The Rent Boxes would be located in popular areas such as grocery stories, Big Box stores, and subway terminals.

Victor has compiled the following financial information related to the Rent Boxes:

- Initial, up-front capital costs of $2,250,000 are required to purchase the 20 Rent Boxes.
- The project is expected to generate future cash flow of $2,500,000 per annum over a five-year period.
- The project is capital intensive, and therefore has relatively little variable costs. Direct variables costs are expected to be $350,000 per annum over the five-year period.
- Advertising costs are expected to increase by 5% from 2020.
- Wages and Benefits costs are expected to increase by 7% from 2020.
- The Rent Boxes will have a CCA rate of 20%.
- OVS has a cost of equity of 12%.

Exhibit IV | Notes from Meeting with Nightingale

Nick Nightingale is the Chief Information Officer for OVS and was responsible for the implementation of the Games By Mail system. He answers the OVS help desk phone, so he has been extremely busy lately because Games By Mail customers have been calling for assistance. He said the following:

"The Games By Mail concept is great, but it has been difficult to get going. Moonwatcher Web Designers (MWD) programmed both the front-end, which is the part the customer sees, and the back-end, which is the database that tracks the games. MWD programmed the website very quickly but has not been available very much since the website went live six months ago. We have had several crashes of the website, and the only advice MWD has provided is to reboot the server. Considering all the money we paid to MWD to develop the site, which at last count was over $8.5 million, I hoped for better service.

"We were able to save money by hosting www.GamesByMail.ca on an existing server. Because the website needs to transfer credit card sales information daily to the accounting system, we used the same server that runs our accounting system.

"Since MWD also programmed an antivirus component right into the website software, we did not have to purchase separate antivirus software for the server. I have been after MWD to provide us with updates to the antivirus software. MWD keeps promising us that updates will arrive shortly. Thank goodness, we have a great firewall, so viruses cannot get access to the system in the first place.

"I am also not too worried because we have a backup that I store off-site, because I know how important that is for disaster recovery. The back up now does both the accounting data and the video game title database. I change the tape every week and whenever I do a backup, it finishes in about 10 seconds and ejects the tape right away. It used to take much longer to do the back up, but the MWD people must have done more than just tweaking when they installed the website.

"One matter I am a little worried about, though, is the shipping report produced by the new system. Each day, the system generates and prints a shipping report and the addressed envelopes. The report indicates which video game gets sent to which customer, and there is one envelope for each customer listed on the report. The idea is that the inventory picker can find the video game and immediately put it in the matching addressed envelope to be shipped. However, I have noticed that sometimes the customer names that the system prints on the shipping report are different from the names it prints on the envelopes. Usually, it is not a big deal because we can correct the information in the system and just reprint the envelope. However, it causes the shipping people to do additional manual work.

"We were also having a problem with the customer login screen. Customers would be denied access, even if they were using their correct username and password. After repeatedly calling MWD, they dialed in to the system last night and applied a service pack to the website to fix the problem. Today, the login screen seems to be working fine."

Exhibit V | Notes from Meeting with Malcom Brodie

Malcolm lamented the fact that the board has not been able to meet more frequently during the year because Victor has been so busy overseeing OVS' expansion plans. The board formally meets twice during the past year—once in February to review Victor's expansion plan and another time in July to approve dividends that Victor wanted to be declared. Victor is the board's secretary and was unable to prepare minutes because of his hectic schedule.

The board of directors comprises the following individuals:

Name	Board Role	Description
Malcolm Brodie	Board Chair	Minority shareholder and long-time friend of Victor Ziegler. Malcolm is an active lawyer.
Victor Ziegler	Board Secretary	Controlling Shareholder and Chief Executive Officer
Nick Nightingale	Director	Chief Information Officer
Muhammad Sanuta	Director	Controller

Malcolm stated that OVS adopted a whistleblower policy in the current year but was unsure if it was working properly as Victor had not received any anonymous calls during the year.

The board is functioning as OVS's audit committee. Malcolm would like to better understand an audit committee's purpose and composition.

Tim's Heating and Cooling

Tim's heating and cooling (THC) was founded in 2003 in Winnipeg, Manitoba. THC specializes in the manufacturing and installation of gas fireplaces and BBQs—both indoors and out. THC has a very large production facility on the same parcel of land as head office and a second large production facility located in St. John's, Nfld. THC products are sold both in Canada and the United States. Sales overseas are limited to only a few countries due to production differences (Hook-up regulations are different).

During their expansion in 2017 to St. John's, the Founder of THC, Owen Horton, decided to take the company public. The initial public offering (IPO) went smoothly. Owen retained 60% of the outstanding common shares of THC, 20% of the shares issued were bought by one investor, and the other 20% of the common shares are widely held.

Your firm has audited THC since they went public in 2017. Your partner has been the lead engagement partner since that time and you, PA, were the staff accountant during 2018 and 2019. It is now February 2021 and you are now the lead senior accountant on the engagement for the audit of the financial statements of THC for the year ended December 31, 2020.

All audit planning was done by you, and materiality was correctly established at $450,000. This was decreased from the previous year due to the increased users, namely, the bank and the preferred shareholders. Exhibits I to VII contain information regarding the current year's audit.

You are currently at the client and you are well into this year's audit. A number of issues have arisen this year and you are unsure of how to address them. As a result, you phoned the partner for some advice. In preparation for a meeting with her, you have been asked by your partner to prepare a memo that discusses any of the issues you have found to date along with any implications, follow-up audit procedures, or anything else you deem important. This includes next steps, if necessary. Given some of the issues that have arisen, your partner wants to take a look at the current summary of accounting and audit differences and has asked you to prepare one as she is concerned that you may be approaching materiality. In addition, your partner has also asked you to prepare a draft management letter. Your draft letter should be organized as: Weakness, Implication(s), and Recommendation(s).

Required

Prepare the required memo and letter.

| Exhibit I | Audit Information |

- In 2018, Owen decided that he needed more money to expand the production facilities at the Winnipeg plant in order to keep up with the increasing demand for fireplaces and BBQs. Not wanting to reduce his ownership further, Owen made the decision to issue preferred shares and obtain a long-term bank loan to finance the expansion. Nothing happened with respect to the expansion during 2018 or 2019 as Owen worked on the details.

- On June 30th 2020, THC obtained a $1,800,000 loan from the Button Bank. The loan will be used to construct an additional manufacturing facility that will be able to produce customer-specific products. Details of the loan can be found in Exhibit II.

- In total, 10,000 preferred shares were issued on April 1, 2020, for $100 per share. The preferred shares pay a dividend of $5 per share. In addition to the dividend, THC enticed investors by including several other provisions into the release of the preferred shares. In any year, if net income does not exceed $1,000,000 before tax, THC will immediately pay a $5 special dividend to the preferred shareholders. This is in addition to any regular dividend that may be paid. In addition, if net income before tax fails to exceed $1,000,000 in three successive years, the preferred shareholders may, at their option, force THC to buy back their shares.

- There was an error posted on last year's summary of accounting and auditing differences (SAAD) in the amount of $150,000. The office building in St John's was painted around year end last year. The invoice was dated January 5th, 2020. Further research revealed that the work was actually done on December 21, 2019. The year-end SAAD entry posted by your firm for the 2019 audit was

Dr. Maintenance Expense	$150,000
Cr. Accounts Payable	$150,000

THC was not asked to correct this error as the cumulative errors for the 2019 audit did not exceed materiality.

| Exhibit II | Other Information |

- THC signed a contract with Homeward Outdoors (HO) for the delivery of an exclusive outdoor fire pit. The production of the pit requires a specially designated production line. The contract was signed on December 1, 2020, and production of the fire pits began on December 15th. The contract called for production of 125,000 pits with a total contract price of $2,500,000. Excerpts from the contract can be found in Exhibit IV;

- THC produces small portable gas BBQs for Muskoka Back County (Muskoka) that are specially branded. These are consumer camping-specific BBQs. In an attempt to get ahead of potential orders, THC produced 15,000 special Muskoka BBQs in August 2020. The price THC sells these BBQs to Muskoka for is $80. Each BBQ costs 50% of the selling price. Muskoka is under no obligation to buy the BBQs, but the normal expectation is that they buy all that THC produces. In September 2020, Muskoka changed its name to Algonquin Outdoors (Algonquin). Algonquin does not want to buy the BBQ stock given that it has the old name on it. While Matthew, the sales manager, tried to negotiate with the newly branded Algonquin, a review of the contract by THC by the company lawyers revealed that there is no contractual obligation for Algonquin to purchase them. When Matthew was asked about the issue, he maintained that he was doing his best to sell them to a discount company at about 40% of cost;

- You have been conducting your audit fieldwork at the Winnipeg office. Yesterday, you came to work and found fire trucks at the back of the property. By midmorning, you found out that one of the temporary storage facilities being used to store some of the inventory burned to the ground.

- The loan from the Button Bank calls for interest only repayments until 2024. The loan carries interest at a rate of 4.5% with principal repayments at a rate of $100,000 per year beginning in 2025.

- Your inventory count completed on December 31st needed to be done twice due to some counting irregularities. THC hired a new inventory management supervisor in October 2020 after the retirement of their previous supervisor. While the new supervisor is slowly gaining an understanding of the system, your junior staff member that attended the count called you with problems over count instructions and segregation of inventory. As a result, you ordered a recount that ultimately was satisfactory. In January, you discussed the issue with the new supervisor and determined that they felt that written count instructions would not be necessary in the future as it simply slowed the process down.

| Exhibit III | Partial Unaudited Financial Statement Amounts (from THC's Trial Balance) |

Account	2020 Amt
Inventory	4,532,450.00
Property, Plant, and equipment	25,436,897.00
Construction in Progress[1]	976,460.00
Accumulated Amortization	−12,345,678.00
Accounts Payable	996,000.00
Unearned Revenue	0
Long-term debt (sharp button bank)	1,800,000.00[2]
Other Debt	3,400,000.00
Preferred Shares	1,000,000.00
Common Shares	1,200,000.00
Net Income (before tax)	1,500,000.00
Retained Earnings (including NI above)	1,400,000.00

[1] Details can be found in Exhibit V (W/P T-5) where your junior accountant completes an audit working paper.
[2] No interest has been accrued on the loan as of year-end.

| Exhibit IV | Excerpts from Homeward Outdoors |

- Total contract price of $2,500,000 specially designed fire engine red fire pit in honor of HO's 75th Anniversary. Delivery is for 125,000 fire pits;

- HO agrees to pay $300,000 on signing of the contract and $200,000 at the end of each month beginning December 31, 2020, with the full remaining balance due and payable June 30, 2021, subject to certain conditions;

- THC agrees to have 10,000 units produced by December 31, 2020, ready to be shipped;

- Shipping is FOB shipping point;

- HO reserves the right to inspect the first 30,000 units for quality and adherence to appropriate colour and specifications. HO has the right to return the first 30,000 units at its discretion with the balance of returns after the first 30,000 based on specified defects

Exhibit V

W/P Ref: T-5
JBG/Jan 2021

Harper Architects Inc.
123 Whisper Lane
H0H 1H0

To auditors of Tim's Heating

We can confirm the following progress payments for the construction of the expanded facilities for Tim's Heating:

Progress payment #1	$150,000	√
Progress payment #2	$486,500	√
Progress Payment #3	$339,960	√

Progress payments are determined and calculated by us based upon our review and approval of work done to date by the construction company. A holdback equal to 10% of each progress payment is calculated in order to account for any construction deficiencies. While the holdback will be payable by Tim Heating, it has not been included in the above progress payments.

If you have any questions, please don't hesitate to contact us.

Harper Architects

Harper

√ - Agreed to invoice and cheque details. Results satisfactory

Exhibit VI

Other Information

- A review of subsequent events by the junior accountant revealed that there were payments made after year-end for invoices and related events that occurred in early 2021. The junior accountant noted that these amounts, totaling $124,000, had been set up as a payable and an expense in 2020. When he asked the accounts payable supervisor, she noted that she wasn't really sure how to deal with some of the payments coming in after year-end and so she guessed at some of them. You had the junior accountant expand their work as a result of this but found no other invoicing cutoff errors.

- The substantive work on accounts receivable involved confirming several balances. The book value of the balances was $567,000. The audit value after all confirmations and alternative procedures was done was $525,000. The total value of receivables for THC is $867,000.

- Your audit work on capital assets revealed that there was $85,000 of expenditures capitalized that were in fact repairs and maintenance. When you questioned the fixed asset clerk, you found out that there have been some accounting policy discussions at THC about what threshold level should be used when capitalizing expenses. Since there was no final decision, she opted to capitalize these amounts.

- THC is considering leasing several large pieces of production equipment next year as a means of keeping these assets and obligations off of the financial statements.

Trapper Run

Madison McKinnon has been an entrepreneur since she was in high school. After studying mechanical engineering at University, Madison went to work at ARC Industries, a company that is heavily involved in the creation of new smart "gadgets." Within two years, Madison realized that she was better as her own boss and decided to combine her passion for running, her knowledge of technology, and her love of entrepreneurship. She opened up her first running store in Simcoe Shores. With Madison's "bubbly" personality, Trapper Run (TR) became a huge success. Over the last five years, Madison has built up a loyal customer base and has opened up two more TR stores in the neighboring GTA areas of Beacon Hill and Yurbury Valley. While Madison hasn't been able to work on her other passion, engineering for some time, she has become a well-known public speaker on tips for running and running for success.

TR is currently a private company. Madison owns 80% of the shares and her two younger brothers each hold 10%. Recently, Madison has been mulling over a number of opportunities and issues and decided it was best to obtain an outside consultant to assist her. As a result, she has hired you, a CPA with extensive experience in company planning, expansion, and strategic management.

Madison would like you to prepare a report to her that fully addresses the issues she has put before you (see the following exhibits), ensuring you state any assumptions that you make.

Required

Prepare the report

Exhibit I — **TR Stores**

Madison made the decision to standardize her three stores in order to maximize marketing synergies. Each store has the following features:

- Each store is in a mall plaza with a minimum of six other stores. One of which must be a major department store or grocery store. Store fronts are leased with a price of $4 per square foot (per month) plus a percentage of annual revenues in excess of $800,000 of 3%.

- Each store has between 1,500 and 2,000 storefront space with 150–200 inventory space. Madison has negotiated with each lessor that the inventory space is excluded from the square foot rate and calculations.

- Leasehold improvements to get the stores ready total $100,000. That includes everything needed to open the store such as shelving, computer registers, and displays.

- Inventory of $100,000 is typically needed to start up the store.

- Each store has one manager that works fulltime and earns an annual salary of $40,000 plus a bonus should the store exceed annual revenues of $1,400,000.

- Each store employs one fulltime staff member in addition to the manager at an annual salary of $30,000 and generally six part-time employees. Part-time salaries generally average $100,000 per year in total.

- Madison does not pay herself a specific salary but rather waits until year-end before deciding how much to pay. Last year, she paid herself a salary of $90,000.

- Other costs such as hydro, Internet, insurance, and others average $1,800 per month.

- Revenues at Simcoe Shores are averaging $1,600,000 per year; Beacon Hill and Yurbury Valley are each averaging annual revenue of $1,350,000. Gross profit on sales for all three stores averages 35%.

- She expects revenues to grow at a rate of 4% per year.

- Madison has a bank loan of $400,000 with monthly payments at prime +1%. She also has access to an operating line of credit up to $500,000.

- Assume that TR's tax rate is 38%.

| Exhibit II | **TR Expansion** |

Madison is trying to determine what her next step should be in trying to grow her TR stores. She knows that her three stores are very popular and she has taken care to make sure they are within traveling distance for her so that she can move between each one. She also knows that she cannot continue to add stores personally and show a presence at each one, especially if she expands beyond her current geographical area. Wimsey, Ontario (southern tip of Ontario, bordering on the United States), Outtawow, Ontario (near the Quebec border), and Niagara Fallen, Ontario have all shown promise for future locations.

Madison needs your help sorting out her best course of action. Should she open up a fourth store herself? Or, should she begin to franchise the stores out? Her friend told her that franchising was the way to go. She's not sure what else she should consider and how each would impact her quantitatively and qualitatively. After some research, Madison found out the following information:

- Given the demographics in the three areas, sales would be projected to be $1,600,000 with revenue growth at 6% per year.

- Shipping of inventory would be cheaper in these areas that would raise the gross profit to 37% of revenues.

- All other costs would be similar to the current stores except that Madison would have to hire a second manager and both managers would command a $47,000 salary.

- If Madison franchised the store, she could charge a $300,000 franchise fee. She would be responsible for setting up the store and stocking the initial inventory. The cost for the inventory would be the same as setting up a store and the physical set-up would also be the same. The franchisee would be responsible for paying for the rent and all the utilities.

- The franchisee would have to buy its inventory through the standard inventory buying done now and reimburse TR.

- The franchisee would pay TR a 5% fee on revenues up to $1,000,000; 3% between 1,000,001 and $1,500,000 and 1% above $1,500,000.

- In addition, the franchisee would pay TR $250 per month for marketing and TR would have full control over the marketing and sales events of the store. This would ensure that the store ran the same as the three owned stores.

| Exhibit III | **TR Internet Site** |

TR has not had an Internet presence to date as Madison has been focusing on setting up her three running stores and the store front. Madison is now looking at a full Internet site in order to sell her products to a larger market. She has made contact with two Internet companies and they have provided her with the following information. She'd like you to analyze the pros and cons of each package for her and recommend.

| Exhibit IV | **Imagine Inc.[II]** |

Imagine Inc. is a full-service provider. In II's response to the request for information they provided the following:

- Development of a full web storefront with backend server support.
- New integrated computer systems and inventory management system. As inventory arrives at each store and entered into the store inventory system, it will automatically link to the II servers. Therefore, when customers are Internet shopping, they will know if an item is in stock.

- Electronic notification system to each store. When a customer makes a purchase, the system notifies the store closest to the customer location. The store then packages the item up and ships directly to the customer. This way no separate warehouse location is necessary to store online inventory.
- Daily backups to the cloud server.
- One week of training at each store.
- Package price of $500,000.
- Monthly fee of $1,000.

| Exhibit V | **Digital Information Yottabytes (DIY)** |

DIY provided the following in their request for information:

- Development of a full web storefront with backend server support.
- Continued use of current computer system—reducing costs. Inventory for the website would be managed separately via the use of a central warehouse.

- DIY owns the central distributing warehouse. TR holds inventory there and DIY charges a lease fee of $2,000 per month. DIY sends TR reports on a weekly basis regarding sales and returns.
- No training is required as the Internet site would be separated from the physical stores.
- Set-up fee is $100,000.

Exhibit VI | The Running Belt

Madison has recently come up with an idea to sell a specialized running accessory through her stores and an online site. This will be Madison's first entrance into the online market. Madison believes that there is a market for this in Canada as running has increased in popularity as many Canadians are much more motivated to get fit. The accessory is a running belt that clips onto the waist and will hold a cell phone as large as the IPhone Plus and was created by Madison. It also has its own fit monitor built in that will measure distance and steps. The cost to make the prototype was $10,000. It will be available in multiple colours and will have lights and reflective strips on it. This is something that other belts do not have.

Madison wants to sell through the Internet in addition to her stores so that she can reach a larger target market. Madison will be competing with big running name stores such as the Running Room and Running Free who also sell a running belt accessory, along with other websites such as Amazon. She believes that there is a potential market base of 320,000 people that are interested in the running belt and that she can potentially capture between 0.5% and 3% of this market for the first year. Madison also provides you with the following information:

- There is no added space cost to holding the belt in her store.

- The cost of the belt regardless of colour is $5 to manufacture and $0.50 per belt shipping.

- Packaging (in shipping to customers) is estimated to be $2 per belt.

- Madison expects that she will sell the belts for $15 each and in order to attract customers, she will offer free shipping (i.e., she will pay the shipping costs).

- The Internet company she is using will charge her 10 cents per belt sold as a commission fee.

- Other fixed selling costs have been estimated at $5,000 per year total for storefront packaging and other (this is for all stores not per store).

- She estimates that 1/3 of the sales will be in-store where she will not have to pay for shipping. The other two-thirds of the sales are estimated to be via the Internet.

Madison is wondering whether this particular product makes sense and wants to ensure that it at least breaks even. Ideally, she would like to make an after tax profit of this product of $20,000.

Vulcanzap Inc. (VZAP)

Vulcanzap Inc. (VZAP) is a high-technology company that develops, designs, and manufactures telecommunications equipment. VZAP was founded in 2017 by the former assistant head of research and development at a major telephone company, Dr. Alec Zander. He and the director of marketing left the company to found VZAP. VZAP has been very successful. Sales reached $8.3 million in its first year and have grown by 80% annually since then. The key to VZAP's success has been the sophisticated software contained in the equipment it sells.

VZAP's board of directors recently decided to issue shares to raise funds for strategic objectives through an initial public offering of common shares. The shares will be listed on a major Canadian stock exchange. VZAP's underwriter, Mitchell Securities, believes that an offering price of 18 to 20 times the most recent fiscal year's earnings per share can be achieved. This opinion is based on selected industry comparisons.

VZAP has announced its intention to go public, and work has begun on the preparation of a preliminary prospectus. It should be filed with the relevant securities commissions in 40 days. The offering is expected to close in about 75 days. The company has a July 31 year end. It is now September 8, 2020. You, CPA, work for Chesther Chathan, Chartered Professional Accountants, the auditors of VZAP since its inception.

You have just been put in charge of VZAP's audit, due to the sudden departure of the senior. VZAP's year-end audit has just commenced. At the same time VZAP's staff and the underwriters are working 15-hour days trying to write the prospectus, complete the required legal work, and prepare for the public offering. The client says that the audit must be completed so that the financial statements can go to the printer in 22 days. VZAP plans to hire a qualified chief financial officer as soon as possible.

An extract from VZAP's accounting records is found in Exhibit I. You have gathered the information in Exhibit II from the client, and your staff has gathered the information in Exhibit III. You have been asked by the audit partner to prepare a memo dealing with the key financial accounting issues.

Required

Prepare the memo.

Exhibit I	Extract from Accounting Records

(in Thousands of Dollars)

	Revenue		Deferred
	Month of July	Total fiscal 2020	Development costs[1]
Product			
Zibor	$815	$8,802	$9,463
Resale components	540	4,715	–
Webstar	700	4,241	359
IDSL 600	–	2,104	1,431
Transact training	2,077	2,077	–
Firewall Plus	402	1,640	1,500
Transact	670	1,350	2,159
700J	–	400	725
ATM 4000	–	394	1,825
Photon phasing project	–	–	691
	$5,204	$25,723	$18,153

[1] Cumulative costs for each product that have been deferred and recorded on the balance sheet.

Exhibit II	Information Gathered from the Client

1. The job market for top software and hardware engineering talent is very tight. As a result, VZAP has turned to information technology "head hunters" to attract key personnel from other high-technology companies. During the year, VZAP paid $178,000 in placement fees, and the company is amortizing the payments over five years. The search firm offers a one-year money-back guarantee if any of the people hired leaves the company or proves to be unsatisfactory.

2. On July 29, 2020, the company made a payment of $100,000 to a computer hacker. The hacker had given the company 10 days to pay her the funds. Otherwise, she said she would post a security flaw she had detected in the VZAP's Firewall Plus software, on the Internet.

3. Alec Zander had been working on a photon phasing project when he left the telephone company. He has moved this technology ahead significantly at VZAP, and a prototype has been built at a cost of $691,000. The project has been delayed pending a decision on the direction that the project will take.

4. VZAP defers and amortizes software and other development costs according to the following formula:

$$\text{Annual amortization rate} = \frac{\text{sales in units for the year}}{\text{total expected sales in units during product life}}$$

5. In line with normal software company practice, VZAP releases software upgrades that correct certain bugs in previously released software, via the Internet.

6. During a routine visit to the AC&C Advanced Telecommunications laboratory in southern California, a VZAP engineer discovered that nearly 600 lines of code in an AC&C program were identical to those of some VZAP software written in 2018—right down to two spelling mistakes and a programming error.

7. The ATM 4000 has been the company's only product flop. High rates of field failures and customer dissatisfaction led VZAP to issue an offer, dated July 30, 2020, to buy back all units currently in service for a total of $467,500. Southwestern Utah Telephone is suing VZAP for $4 million for damages related to two ATM 4000 devices that it had purchased through a distributor. The devices broke down, affecting telephone traffic for two weeks before they were replaced.

8. VZAP also resells components manufactured by a Japanese telecommunications company. The effort required to make these sales to existing customers is minimal, but the gross margin is only 12% versus an average of 60% for the company's other products, excluding the Transact and 700J lines.

9. During the first two years of operation, VZAP expensed all desktop computers (PCs) when purchased, on the grounds that they become obsolete so fast that their value after one year is almost negligible. In the current year, VZAP bought $429,000 worth of PCs and plans to write them off over two years.

10. Revenue is recognized on shipment for all equipment sold. Terms are FOB VZAP's shipping location.

11. VZAP's Director of Marketing, Albert Buzzer, has come up with a novel method of maximizing profits on the Transact product line. Transact is one of the few VZAP products that has direct competition. Transact routes telephone calls 20% faster than competing products but sells for 30% less. VZAP actually sells the product at a loss. However, without a special training course offered by VZAP, field efficiency cannot be maximized. Customers usually realize that they need the special training a couple of months after purchase. Buzzer estimates that the average telephone company will spend three dollars on training for every dollar spent on the product. Because of the way telephone companies budget and account for capital and training expenditures, most will not realize that they are spending three times as much on training as on the product.

Exhibit III	Information Gathered During the Audit

1. Materiality has been set at $300,000.

2. In testing of revenue cutoff, one item in a sample of 60 showed that revenue was recorded on July 30, 2020, for 44 boxes of Zibor units at $2,200 each. There were no shipping documents showing that the units were shipped from the warehouse. The shipper claims that the customer said they would pick the goods up at the shipping dock on July 29 or 30 since they had a truck passing by. The goods were picked up by the customer on August 3, 1998. The audit junior who did the testing prepared a memo to the file stating that fraud may have occurred.

3. During the search for unrecorded liabilities, it was found that purchase orders totaling $318,202 with expected receipt dates before year-end had not yet been accrued. Most related to services. This situation is being investigated.

4. The IDSL 600 equipment was sold to customers in May 2020. In September 2020, VZAP provided the custom software required to operate the IDSL 600 equipment. The software was "shipped" via the Internet.

5. VZAP's total staff has increased from 49 to 123 during the fiscal year. To verify payroll in VZAP, the audit staff performed two tests and found no errors. For 20% of the employees, the 2019 T4 summary filed with the Canada Revenue Agency was agreed to the December 2019 payroll register and to the employee's original offer of employment. Then, for 20% of the employees, the amount as shown in the human resource database was agreed to a weekly pay run.

6. On June 30, 2020, VZAP issued from treasury 50,000 common shares, with a stated capital of one cent each, to another high tech company. On the basis of an oral agreement that company provided design services to VZAP in exchange for the shares.

7. After lengthy negotiation, VZAP received a $900,000 grant from the provincial government to help finance a new facility. The terms of the grant require VZAP to maintain certain employment levels in that province over the next three years or the grant must be repaid. The new facilities became operational on May 1, 2020, and VZAP has recorded the entire $900,000 as revenue in the current fiscal year.

8. During the year, Vulcanzap was involved in various transactions with JDP. JDP is controlled by the same shareholder group as the Vulcanzap.

Zuke's Productions Inc.

Quasi Montgomery founded the beginnings of Zuke's Productions in 2011 out of the basement of his parent's home primarily making special event costumes for his high school friends. Quasi always had a knack for creativity, a skill he attributed to his hours and hours of research on his electronic games, cellphones, and tablets. Quasi continued to hone his creative skills while in art school and after graduation worked for a few years at a major art production company that specialized in creating stage backdrops for major theatrical productions throughout North America and Europe. In 2017, Quasi decided to form his own creative production company, Zuke's Productions Inc. (ZP).

ZP has three main sources of revenue:

- ZP bids on contracts that call for the creative development and manufacturing of the theatrical back drops of stage productions throughout North America. For example, when the stage show *Dancing Skeletons* came to the Scary Harry Theater, ZP bid to create, manufacture, and install the stage for the production. ZP is currently a small creative production company managing one or two small productions per year.

- ZP also obtains contracts for creative advertising that could be in print, electronic delivery, or TV. In 2018, ZP won an award for their TV advertising campaign for a major election in another country.

- The third way, and one that Quasi is very interested in, is the burgeoning commercial market for costumes. Once only for kids on Halloween, costumes have risen in popularity. The costumes are also becoming more creative, with customers wanting Bluetooth integration and other added features.

You, CPA, are the audit senior on the ZP audit. Your firm has audited ZP since its inception in 2017, but this is the first year that you have been assigned to the audit. ZP has a December 31st year end. Exhibit I provides more general details about ZP. Your audit partner has asked you to provide a full planning memo for the upcoming ZP engagement, including, but not limited to, an assessment of risk and a materiality calculation. You have obtained information from the meeting that your partner had with Quasi [See Exhibit II]. Financial statement information can be found in Exhibit III. In addition to the planning memo, your partner would like you to discuss any potential issues that you believe will need to be addressed in the upcoming audit. In doing so, the partner would like you to ensure you draft four substantive audit procedures based on the issues and two potential tests of controls (specific to the issues at hand, not generic ones).

Required

Prepare the report

| Exhibit I | Zuke Productions Inc. |

- ZP is owned 80% by Quasi with a 20% ownership being held by Quasi's parents. ZP prepares its financial statements using ASPE.

- Financial details for 2019 and the unaudited 2020 figures are found in Exhibit III.

- The note payable was a loan when the company was owned by Quasi's Uncle Moto. The loan does not need to be repaid until 2032 as long as the current ratio is maintained at a minimum of 2.5:1. Should it fall below that, Moto can demand immediate repayment. Interest is payable at 5% per year on the loan balance.

- Uncle Moto owns a large construction company and Quasi often uses him when the theatrical sets are built.

- The set production industry is relatively small. It is very difficult to gain entry into it and to be successful at contracts. The industry is known for providing the contracts to "well known" companies or "friends of friends." If something were to go wrong with a set production, it typically results in that company not being awarded any future contracts.

- The retail costume market is very competitive with many players in the industry. Price point is critical as is knowing what is trendy at the moment. Otherwise, the inventory cannot be sold.

- Media advertising accounts for about 20% of ZPs revenues. Quasi sees this as a growing area, especially in the web or phone-based markets, where ads can pop up in apps or sites.

- There are approximately 30 employees at ZP including Quasi. The creative team comprises a significant portion of the employees with only five administrative staff on hand to handle the day to day accounting. Salaries are a large component of the administrative expenses.

- ZP doesn't own the building or land they operate in. They are both currently leased for a very good rate at $300,000 per year.

- Property, plant, and equipment are comprised of the creative equipment necessary to design the costume model, and the stage sets. It is net of accumulated amortization.

- Development costs may comprise two amounts. One amount would be any preproduction costs for current contracts. In other words, partially completed theatrical sets. It may also contain

Exhibit I | Zuke Productions Inc. (Continued)

amounts for some of the special projects that Quasi has, including the development of priority Bluetooth electronics that are embedded into the ZP costumes.

- Historically, the five office staff have shared most of the accounting duties. Quasi has always believed that this was helpful should someone leave or get sick. All members have completed the payroll, collected cash, and billed clients and paid bills.

- Good creative staff are hard to hire and will quickly move to another company should they obtain a better salary and/or benefits.

- Last year there was a revenue amount of $50,000 recorded in 2019 that your audit firm felt should not be recorded until 2020. The amount was sent to the error summary sheet and was not adjusted on ZPs financial statements. Since it did not exceed materiality, the statements received an unmodified audit opinion.

- Current risk-free interest rates are approximately 4%; present value of an annuity at 4% for 10 years is 8.11.

Exhibit II | Details of Meeting with Quasi

- Year 2020 was a great year for ZP according to Quasi. It was able to successfully obtain some lucrative contracts that will extend into 2021 and possibly 2022.

- One of Quasi's masterpiece costumes ended up being recalled in October due to a faulty embedded Bluetooth device. The costume was a zombie costume that had the ability to have changing eye colours, and LED lighting and sounds that could be customized. Unfortunately, there was an issue with the electronics. When the costume became connected via Bluetooth to the person's phone, it would randomly use the phone and dial a person from the person's contacts. Once connected, it would then randomly send the zombie sounds and other random sentences through the phone to the person who picked up. This has resulted in some embarrassing situations for customers. One such customer is suing ZP as a result of the issue, claiming that the device phoned his boss in the middle of their Thanksgiving dinner and it resulted in a suspension. The customer is suing ZP for $450,000. Quasi doesn't think the case has any merit.

- During 2020, ZP installed a new computer system to track production costs and to streamline billing. The computer system was installed in June and ZP moved to it fully on August 1st.

- Receivables are higher this year as some retailers are upset with the costume malfunction and have held back payment. About 60% of the receivables are typically from retailers and the other 40% from theatrical production and advertising. The largest receivable is a $200,000 receivable from the Elpin Stage Company for a contract signed by ZP in November. ZP expects to start manufacturing and producing the set in January.

- In 2020, ZP obtained a $300,000 bank loan from the Power Bank. The $300,000 was to be used to purchase a small building on the East side that ZP could move into. Due to zoning restrictions, the purchase fell through. Quasi said they are currently looking for a new site.

- One of the main printer units owned by ZP is not being used as it is unable to produce the images that ZP is now creating. The

equipment cost $150,000 in 2018 and was being amortized over 10 years. There is a smaller production shop that is interested in buying it for $35,000, or ZP could sell it for scrap for $28,000.

- A letter from ZPs lawyers was found in the legal file suggesting that the outstanding legal case would most likely be successful with a range of somewhere between $150,000 and $450,000. The lawyers are concerned that other suits might come forward. ZP does not have liability insurance for this type of lawsuit.

- According to Quasi, inventory is higher this year as he has a number of new products available for the upcoming festive season. Costumes and novelty production items for the consumer festive holiday have increased significantly over the past two years. There is also a number of inventory items in inventory that have the faulty Bluetooth chip. Quasi is trying to see if he can fix the chip. If he does, the inventory can be sold. If not the inventory is most likely worthless. He estimates that roughly $500,000 of inventory has the new Bluetooth chip.

- The investment was an investment in a small public production company. ZP sold it for $150,000.

- Capitalized production costs include theatrical sets in process as well as costs capitalized as a result of ZPs research into new technologies for enhanced costumes. A total of $150,000 of the production costs this year is for the Bluetooth chip embedded in the costumes. Another $200,000 is for a new latex covering for costume masks. Quasi thinks this could be the next new thing in costumes.

- Quasi had to fire one of the administrative employees in September after finding out they stole approximately $8,000. The money has not yet been recovered, and Quasi has not pressed charges as he didn't want the negative publicity.

- The intangible asset is a patent purchased by ZP for certain facial molds. It is expected that the patent will provide benefits for another 10 years with cash flows of approximately $50,000.

Exhibit III	Zuke's Productions Inc—Selected Financial Information (2020 unaudited)

	2020 (to Nov 30th)	2019
Revenues	$4,587,987	$3,576,345
Administrative expenses	1,237,655	988,564
Research expenses	191,345	325,987
Other expenses	956,879	724,578
Operating expenses	854,432	786,345
	3,240,311	2,825,474
Net income	$1,347,676	$750,871
Balance Sheet Information		
Cash	101,342	154,689
Accounts receivable	698,345	452,907
Inventory	1,454,986	643,245
Investments	0	120,000
Property, plant, and equipment	943,765	654,876
Production development costs	853,931	260,000
Intangible assets	450,000	450,000
	4,502,369	2,735,717
Accounts payable	554,654	435,678
Note payable	350,000	350,000
Long-term debt	300,000	0
Common shares	1,000	1,000
Retained earnings	3,296,715	1,949,039
	4,502,369	2,735,717